THE NEW
Miniature Schnauzer

The Breed Since
Ch. Dorem Display

Ch. Skyline's Blue Spruce

The sire of 52 Champions, carries several hundred lines to this breed's great Super Sire, CH. DOREM DISPLAY. Although 30 years and many, many generations separate these outstanding sires, note the striking resemblance.

THE NEW
Miniature Schnauzer

The Breed Since
Ch. Dorem Display
by DAN KIEDROWSKI

First Edition

HOWELL
BOOK HOUSE
New York

HOWELL BOOK HOUSE
Macmillan Publishing Company
866 Third Avenue, New York, NY 10022
Collier Macmillan Canada, Inc.

Library of Congress Cataloging-in-Publication Data

Kiedrowski, Dan, 1936-
      The new miniature schnauzer.

      1. Miniature schnauzers.   I. Title.   II. Title:
Ch. Dorem Display.
SF429.S375K54   1986   636.7'55   86-21494
ISBN 0-87605-240-5

Macmillan books are available at special discounts for bulk purchases
for sales promotions, premiums, fund-raising, or educational use.
For details, contact:

                    Special Sales Director
                    Macmillan Publishing Company
                    866 Third Avenue
                    New York, NY 10022

10 9 8 7 6 5 4

Printed in the United States of America

To
John T. Knight

KNOWN TO ME as John "The Knight", he has for over two decades kept incredibly accurate records on all aspects of the breed which have been used in this book as well as in the monthly magazine, *Schnauzer Shorts*. It was John who devised a "system" to rate show dogs according to the numbers defeated in breed competition only. To this day it is still known as the **Knight System,** and has been taken up by countless other breed statisticians over the years. More importantly, John has developed a unique system which delineates lines of champion descendency so that a complete picture of many generations can be drawn from any producer of note. These have been a frequent feature in *Schnauzer Shorts,* and this system, too, has been taken up by other breed historians in providing similar records on top producers.

Thank you, John, for this and so much more.

Contents

About the Author

DAN **KIEDROWSKI** has enjoyed a vicarious love affair with the Miniature Schnauzer for nearly half of his lifetime. His introduction to the breed came in 1955, through an association with Chris and Bob Snowdon of the Glenshaw Kennels.

In 1960 he began publishing the monthly breed magazine, *Schnauzer Shorts,* continuing to do so after more than a quarter-century. Since 1962 he has broadened his scope as publisher of the monthly group magazine, *Terrier Type,* producing between them over 2,500 pages annually.

An accomplished artist, Mr. Kiedrowski fills his spare time painting and sculpting. The oil painting featured on the back cover is an example of his work.

Judging became a natural bi-product of his total involvement in dogs, although AKC rulings limit this to Sweepstakes classes in the United States. Members of the American Miniature Schnauzer Club have thrice honored him as their selection of Sweepstakes judge for their National Specialty (a gap of five years must intervene between nominations). His 1976 Sweepstakes entry continues a breed record. In addition, he has judged Sweepstakes classes for many Regional Clubs from coast to coast, some as many as three times.

Today he is considered one of the world's most respected Miniature Schnauzer authorities.

Dan Kiedrowski with Ch. Regency's Right On Target, the leading sire of 1984, 1985 and 1986, bred and owned by Beverly Verna (Regency).

Acknowledgements

THE WRITING OF THIS BOOK would not have been possible without the assistance given from the many breeders throughout the world who furnished pictures and information on their dogs.

The breed's early history was so well documented in the late Anne Eskrigge's breed classic, *The Complete Miniature Schnauzer* (Howell Book House), all that was necessary was a condensation of the highlights, as most real students of the breed will have this fine effort in their personal libraries.

The chapters on the breed outside of the United States required many sources. Our sincere thanks especially to Dr. Martin DeForest of Canada, Peter Newman of England and Joan Lamping of Australia, each doing yeoman service in providing information on activities in these countries. The late Dolores Walters was instrumental in gathering information on European activities.

The many dog show photographers over the years have contributed much in depicting the changes in the breed visually from its earliest to latest stages in both type and presentation. The handsome photos by the late Rudolph Tauskey and William Brown show the wonderful Dorem and Phil-Mar dogs in all their glory. More recently, John Ashbey, Martin Booth, William Gilbert, Joan Ludwig, Evelyn Shafer, Missy Yuhl and others have contributed much to making this book a visual pleasure.

Last but far from least, our thanks to Denis Shaw for his monumental effort in achieving and presenting the host of drawings depicting breed type and grooming. They are truly wonderful.

The foregoing are but a few of those who aided in this work, as will be seen by references to others in the course of the book.

As is inherent in any book of this nature, many people and many dogs, unfortunately, have had to go unmentioned. We are deeply indebted to all Miniature Schnauzer fanciers whose industrious efforts have advanced breed type while maintaining its unique and most satisfying character.

—DAN KIEDROWSKI

Prologue

THE PURPOSE of this book is to give the reader, whether a novice or seasoned breeder-exhibitor, a complete and accurate source of information on all facets of interest concerning the Miniature Schnauzer.

The last two decades have witnessed a dramatic rise in popularity for this stylish, active and intelligent breed. The challenge offered by this preferred position has been enthusiastically accepted by breed fanciers throughout the world, and we have today a much improved version, both physically and mentally—a dog for all reasons.

The Miniature Schnauzer is singularly unique in that all breeding stock throughout the world can trace its roots to one remarkably current super sire—the great CH. DOREM DISPLAY (March 5, 1945-February 28, 1959). Therefore, every effort has been made to outline the breed from this one source, dividing it into various branches, lines and families. As many illustrations as possible have been used to more clearly delineate breed type as it has developed to the present.

You will note that statistics are liberally used to designate the producing records of the great sires and dams of the past and present. Represented are their producing records through mid-1986. Any male that has produced five or more champions, and any female that has produced three or more champions, is considered a Top Producer. The figure in parentheses ( ) after a dog's name will indicate the number of champions produced up to the time of publication. Example: CH. DOREM DISPLAY (42 Chs.).

Be mindful of the fact that a dozen or more new champions in the breed are finished each month, and that producing records on current sires and dams are constantly growing.

1

The Type and
Character of the
Miniature Schnauzer

O N APPEARANCE ALONE, the Miniature Schnauzer deserves the popularity he enjoys. It is, however, his lively, inquisitive character which launched him into the top ten ranking among all breeds in recent years. The Miniature Schnauzer is big enough to really be a dog, and small enough to share your comfortable chair. Most people will select this breed for its total livability. A good one is by nature alert, friendly, intelligent, vigorous and, most important, long-lived.

Over 30 years ago, Dorothy Williams of the famed Dorem Kennel wrote the following appraisal of the breed.

> The Miniature Schnauzer is of terrier outline with the same beauty of balance and with the typical style and spirit. But in all other respects, this breed has a distinct individuality from the other members of the Terrier Group. The combination of cropped ears and short tail is most unusual. Also the gray salt and pepper color is found in the Schnauzer family alone. People unacquainted with this breed often object to the bother of cropping, not realizing that the ears are healed completely in two weeks and that there is no further trouble of setting, which can go on for months in some breeds and often unsuccessfully.
>
> Miniature Schnauzers are plucked in the same manner as wire coated terriers. But a good coat in this breed can be kept going continually without stripping down to rock bottom. Plucking is also easier as the hair comes out much more readily than other wire coats.

Four-year-old Erik Parker with Ch. Orbit's Lift Off, CDX.

Miniatures have the same spirit and showmanship of most terriers, but are much more responsive to the owners' wishes and are noted for great intelligence. I have raised hundreds of these dogs and have never had a crazy one—no spinners and no cribbers. Nor have I ever heard of a stud fainting. They never have convulsions or fits except from serious diseases. In other words, they are not prone to nervous disorders of any kind. They do demand human companionship and have great devotion. Schnauzers were originally very much a one-man dog, resenting strangers, but this tendency has practically been bred out in the Miniature.

Miniature Schnauzers have great stamina and, in fact, will show no signs of illness until they are quite sick, and then they are fighters and will not give up. They are also easy whelpers and most careful and devoted mothers.

The responsiveness and intelligence of Miniature Schnauzers makes them ideal for obedience work, enhanced by the fact that they love to please their owners.

How fortunate that what was so three decades ago has, by careful breeding, been maintained.

Dogs, like people, differ greatly in character, even when they belong to the same breed. The Official Standard of the Miniature Schnauzer includes these comments regarding temperament: The typical Miniature Schnauzer is alert and spirited, yet obedient to command. He is friendly, intelligent and willing to please. He should never be over-aggressive or timid. *Faults:* shyness or viciousness.

For decades, breeders have given far more attention to character and temperament than what may have been suggested by the Official Standard, and have developed an all-purpose dog—a dog for all reasons.

The Schnauzer's intelligence expresses itself in many ways. One look into his face is to sense his ever-active mind and fun-loving personality.

The learning capacity of the Miniature Schnauzer is proverbial, and limited only by the patience of the teacher. The breed's performance on all levels of obedience is exceptional, and ranks among the highest in numbers of dogs that achieve obedience titles. Schnauzers learn quickly as a rule, and in time can be taught almost anything a dog is capable of learning. The only requirements are firmness, repetition, patience and, above all, *kindness.*

Frequently called "the dog with the human brain," their reasoning faculties are uncanny. Whereas most breeds think in a doggy way, Schnauzers react in a much more human fashion, and in a way we humans can better understand. Schnauzers are, in fact, pathetically dependent upon human companionship and understanding. Without it they become mistrustful and dull. Once a Schnauzer makes up his mind about you and places you in his world, he seldom changes his idea of your worth. When closeness is achieved, he gives you his full devotion, and from that point on your moods and your commands are his chief concern in life.

Although Miniature Schnauzers are quick to adapt, they love a routine. The typical companion takes pride in knowing, practically before you do, what your next move will be. Schnapps, who has been trained not to be a nuisance during mealtime, comes from under the table just as soon as he hears the sound of the first napkin being crumpled. He quickly takes a position next to that person, knowing this will be the first plate to clean. The process is repeated as each member of the family completes the final napkin maneuver.

Heide seems to know exactly when her next walk will come, regardless of the time of day. Her mistress, a fastidious young lady, always checks her appearance at the hall mirror beforehand, and Heide always meets her at the front door.

Schnauzers have good memories and will recognize friends or former owners after a long period. As he is not a jealous dog, he will gladly share his people with others, both human and canine, and even give space to the family cat.

Although not known essentially as a one-man dog, his full devotion is usually for one person, after which he includes the immediate family in various gradations of affectionate regard. Schnauzers seem to understand children, are infinitely gentle with them, and will delight them for hours with their clever antics without becoming impatient or intolerant. Children who are taught to handle them properly will particularly enjoy their whimsical character.

Miniature Schnauzers are not by nature aggressive, as are some of their terrier cousins. They should, however, be relatively fearless. Once mature, the

Ch. Benrook Ben-Gay relaxes with a cup of coffee.

Schnauzer has a strongly developed territorial instinct. He is an ideal guard dog as he defends vocally rather than physically. There is a meaningful difference between being quick to defend and quick to attack. A good Schnauzer will bark at anyone who may appear a threat to his home. He barks until the caller leaves, if you are not at home, or until you arrive on the scene. Once you are there, he accepts that you are in control of the situation and is silent. For all his boldness, the Miniature Schnauzer will display a natural kindness and charm for those who show themselves as friends.

Schnauzers are not random, incessant barkers. They are discriminating and intelligent guard dogs that assume this duty naturally. Too intelligent to be argumentative, they are positive thinkers, know their territorial rights, and will defend them.

Basically, the Schnauzer disposition is sweet, loving and loyal, but he is not at all subservient or overly sensitive. People who want a lie-at-your-feet type dog, or one that is aloof, would not enjoy a Miniature Schnauzer. Wanting your affection, he may climb into the middle of your newspaper or put his head under your arm with a prodding motion. It would never occur to him that you might be too occupied to pet him. A great sense of self is one of his most endearing qualities.

Schnauzers enjoy the outdoors in all kinds of weather. This need to be a part of their local surroundings should be satisfied. They enjoy long walks, and in pairs will run lively races with each other. Usually they like to swim, too. On the other hand, they exist quite happily on a moderate amount of exercise, and therefore are an excellent breed for the city dweller. The Schnauzer kept mostly indoors would be happiest when provided with a window or door from which to view the world outside.

Whether a dog or a bitch (female), the Miniature Schnauzer rates high as a totally reliable companion. Individual disposition is far more important than sex in a pet, both males and females being equally lovable. Many owners maintain that bitches are more affectionate, quieter, less inclined to wander and easier to train. The fact that a bitch comes in season (is breedable) twice a year, as a rule, must be considered. Confinement for two to three weeks during these periods is essential. A bitch, however, may be spayed (her reproductive organs removed), and the problem eliminated. Males may be attracted by a bitch in season at any time, and will react accordingly. He may find that a selection of potential mates live in the neighborhood, and on occasion will want to check them out if given the opportunity. Castration (his reproductive organs removed) offers the same sense of security as spaying does for females, although comparatively few owners of males feel this more drastic measure necessary.

Miniature Schnauzers are quick to adjust to new situations, and are particularly suitable to a change of homes and people at any age. Many have shown that at six or seven years and beyond they will learn to enjoy completely their new family. Selecting an older dog as a pet can be just as rewarding as taking on a new puppy, as the Miniature Schnauzer's average life span is from 12 to 15 years.

The best advice in determining the age at which to buy is to consider all the circumstances involved. If you have not had previous experience in raising a puppy, are you willing to learn? Have you the time and patience to train one? Have you the facilities? You cannot expect to train a puppy properly unless he is with you. If puddles on the floor upset you, if you are away from home most of the time, if you cannot control your small children, do not expect to successfully train a young puppy. In many cases the older dog will prove more satisfactory, particularly if he has been raised in the family, is friendly with strangers, behaves on a leash and in the car and, of course, is in good health.

A wire-coated breed such as the Miniature Schnauzer loses much of its distinction and charm if not kept in a neat, well-groomed state. This is almost a basic requirement, and only those who are conscious of these needs should consider owning a dog of the breed.

The wire hair of the Schnauzer coat is not at all like human hair. It grows for a certain period, and to a particular length, and then dies. It does not immediately shed, as in many breeds, but tends to cling half-heartedly until it is pulled out by brambles, household play, or more specifically in the grooming process. Many owners will choose to totally maintain their own pets, but most plan on three or four trips annually to a professional grooming shop. All will want to learn how to keep the family dog looking smart, if only between visits to a professional.

Good health and good character should always come first in selecting a companion dog, but if you are particularly conscious of the physical attributes of the breed and are interested in a future involving showing and breeding, you will want to study and understand what a good Miniature Schnauzer should look like—and why.

Why the Miniature Schnauzer Is Classified as a Terrier

The Schnauzer began his recorded history as a yard and stable dog. With a substantial infusion of cattle droving blood, he was not only a good ratter and vermin killer, but also helped herd livestock. The United States and Canada are the only countries in which the Miniature Schnauzer is classified in the Terrier Group. In England, and throughout most of the show-giving countries worldwide, he is classified in Non-Sporting (or Utility). Originally, all three sizes, Giant, Standard and Miniature Schnauzers competed in the Working Group here, and no one seems to know how or why the move to the Terrier Group was made. In the late 1930s, the larger varieties were moved back to the Working Group while the Miniatures remained among the Terriers.

In general character and type, Miniature Schnauzers do resemble terriers more closely than breeds in other Groups. He is an excellent ratter, and probably would "go to ground" as readily as most terriers, given the opportunity. In temperament, he is closer to the alert, active terrier than to gun dogs, hounds or toys. Nevertheless, a typical Miniature Schnauzer carries a dash of working temperament, and this "big dog" quality is a decided asset in making him the total companion that he is today.

Although the original intent to produce a small scale Standard Schnauzer remains a challenge, the "terrier type" seems to have taken hold. There is ample reason for this. For decades, at most all-breed shows, a terrier specialist judges Miniature Schnauzers along with the rest of the terrier breeds, and then often picks the Group winner. This is bound to have its affect on type over the last four decades. Judges are bound to be influenced unconsciously by a mental picture that closely relates to a terrier ideal. Sloping shoulders can easily give way to a "terrier front" with its corresponding, somewhat stilted action. Good spring of rib yields to flatter, slab sides. The head becomes increasingly longer and narrower.

Using the Official Standard as our guide, it is clear that we have gone just about as far as we safely can in the direction of "terrier type." The challenge now is to produce a good terrier of Schnauzer type—a dog for all reasons.

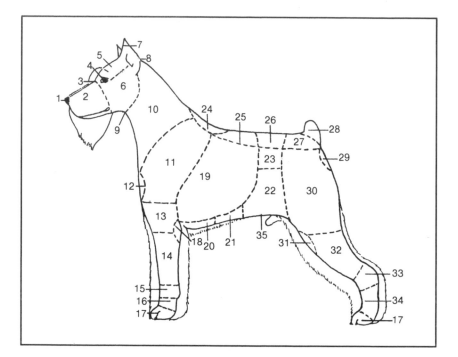

POINTS OF THE DOG
AS SHOWN ON THE MINIATURE SCHNAUZER

1—Nose	13—Upper arm	25—Back
2—Muzzle; foreface	14—Forearm	26—Loin
3—Stop	15—Knee	27—Croup; rump
4—Eye	16—Front pastern	28—Tail; stern
5—Skull; forehead	17—Foot; paw	29—Point of buttock
6—Cheek	18—Elbow	30—Thigh
7—Ear	19—Ribs	31—Stifle
8—Occiput	20—Brisket	32—Gaskin; second thigh
9—Throat	21—Abdomen; belly	33—Hock
10—Neck	22—Flank	34—Back pastern
11—Shoulder	23—Coupling	35—Tuck-up
12—Point of Shoulder	24—Withers	

LENGTH of the Schnauzer is measured from point of shoulder (12) to point of buttock (29).

HEIGHT of the Schnauzer is measured from withers (24) to ground.

LENGTH should approximate HEIGHT on the Schnauzer.

FOREQUARTERS consist of the area beginning at the withers (24) and include 11, 12, 13, 14, 15, 16 and 17.

HINDQUARTERS consist of the area beginning at the croup (27) and include 30, 32, 33, 34 and 17.

BACKLINE includes the withers, back, loin and croup.

2

What Makes a Good
Miniature Schnauzer?

IN ORDER TO accurately assess the physical attributes of a particular breed, early devotees found it necessary to develop a word picture that would serve as a Standard. In the early days that Standard of Perfection would more likely represent a breeder's ideal—striven for but not entirely realized. As the breed improves, through careful selection, the Standard may require revision as a particular type gains favor.

The Miniature Schnauzer Standard has had several revisions over the last half-century, the major changes relating to size. The original American Standard set a maximum shoulder height of 12 inches for both sexes. By 1934 this had been changed so that the rule read 10½ to 13½ inches for males and 10 to 12½ inches for females, but no male was to be disqualified for oversize unless over 14 inches, and no female unless over 13 inches.

During 1956 a committee of the American Miniature Schnauzer Club (AMSC) made a study of the breed Standard and presented a revision which was accepted by a mail vote of the members, and approved by the American Kennel Club (AKC) in the spring of 1957. The principal difference was again related to size, changing the minimum to 12 inches, maximum to 14 inches, and the ideal size 13½ inches. In the show ring, dogs or bitches under 12 or over 14 inches were to be disqualified.

It was more than two decades later that a further revision was made. Again, a ballot noting the AMSC committee recommendations was mailed to the entire membership numbering over 500. It was necessary to have an affirmative vote of more than two-thirds of all members. It is interesting to note that all the proposed changes were approved except the one deleting the words "Ideal size to be 13½ inches." This item missed being accepted by only two votes. The major change was the addition of a paragraph describing temperament. Other changes involved a clearer description of body and coat, and a new paragraph on movement. These revisions were approved by the AKC on March 13, 1979, and are included in the current Standard of Perfection which follows.

OFFICIAL STANDARD OF THE MINIATURE SCHNAUZER

General Appearance — The Miniature Schnauzer is a robust, active dog of terrier type, resembling his larger cousin, the Standard Schnauzer, in general appearance, and of an alert, active disposition. He is sturdily built, nearly square in proportion of body length to height, with plenty of bone, and without any suggestion of toyishness.

Faults: Type — Toyishness, raciness, or coarseness.

Temperament — The typical Miniature Schnauzer is alert and spirited, yet obedient to command. He is friendly, intelligent and willing to please. He should never be over-aggressive or timid.

Faults: Temperament — Shyness or viciousness.

Head — Strong and rectangular, its width diminishing slightly from ears to eyes, and again to the tip of the nose. The forehead is unwrinkled. The top skull is flat and fairly long. The foreface is parallel to the top skull, with a slight stop; and it is at least as long as the top skull. The muzzle is strong in proportion to the skull; it ends in a moderately blunt manner, with thick whiskers which accentuate the rectangular shape of the head.

Faults: Head coarse and cheeky.

Teeth — The teeth meet in a scissors bite. That is, the upper front teeth overlap the lower front teeth in such a manner that the inner surface of the upper incisors barely touches the outer surface of the lower incisors when the mouth is closed.

Faults: Bite — Undershot or overshot jaw. Level bite.

Eyes — Small, dark brown and deep-set. They are oval in appearance and keen in expression.

Faults: Eyes — Light and/or large and prominent in appearance.

Ears — When cropped, the ears are identical in shape and length, with pointed tips. They are in balance with the head and not exaggerated in length. They are set high on the skull and carried perpendicularly at the inner edges, with as little bell as possible along the outer edges. When uncropped, the ears are small and v-shaped, folding close to the skull.

Neck — Strong and well arched, blending into the shoulders, and with the skin fitting tightly at the throat.

Body — Short and deep, with the brisket extending at least to the elbows. Ribs are well sprung and deep, extending well back to a short loin. The underbody does not present a tucked-up appearance at the flank. The topline is straight; it declines slightly from the withers to the base of the tail. The overall length from chest to stern bone appears to equal the height at the withers.

Faults: Chest too broad or shallow in brisket. Sway or roach back.

Forequarters — The forequarters have flat, somewhat sloping shoulders and high withers. Forelegs are straight and parallel when viewed from all sides. They have strong pasterns and good bone. They are separated by a fairly deep brisket which precludes a pinched front. The elbows are close, and the ribs spread gradually from the first rib so as to allow space for the elbows to move close to the body.

Faults: Loose elbows.

Hindquarters — The hindquarters have strong-muscled, slanting thighs; they are well bent at the stifles and straight from hock to so-called heel. There is sufficient angulation so that, in stance, the hocks extend beyond the tail. The hindquarters never appear overbuilt or higher than the shoulders.

Faults: Bowed or cowhocked hindquarters.

Feet — Short and round (cat-feet) with thick, black pads. The toes are arched and compact.

Movement — The trot is the gait at which movement is judged. When approaching, the forelegs, with elbows close to the body, move straight forward, neither too close nor too far apart. Going away, the hind legs are straight and travel in the same planes as the forelegs.

Note: It is generally accepted that when a full trot is achieved, the rear legs continue to move in the same planes as the forelegs, but a very slight inward inclination will occur. It begins at the point of the shoulder in front and at the hip joint in the rear. Viewed from the front or rear, the legs are straight from these points to the pads. The degree of inward inclination is almost imperceptible in a Miniature Schnauzer that has correct movement. It does not justify moving close, toe-ing in, crossing, or moving out at the elbows.

Viewed from the side, the forelegs have good reach, while the hind legs have strong drive, with good pickup of hocks. The feet turn neither inward nor outward.

Faults: Single tracking. Sidegaiting. Paddling in front, or high hackney knee action. Weak rear action.

Tail — Set high and carried erect. It is docked only long enough to be clearly visible over the topline of the body when the dog is in proper length of coat.

Faults: Tail set low.

Coat — Double, with hard, wiry, outer coat and close undercoat. Head, neck and body coat must be plucked. When in show condition the body coat should be of sufficient length to determine texture. Close covering on neck, ears and skull. Furnishings are fairly thick but not silky.

Faults: Coat—too soft or too smooth and slick in appearance.

Size — From 12 to 14 inches. Ideal size 13½ inches. (See disqualifications.)

Color — The recognized colors are salt and pepper, black and silver, and solid black. The typical color is salt and pepper in shades of gray; tan shading is permissible. The salt and pepper mixture fades out to light gray or silver white in the eyebrows, whiskers, cheeks, under throat, across chest, under tail, leg furnishings, under body, and inside legs. The light under-body hair is not to rise higher on the sides of the body than the front elbows.

The black and silvers follow the same pattern as the salt and peppers. The entire salt and pepper section must be black.

Black is the only solid color allowed. It must be a true black with no gray hairs and no brown tinge except where the whiskers may have become discolored. A small white spot on the chest is permitted. (See disqualifications.)

Disqualifications

Dogs or bitches under 12 inches or over 14 inches.

Color solid white or white patches on the body.

Breed Standards were developed for breeders and judges as a guideline or blueprint for evaluation. Accurate assessment of your own dog or those of others requires a clear understanding of the fine points illustrated by the written words. This requires experience and does not come easily unless you are one of those rare individuals possessing a gift frequently called "an eye for a dog"—the ability to appraise the qualities of a specimen at a glance. Most of us were born without that power and must learn through constant study as well as considerable familiarity with dogs of good type.

The balance of this chapter is a point by point analysis of the word picture of Miniature Schnauzer perfection as outlined by the Standard. Careful study will give the reader an excellent basis for understanding the qualities which give the breed its unique "type."

The Miniature Schnauzer is a dog of normal conformation, and in basic points is similar to many other breeds. To the novice, Miniatures look much alike except for decided variations in color. Gradually, with study and experience, the differences in type become clearer and the finer points more obvious.

Since Miniature Schnauzers in the show ring are highly styled, requiring skillful grooming and presentation, those who attempt to assess their real quality must look beyond outward characteristics *applied* by exhibitors. Individual trimming styles can greatly affect the total picture. Our able professional handlers best exemplify this influence as they consistently have Schnauzers in the ring month after month. These handlers normally will be showing dogs of widely diverse bloodlines. The type may vary, but their "stamp" will be evident, and with it will cover much of the variation in type which might otherwise be obvious. The dog has not changed, only the surface qualities have been manipulated according to the individual preferences of the exhibitor. I am quite sure that given the same Schnauzer and presented by one handler on one coat and by another on the next, the average breeder would not even recognize the specimen as the same individual. Has the dog changed? A different "stamp" has been placed on the outward characteristics. The dog, essentially, is the same. This is one of the reasons why "ringside judging" has its shortcomings. Any comment concerning a particular specimen should be reserved until he has been examined more closely and completely.

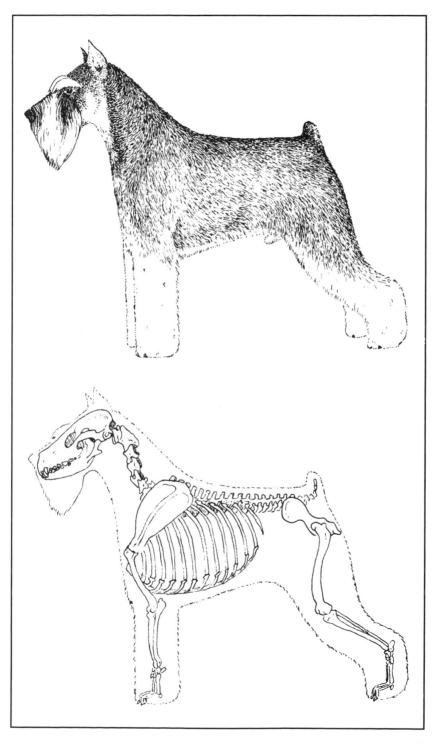

If we are to understand and identify correct type regardless of the stamp given the Schnauzer by his handler, we must look beyond the finishing touches which may be so skillfully applied.

Type cannot be limited to any single part of the Schnauzer, as variables are possible in all areas of his anatomy. Often a judge is faced with as many types as there are dogs in the ring. His job is to select that individual who possesses the characteristics closest to those defined by the Standard.

General Appearance

The first statement in the Official Standard of the Miniature Schnauzer attempts to give a general picture of the breed. The key phrases, "of terrier type" and "resembling his larger cousin, the Standard Schnauzer" ask the reader to have already formed impressions about these other breeds. "Without any suggestion of toyishness" also presumes previous knowledge. It is, of course, only a brief preamble to the more precise definitions that follow.

Essentially the Standard suggests a small, stylish dog of nearly square proportions with good bone and substance. Nearly square is defined by comparing the height at the withers with the length of body, the distance from the chest to the buttocks. In no way should the breed be toyish, delicate or have fine bone. A slightly made, racy look or, at the other end of the scale, a heavy, overbuilt look are considered serious faults.

No mention is made of sex characteristics, although it is accepted in most breeds that the bitch is more refined throughout. Given a male and female of equal size, make and shape, the bitch must be just as feminine as the dog (male) is masculine. A *doggy* bitch is generally coarse in head and thick in neck. A *bitchy* dog lacks strength of head for his size and substance, and may also have a less aggressive attitude. Most Standards suggest that bitches may be a little longer in loin than dogs, the neck may be lighter and more elegant, and the rump more shapely.

Temperament

"Alert, spirited, obedient, friendly, intelligent," are all terms found in the paragraph on temperament, and are easily understood. They are, in fact, terms that should apply to virtually all canines that expect to be well-received as human companions. Likewise, shyness or viciousness would be considered faults in any family dog.

Miniature Schnauzer temperament is less volatile than that of most of its terrier cousins. He is essentially a companion dog, with an outgoing personality that copes with all situations in a sensible and reliable way.

In the show ring, a Miniature Schnauzer is expected to display an animated, inquisitive attitude, without rowdyism or savagery, and certainly with no suggestion of meekness or shyness. Allowing for youth, inexperience or strange surroundings, a first meeting with the breed should always prove positive. In competition, they should be able to put up a good show whether facing off against another dog or just to please their handlers.

External Head Characteristics

The most distinguishing characteristic of the Miniature Schnauzer is his head. The neatly cropped ears set him apart from the other members of the Terrier Group. His wedge-shaped head is accentuated by full whiskers which impart an over-all rectangular look. External qualities such as ear shape, whiskers and eyebrows are manipulated by the human element, and often in such a clever way that one must all but ignore them if he is to gain a clear understanding of head type.

Fortunately, the rather "houndy" ears presently being bred can be cropped in such a way that what otherwise might be a fault can be turned into a virtue. This may not always be true, however, as many otherwise excellent specimens never see the show ring because of unsuccessful ear cropping, and those with mediocre ear crops suffer in competition.

An ear with too much bell (outer edge) left on can make the skull appear to be broader; not enough bell may accentuate cheeks which are too full and/or a skull which is too rounded. An ear which is too long gives a coarser look to an otherwise good head; too small an ear, ironically, can produce the same effect. Be sure this man-made condition is not overly influencing your evaluation of head type.

After several decades in which only cropped specimens earned titles in America, the 1980s have seen a few Miniature Schnauzers with uncropped ears become Champions of Record. In each case these individuals possessed excellent head properties, with ears that were not only small enough, but well-placed, well-cared-for in their early development, and most importantly, used well in the show ring.

Whether cropped or natural, it is the placement and carriage of the ears which must be considered as most important. Low set and/or lazy ears detract from the look of alertness which is desired. I have seen many Schnauzers faulted, even left out of the ribbons, because of the "dead-pan" expression produced by poor use of the ears.

The more obvious external head characteristics involve whiskers and eyebrows. These are placed and trimmed in a variety of ways, the object being to accentuate good qualities and give less emphasis to faults. If the longer and lighter hairs of the eyebrows are set too far back from the eyes, it can cause the skull to look shorter and broader. Eyebrows left too long, perhaps in an effort to cover a light or prominent eye, may also cause the foreface to look shorter.

The whiskers essentially play the same role and can also be manipulated and trimmed in a variety of ways. Some exhibitors simply let them grow and grow to a point where the extra length distorts whatever balance the head may have had. The object, of course, is to achieve a balanced, rectangular look that will enhance expression.

Head

The external head characteristics have little to do with head type, which is actually based on the size, shape and position of the bones and muscles of the skull. Head balance is based on the proportions of skull length and width compared with muzzle length, width and depth. The inside corner of the eye is considered when measuring length of skull and length of muzzle (foreface). The Standard requires the foreface to be "at least as long as the top skull." A slightly longer foreface seems permissible, but a shorter foreface must be considered as less desirable.

The most common type deviations currently found on Schnauzer heads are rounded or bumpy top skulls and weak muzzles. When viewed from the side, the top of the ideal head should appear to be like two flat planes, the skull only slightly higher than the muzzle, separated by a slight stop. The most obvious deviation is a rounded top skull and prominent stop. Less obvious is a weak muzzle, lacking eye fill, as this fault can be somewhat concealed by thick whiskers. A muzzle that is dished below the eyes is a weak formation, and not worthy of a terrier.

There seems to be a tendency toward breeding narrower and longer heads, of the type found on several terrier breeds, and lacking the wedge shape described in the Standard. There are some breeders who feel that in the case of the foreface, longer is better. The nature and character of the breed would indicate otherwise, if it is to remain unique among the dogs in the Terrier Group.

The Standard is similar to many others in regard to teeth and eyes. The Miniature Schnauzer's teeth are large for the size of the dog. At the front of each jaw should be six small incisors with a canine tooth (fang) at either side. The incisors of the upper jaw should slightly overlap those of the lower jaw for a tight "scissors" bite. When the upper incisors meet the lower ones end to end, this is called a "level" bite, and should be faulted. If the upper jaw is longer, causing an "overshot" mouth, or if the lower jaw is longer, causing an "undershot" mouth, these are considered serious faults. A "wry" mouth is one in which the upper and lower jaws fail to meet in parallel alignment; it is usually the lower jaw that is affected.

Many judges will dismiss entirely any terrier that has a faulty mouth, feeling that it renders the dog unfit for the work for which he was bred. Even though no mention is made regarding the need for a full complement of 42 teeth, many judges will penalize a dog with fewer than six incisors. Missing molar or premolar teeth are usually ignored.

The eyes are well described in the Standard, and the subject needs little clarification. They are set at the level of the stop and should be widely spaced. Eyes that are too closely set generally appear in a skull that is also too narrow. Occasionally the eyes will be too small, or "beady," and detract from the desired expression. Light and/or prominent eyes are far more common and are considered major faults.

26

The nose goes unmentioned, but should be black and not too small. Breeders are occasionally worried by the appearance of a partially pink nose on a puppy. Ordinarily the nose turns black by the time the puppy begins to teethe. Occasionally a mature dog will incur a seasonal change in nose color. Frequently, in winter, the nose fades slightly, and has a washed-out appearance. This is a minor point and should not be penalized.

The last point is expression, and this is a combination of several factors: size, shape, color and placement of eyes; size and carriage of the ears, together with the general shape of the head. The expression of the Schnauzer is less hard-bitten than that of his many terrier cousins. It is more a sharply alert, quizzical look.

Neck

The neck consists of seven large cervical vertebrae, the first two immediately behind the head differ in shape from the others. It is the manner in which they are joined that governs the arch. The neck should be well arched and approximately equal in length to the head. An arched neck gives a flexibility to the head, allowing it to be carried high in a proud, elegant manner.

The skin fits tightly over well-developed, but flat muscles which blend smoothly into the shoulders. When viewed from above, the neck is of about the same width throughout until it reaches the shoulders. Any suggestion of throatiness (dewlap) as seen in certain hound breeds is objectionable. The desired clean throat, free from folds of loose skin is called "dry," with a "wet" throat being the houndy sort. The most objectionable variation is the "ewe neck," in which the neck sags instead of arches.

Body, Topline and Tail

The body consists of the spinal column and rib cage. The spinal column forms the topline and tail and is divided into six parts, beginning with the seven bones of the neck. The next eight bones form the withers, the next four comprise the back, followed by seven bones which form the loin. Just above the croup are the three fused bones of the sacrum, forming the base of the remaining bones of the docked tail.

The Standard calls for a straight topline, declining slightly from withers to tail. Any deviation is fairly obvious even to the untrained eye. There should be no upward arch (roach) and the muscles give strong enough support so that the back does not sag (sway). The tail should be set on high enough so that there is no dip in the topline at its base. A low set tail is an obvious fault and is severely penalized by most terrier judges. This firm, correct topline should be evident both standing and on the move. Of the terriers that require docking, the tail of the Miniature Schnauzer is the shortest, but should always be of sufficient length to be clearly visible.

The remainder of the body proper is formed by the ribs. The shape of the rib cage varies tremendously in the different breeds. At one extreme is the round, full-bodied Bulldog—at the other the deep, slab-sided Greyhound or Whippet. Requirements for the Miniature Schnauzer lie somewhere in between. The ribs are long and elliptical in shape. They angle back from the spinal column, with the first five ribs being slightly flatter to allow free movement of the forelegs. They slope steeply to the sternum and brisket, extending at least to the elbow. In a mature dog, the depth of the chest should equal the length of the foreleg, from elbow to ground. There is a definite widening quality, or "spring," from the fifth rib to where the floating rib begins the formation of a rather short loin.

The section between the last rib and the pelvis is called the loin, or "coupling." Dogs in most breeds are shorter coupled than bitches. An overlong loin in either sex is a fault, although the bitch can be forgiven more length since she will need space in which to carry a litter. Although rounder in shape than most of the leggy terriers, the body of the Miniature Schnauzer should in no way be broad in chest or round (loaded) in shoulder. A rib cage that is too round also adds to such faults as out-at-the-elbows, bowed legs, and rolling or paddling movement. A rib cage that is too flat produces "pinched" fronts and equally untypical movement.

Forequarters

The forequarter assembly begins with the shoulder blades (scapula), which slope both to the rear and toward each other. They should be closely set at the withers, about one inch apart. A correctly placed shoulder is laid well back on the rib cage, with the point of the sternum slightly ahead of the front of the upper arm (humerus). The scapula and humerus are nearly equal in length, meeting at approximately a 90 degree angle.

The forelegs (radius and ulna) are well-boned, strong and straight. The elbows are set close to the body and point directly backwards. The pasterns are only slightly bent to assure springy action. Any looseness of elbow or pastern will negatively affect movement.

One of the most obvious deviations from correct type in today's Schnauzers has to do with incorrect shoulder angulation. The 90 degree angle is the most universally accepted formation for most of the working breeds, allowing as it does for good length of stride. When the angle is greater, and the shoulder blade more upright, the look is the "terrier front." The outline achieved can be quite elegant in a straight-shouldered dog, but he will always fail the test of movement. Straight shoulders produce a shorter stride, more typical of terriers.

Correct forehand movement depends on two basic factors. The bones must be of correct length and must form the correct angles to each other. Variation of lengths and angles account for the multitude of type deviations possible in the forequarter assembly. Any imbalance will directly affect movement.

28

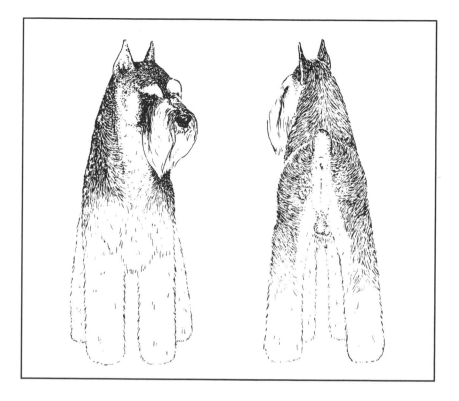

Hindquarters

The hindquarters, like the forehand, must have bone lengths and angles that complement each other. It is mainly the hindquarters that give the propulsion for movement. Historically, the well-angulated rear, which increases length of stride, was useful in the Schnauzer's work as a drover. When angulation, both front and rear, is in balance, the resulting action is very fluid and well-coordinated.

Generally, the degree of hindquarter angulation, or bend of stifle, depends on how much longer the bones of the gaskin (tibia and fibula) are, compared to the thigh bone (femur). When the bones are nearly equal in length, the dog will appear to be rather straight in stifle. A longer gaskin will produce proportionately more angulation.

Although the Standard makes no mention of the length of the hocks, a short hock creates better overall balance. A longer hock not only restricts rear movement, but also has an adverse affect on the topline, making it high in rear.

The overlay of muscles completes the picture. Although the hindquarters are strongly muscled, they should in no way be over-built, as in some of the running breeds.

Viewed from behind, the hind legs are straight, in that an imaginary line drawn through the point of the buttocks, hock and foot should center all three.

29

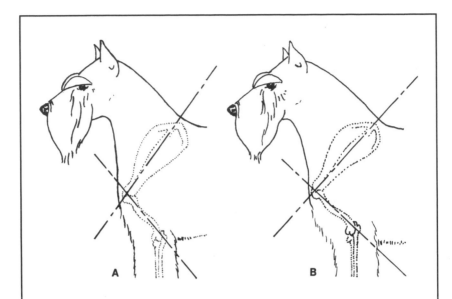

A - illustrates correct formation of shoulder with layback. B - illustrates a formation more typical of a working or sporting dog, with too much layback of both shoulder blade and upper arm. C - illustrates a well-placed shoulder blade coupled with a rather straight upper arm so that the angle between these bones is greater than desired, resulting in a "ewe" neck. D - illustrates a rather straight shoulder blade coupled with a well-placed upper arm, resulting in a "swan" neck and bumpy shoulder.

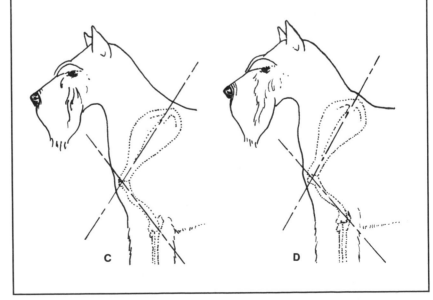

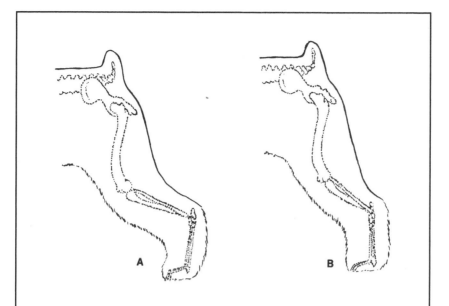

A - illustrates proper angulation, but a hock that is less than straight. B - illustrates an assembly with a short gaskin (tibia and fibula) and the resulting lack of angulation. C - illustrates an over-angulated hindquarter assembly coupled with a less than straight hock. A dog with this assembly is commonly referred to as "sickle-hocked." D - illustrates proper angulation, but with a steep croup, resulting in a low tail-set.

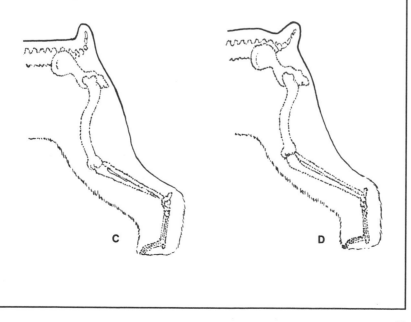

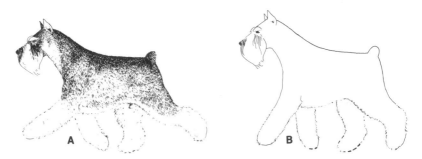

A - illustrates proper movement with correct reach and drive. B - illustrates incorrect short stride and mincing action.

Weak hocks that turn in (cow-hocked) or out (open-hocked) are obvious faults. The inefficient action that either condition produces compounds the problem.

Feet

The feet are well-arched and compact, with the two center toes only just forward of the others. Thick black pads ensure that the feet will be able to cope with varied ground conditions. Deviations include the "hare" foot which is flat and long, and the "splayed" foot in which the toes are spread out.

Set on fairly straight pasterns, the feet should point forward, turning neither in nor out. Nails should be kept short to ensure a tight foot.

Tail

The tail is docked to three joints and carried nearly perpendicular to the backline, at about 1:00 o'clock. A low-set tail prevents the dog from carrying it proudly and properly. The other extreme is called a "squirrel" tail, when carriage is almost over the back in a marked forward curve.

Movement

The most difficult area of the Standard to appraise accurately is movement or gait. Proper movement requires correct structure and muscle coordination. Remember that the Miniature Schnauzer is an all-purpose dog; his ancestors were drovers' dogs with the emphasis on utility of function.

All the faults of movement, such as sidegaiting, paddling or high hackney knee action cause wasted motion. It is for this reason that most Standards for "working" dogs give emphasis to gait.

32

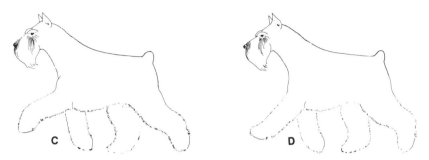

C - illustrates incorrect hackney action. D - illustrates incorrect goosestep action.

The Miniature Schnauzer has a working dog gait, with forequarters and hindquarters working in such perfect harmony that the profile of the moving back appears level. The length of stride is moderate, not nearly that achieved by the German Shepherd, nor as brisk and business-like as most terriers. Although not greatly extended, the gait should not be mincing, stiff or stilted. At full extension, forearm, pastern and foot should form a continuous straight line, which is maintained through the full arc of the downward swing. In traveling, the object of the foreleg is to reach as far forward as is structurally possible. Any tendency toward the high, prancing action of the Hackney Pony, or the high, stiff "goose step" is totally incorrect.

Often the lift and fall of the front furnishings make it difficult to evaluate movement. Look at the feet—they should be in direct line with the points of the elbow. When a dog is out-at-the-elbow, the feet have a tendency to move towards each other (pigeon-toed). The reverse is so when the dog is "pinched" in front, the forelegs appearing to come from the same hole. The feet, themselves, should turn neither in nor out.

At no time do the forelegs pull the body forward. The Miniature Schnauzer is strictly rear-drive! The hindleg swinging forward contacts the ground at approximately mid-length of the body, the foot strongly pushing back and thrusting the body forward. As the leg moves beyond the line of the body, the foot is quickly lifted, creating a "snatch of hock" so desirable in achieving full extension. When viewed from the rear, the dog should be somewhat wider through the hips than he is through the shoulders, the hind legs tracking slightly outside of the front legs. The hocks are parallel when moving, and any deviation inside or outside these parallel lines is a fault.

Perhaps the best way to understand what is correct in a Miniature Schnauzer gait is to be aware of what is not. An appropriate group of illustrations is included so that this may be more easily accomplished.

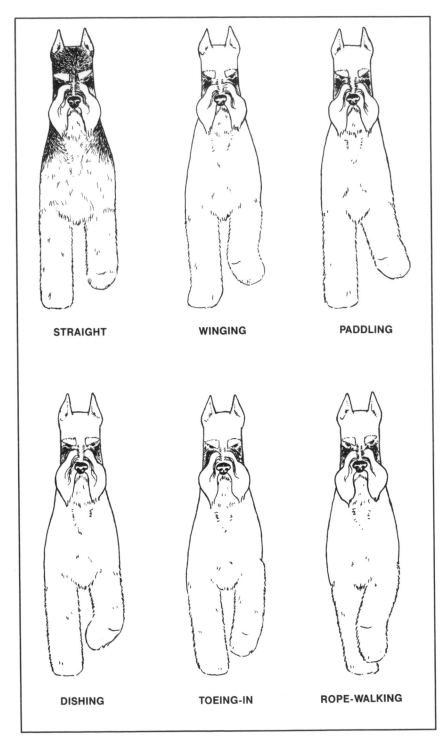

STRAIGHT WINGING PADDLING

DISHING TOEING-IN ROPE-WALKING

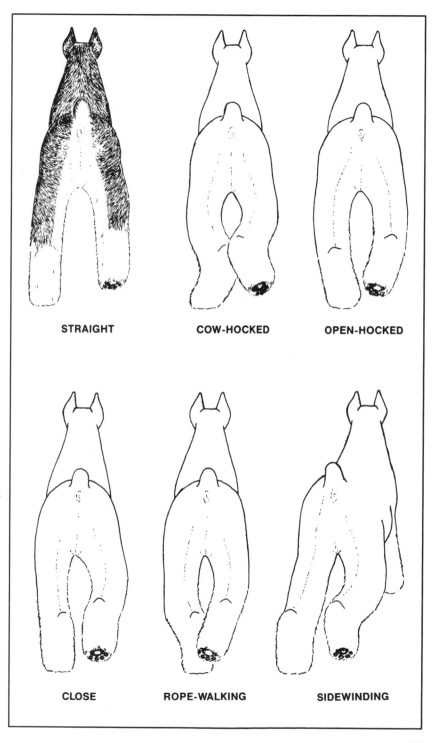

STRAIGHT   COW-HOCKED   OPEN-HOCKED

CLOSE   ROPE-WALKING   SIDEWINDING

Size

"Ideal size 13½ inches. . . . Dogs or bitches under 12 inches or over 14 inches" to be disqualified. What could be more specific! The Standard makes a strong and solid statement in its effort to maintain this medium-sized breed.

With such a definitive statement, one might expect that breeders, exhibitors and judges would find adhering to the limits a matter of fact. Not so! If you were to ask contemporary breeders what is the most serious problem within the breed, they would unanimously say "size."

As recently as the summer of 1985, one of our more astute judges, Robert Moore, an all-arounder whose initial breed was Miniature Schnauzers, made the following plea, published in *Schnauzer Shorts.*

The time has come for the breeders and handlers to do something about the dogs that are being shown today that are entirely too tall for the Standard. At a show some time back, three of the four dogs in the open class were measured out and disqualified by me. One of these dogs had to have been at least 15½ inches and had nearly finished his championship. These dogs were handled by handlers who are Miniature Schnauzer breeders. Three of the four handlers thanked me for measuring the dogs out, and when asked why they showed dogs that were so large, it was explained that everyone else was showing big dogs, too.

Now is the time for breeders and handlers to get together and develop some ethics for the welfare of the breed. A breeder or a handler should not take a dog into the ring that has a disqualifying fault. Although, to my knowledge, your parent club does not promote a "Code of Ethics," this size thing is getting to be a "Moral" issue.

Over the years, many people have said that size disqualifications should be abolished. If this is done, it will not be many years until one cannot tell the difference in Miniature and Standard Schnauzers. A couple of years ago, while judging in another country, a dog was shown to me that was as big as, and coarser than Standard Schnauzers in our country. This dog was sent over by one of our leading breeders. Fortunately, he was not producing his size there, but what will this do to future generations?

Please, you breeders and handlers of the Miniature Schnauzer, do give some thought to what is happening to the breed. Get together and agree to show only dogs within the breed Standard—and prove that you care about the breed, other than today's wins, while there is still time.

It serves little purpose to ask how we got this way. The question is how can corrective actions be taken. It starts with the breeder, of course, but judges need to be better informed, and more measurements need to be taken in the show ring. Above all, exhibitors must take a firm stand on the question of size, vowing to show only those that *measure* up to Standard requirements.

Coat

The Miniature Schnauzer has a double coat, combining a hard, wiry outer coat with a dense soft undercoat. The outer coat provides weather protection; the undercoat provides warmth. Hand stripping is required to bring a dog into show condition. In the show ring the coat is required to be at least a half-inch in length on the body, so that texture and color can be evaluated fairly.

Some coats have a slight wave, particularly as the coat lengthens. Coats of proper texture should never curl, even when wet. An open coat, one that does not fit the body tightly, is undesirable. Although the Standard requires under-coat, the density and length must be controlled in order to keep a dog in show condition. Left unchecked, it quickly spoils body contour as well as color.

Leg hair (furnishings) should be fairly thick. Although in no way as harsh as the body coat, the furnishings may not be silky in texture. The length or fullness of beard and leg furnishings seems to be a matter of taste. The object should always be a trim, smart look, not unlike that of the Schnauzer's terrier cousins.

Color

The acceptable colors and patterns allowed by the Standard give Miniature Schnauzers great variety. The large majority are of the distinctive and unique salt and pepper color, based on a "banded" harsh outer coat. The color is produced by each hair having three bands of light and dark shades of gray. Dark dogs will have the majority of the hair ends dark, while in the lighter-colored dogs there are more lighter ends. In a true salt and pepper, each hair will be banded, not just some. Any suggestion of tan or red banding should be discouraged.

Black and silvers follow the same pattern as the salt and peppers, excepting that the salt and pepper section must be pure black.

Black is the only solid color permitted, and must be pure in color, with no suggestion of a gray or brown tinge. A small white breast spot is permitted.

A final word about QUALITY and BALANCE seems appropriate here. Quality is that indefinable "something" that sets a dog apart from his competitors. Balance is that "something" that makes him appear "all-of-a-piece," both in stance and in action. Understanding all the pieces is no small feat in itself. Recognizing how and why they fit is a continuing challenge.

3

Breed Origins
and Early History

THE MINIATURE SCHNAUZER is of German derivation, the only breed recognized in the Terrier Group without British roots. There is little data to indicate exactly how the breed originated, but it appears to be the result of considerable experimentation in Germany during the last decade of the nineteenth century.

Originally known as a *Pinscher,* the name Schnauzer (pronounced *Shnowtser*—the German z always sounds like ts) came from the German *schnauze* (meaning snout), applied because of the heavy whiskers on the muzzle.

Records indicate that the Standard Schnauzer was developed first, appearing as early as 1879 in the first volume of the Pinscher-Schnauzer-Zuchtbuch (PSZ). The Pinscher-Schnauzer Klub (PSK), founded in Cologne in 1895, published the first independent Schnauzer stud book. The oldest Miniature Schnauzer registered was a black bitch, Findel, whelped in October 1888. She was of unknown parentage. Of the eight bitches registered in this first volume, three were black, three were yellow, one black and tan and only one was described as pepper and salt. The six males included no blacks. Four were yellow of various shades, one was black and tan, and again only one was pepper and salt (this color now commonly referred to as salt and pepper). Four of the eight bitches were of unknown breeding, and the sire of a fifth was also unknown. Most were recorded as having Wire-haired Miniature Pinschers as parents.

Jocco Fulda Liliput

Jocco Fulda Liliput, whelped December 6, 1898, was the first Miniature Schnauzer to be registered in the PSZ. Jocco's picture appears in *Gebrauchs- und Luxushunde,* a book on German dogs by Emil Ilgner, published in 1902. It differs very little from another illustration of Fritzle, which is labeled as an Affenpinscher.

The theory regarding the origin of the Miniature Schnauzer is that the breed resulted from the crossing of Standard Schnauzers with Affenpinschers. The fact that so many of the earliest Miniatures were solid black seems to confirm the theory. Other indications point to the possibility that the black color may have been derived from the Toy Spitz, otherwise known as the Pomeranian. Ilgner's book illustrates a group of these, all blacks, owned by the Heilbronn Kennel, and Heilbronn had long been a center for black Miniature Schnauzers. If the large Spitz was used in the development of the Standard Schnauzer, as has been suggested, it would seem logical to make use of the Toy variety to produce Miniatures.

Several other breeds may have played a part in the development of the Miniature Schnauzer. It was still an experimental period at the turn of the century, with various crosses being made to improve certain characteristics. The occasional appearance of parti-colors, even today, in pure-bred litters of Miniature Schnauzers gives rise to the theory that Fox Terriers were used, even as late as the 1930s. However, the Standard for Miniature Pinschers, as late as 1924, listed parti-colors as permissible, and may be the more likely source.

Ch. Peter v. Westerberg

In early volumes of both German and Swiss stud books, there are several cases where puppies from the same litter are registered some as Miniature Schnauzers, some as Miniature Pinschers and even some as Affenpinschers. Individual type appears to have counted as much as did their breeding. As late as 1920, Michel Chemnitz-Plauen, registered as a Miniature Pinscher, was sired by a Miniature Schnauzer Sieger (a male German Champion) Trumpf Chemnitz-Plauen, out of a Miniature Schnauzer bitch, Resl Chemnitz-Plauen. Both parents played an important part in the breed's early development. Trumpf, whelped March 21, 1912, was a great grandson of the most significant of the "Big Three" cornerstone sires, Prinz v. Rheinstein.

Whelped July 12, 1903, Prinz was bred by Herr Kissel of Frankfurt and owned by Herr Trampe of Berlin. He was described as being a very sound dog, black with yellow markings. Prinz's picture indicates a sturdier build and heavier bone than his nearest competitor of the period, Sieger Peter v. Westerberg, born in November 1902 and the oldest of the "Big Three" sires. Sieger Lord v. Dornbusch, youngest of the trio, was whelped two years later.

Lord's breeding is uncertain. Various early pedigrees give his sire as Bubi or Mobi, and his dam as Guss, or (more probably) Suss, the latter by Poppi out of Lottchen, the parents ascribed to Prinz v. Rheinstein in early Dutch pedigrees. Since Poppi's parents are given as Bubi and Hexe, it appears that Lord was inbred to Bubi.

Lord left three producing sons who founded male lines, and three daughters who may be found at the back of most early pedigrees.

Peter v. Westerberg and Prinz v. Rheinstein, most important of the "Big Three," were in direct competition, both in the show ring and as producers. Peter was the more successful show dog, his owner, Herr Max Woch claiming that he always defeated Prinz when they met. Herr Woch described Peter, a

Ch. Lord v. Dornbusch

Prince v. Rheinstein

solid black, as "a foundling without a pedigree." In spite of this, he was a most popular sire, recorded by the PSK as having produced 55 litters, the last sired when he was 12 years old.

A line drawing by Richard Strebel shows Peter at the age of five. Berta, an early breed authority, described him at the time as having "good length of head, no longer recalling the Affenpinscher in form or expression, with heavy, close coat, sound bone and harmonious appearance." Apparently Berta accepted the fact of an Affenpinscher cross before 1907.

Peter's popularity may account for the fact that the large majority of Miniature Schnauzers during that period were solid black. His importance is immeasurable. I doubt if there is a single Miniature Schnauzer today that does not go back to Peter hundreds, even thousands of times over. His tail-male line comes principally through four producing sons, and most importantly, Sieger Cito v.d. Werneberg, bred by Herr Woch of the Werneberg Kennels.

It is to Prinz v. Rheinstein that American bloodlines owe the most, as all tail-male lines of today trace to him. Although he died at the early age of four, he left three champions, most notably Ch. Perle v.d. Goldbach, out of (ex) Nettel v.d. Goldbach, whelped December 14, 1904. Perle was bred back to her sire and produced Ch. Gift Chemnitz-Plauen, a black and tan like Prinz. All present day male lines come through Gift, doubling the importance of his sire.

Gift, foundation sire for Herr Stocke's Chemnitz-Plauen Kennel, produced 40 litters, from which came seven champion sons, one champion daughter, plus ten non-champions who were producers. Shown under Herr Berta when six months old, Gift was described thusly in the judge's report:

An inquisitive fellow; typey, strong bone, solid if somewhat narrow front, good coat, very good in head and expression, full muzzle, luxuriant whiskers, excellent carriage and temperament.

Siegerin (female German Champion) Mirzl Chemnitz-Plauen was the only bitch among Gift's champion get. Bred to her half-brother, the Gift son, Ch. Fips Chemnitz-Plauen, a daughter, Resl Chemnitz-Plauen, was the grand-dam of Am. Ch. Cuno v. Burgstadt, one of the most important of the early American sires.

Ch. Fips Chemnitz-Plauen, whelped June 6, 1911, was unlike his sire Gift in that he carried on through daughters rather than sons. He sired 29 litters, as compared to his sire's 40. In almost all cases, the producers from Fips were strongly inbred to Gift, with several of them double granddaughters. The picture of Fips indicates that he was considerably lighter in color than his sire Gift, and could be called a medium salt and pepper, probably with yellowish furnishings. His daughter Goldjungfer (Golden Girl) and son Goldjunge (Golden Boy) bore names suggesting the tawny yellow color characteristic of the breed at this point. Yellow or red was also found in many of the near descendants of Fels v.d. Goldbachhohe and Ch. Cuno v. Burgstadt, who were both unusually strong in Fips blood.

The Chemnitz-Plauen team in 1911. (L to R) Taps Chemnitz-Plauen, Ch. Gift Chemnitz-Plauen, Ch. Fips Chemnitz-Plauen and Ch. Mirzl Chemnitz-Plauen.

It was the Gift son, Ch. Trumpf Chemnitz-Plauen who was by all odds most important. From him comes practically every male line that traces to Prinz v. Rheinstein. Trumpf's most important breedings were to the Fips daughter Motte v. Goldbachtal, from which came Linus, Heinerle and Kalle Chemnitz-Plauen, the latter a Swiss champion.

Linus was whelped in 1915, while his full brother Heinerle arrived four years later. Although not himself a champion as was Heinerle, Linus was the more successful sire of the two. It was reported that after Linus appeared on the scene, the famous Heinzelmannchen Kennel virtually scrapped their existing stock and began over again. Linus' most notable son, Bolt v. Annenhof, was whelped April 27, 1920, and sired 26 litters during the next nine years. Bolt's get include the double Linus grandson Fels v.d. Goldbachhohe. The Fels son Mack v.d. Goldbachhohe and daughters Ch. Lotte and Lady v.d. Goldbachhohe were cornerstones of the breed in America.

Virtually all the early American imports carried lines to Linus and Heinerle, and the most notable, Ch. Cuno v. Burgstadt, is intensely linebred through them to Gift.

Although these oldtimers may seem of little consequence with the passing of time, their influence on the modern Miniature Schnauzer is immeasurable. All present day stock descends from the foregoing individuals over numerous lines. Some were so often repeated, as was Gift, that the cumulative effect cannot help but be recognizable throughout the breed's development in the United States during the past 60 years.

4

Breed Beginnings
in America

DURING THE FIRST TEN YEARS of Miniature Schnauzer breeding in the United States (1925 - 1935), 108 dogs and bitches were imported from the Continent, nearly all from Germany. All the American-bred Miniature Schnauzers descend entirely from these initial imports. By 1935, the 54 American-bred Champions finished up to that time traced to only ten of the imported dogs and 11 of the bitches.

The real beginning of the Miniature Schnauzer in America came in the summer of 1924 when Rudolph Krappatsch sent over four Miniatures to Marie Slattery. They would become the foundation, not only for her Marienhof Kennel, but for the breed itself.

Amsel v.d. Cyriaksburg, whelped June 12, 1921, and her two puppy daughters, Lotte and Lady v.d. Goldbachhohe, whelped July 7, 1924, came across the Atlantic, along with their future mate, Mack v.d. Goldbachhohe. It is safe to say that there is no American champion today that is not descending from them thousands of times over.

Amsel was the dam of the first American-bred litter, whelped July 15, 1925, and sired by Mack. It contained Ch. Affe of Oddacre, who sired the first American-bred champion in Mrs. Slattery's Ch. Moses Taylor. Virtually all the early "firsts" would be earned by Marienhof dogs. During nearly a half-century of activity, more than 100 champions would emerge from Marienhof, and Mrs. Slattery would earn the title of "Breed Matriarch."

The Amsel daughter, Ch. Lotte v.d. Goldbachhohe, held the breed record for 25 years as the dam of 12 champions. Nine of these were from three litters sired by Ch. Cuno v. Burgstadt, including a record-setting litter of five that all became champions. The "star" from the Cuno-Lotte breedings was clearly Ch.

Ch. Amsel
v.d. Cyriaksburg

_____

Ch. Cuno v. Burgstadt

Aennchen of Marienhof. She was one of the top winners of her day, being the first American-bred and first bitch to win a Group. Aennchen remains the only bitch, and until CH. DOREM DISPLAY in 1949, the only Miniature to go Best of Breed at both Westminster and Morris and Essex, the two premier events of the period. She was described thusly by her original owner, Anne Eskrigge:

> Almost black and cream as a puppy, but became greyer as she matured, though always retaining a strong reddish tinge derived from her dam. Aennchen had a beautiful head and expression, and was a natural shower with a lovely disposition.

Two years after the untimely death of Mack v.d. Goldbachhohe in 1925, Mrs. Slattery imported the three-year-old male Cuno v. Burgstadt, who was to make breed history and to have a more far-reaching effect upon the development of the breed in this country than any other imported sire. Cuno sired 14 champions, a record which only stood a few years until broken by his great-grandson Ch. T.M.G. of Marienhof.

Although he gained his American title, Cuno's record as a show dog was undistinguished. He was described as a dark salt and pepper with cream markings, short in body, with lots of beard and furnishings. The last characteristic he passed on to his get in a day when sparse whiskers and leg hair were the rule. He was an upstanding dog, but light in bone, making him appear smaller than his 12 inches at the withers. Cuno sired few litters outside of his home kennel, used almost exclusively with Amsel and her daughters. Before his value was generally realized, he was killed in a dog fight with a Setter.

Shortly after Cuno's death, Leda Martin imported the breed's next significant sire, Flieger Heinzelmannchen. Mrs. Martin's specifications included small size, gray color, and a pedigree suitable for use with Cuno daughters. Herr Walther of the famed Heinzelmannchen Kennel in Germany complied with the request and Flieger arrived at Ledahof.

Leda Martin recalled Flieger as follows:

> In 1930 I imported Flieger Heinzelmannchen. He died before he gained his title, but fortunately sired a few puppies. He was a lovely gray salt and pepper, and threw this color in a day when the majority of our dogs were cinnamon, black and tan or black and silver, or a rather unpleasant combination of all three. He was also a very short-backed dog which at the time was not a common attribute. He threw very well-set tails in a day when most were set and carried at half-mast.

Like Mack and Cuno, Flieger's short life span allowed a limited return. He left only eight litters, from which came five champions, including four out of Galloper of Marienhof. Mrs. Martin shared in this litter, selecting and finishing Chs. Flieger and Freifrau of Edgeover. The younger Flieger was described as a small dog of good color and unusual bone, with a lovely disposition. He lived to

(L to R) Ch. Handsome of Marienhof, Ch. T.M.G. of Marienhof and Ch. Kubla Khan of Marienhof.

(L to R) Ch. Hermione of Marienhof, Primrose of Marienhof and the import, Flieger Heinzelmannchen.

11 and was a popular stud, leaving five champions plus eight non-champions who were producers.

The breed's progress from this point forward would be based on the blending of offspring from Ch. Cuno v. Burgstadt and Flieger Heinzelmannchen. Two decades later, the breed's "super sire," CH. DOREM DISPLAY, would carry 32 lines to Cuno and 12 to Flieger.

Pleased with the quality Cuno was producing, and needing another stud for line-breeding, Mrs. Slattery imported the five-year-old Cuno son, Marko v. Beutenberg. He was shipped initially to Tom and Kay Gately, professional handlers at the time, and currently among our most respected judges. The Gatelys were responsible for finishing over 20 Marienhof champions, including Marko. Tom's description of Marko gives us a first-hand impression of the breed at this time:

> Marko was entirely different from anything in the breed today. He was a large dog, oversize in fact, but a true Schnauzer with small, dark, well-shaped eyes, a long head with a flat skull, strong foreface, sound running gear and a resolute disposition. Every hair was as harsh as wire, right down to the toes. His furnishings were not as profuse as those seen today—every hair was hard. His color was a dark salt and pepper, with the furnishings just slightly lighter.

Ch. Marko v. Beutenberg sired nine American champions, including three from an outstanding litter out of Mehitabel of Marienhof II. This Marienhof litter produced a number of "firsts." Ch. Mussolini of Marienhof was the first Miniature Schnauzer shown in obedience and won the Novice Class at Philadelphia in 1935. His sister, Ch. Mehitabel of Marienhof III, was the first uncropped Group winner and was runner-up for Best in Show in 1934. The other male, Ch. Marko of Marienhof was chosen as heir apparent, and became the first American-bred to sire over ten champions. His record of 13 champions equaled the American-bred get of his grandsire, Cuno, and continued this strong tail-male line by leaving the outstanding son, Ch. T.M.G. of Marienhof.

Thomas Michael Gately's connection with T.M.G. is obvious, and his story tells so much about the times.

> Some time along in the early thirties, when the depression was about at its worst, I telephoned Marie, saying that I had a customer who would pay $50 for a male puppy. I stated that I would like to make about $15, so could pay $35. She was coming to a nearby show and said she would bring a puppy along. When Marie set the puppy down in our living room, I exclaimed, "Gosh, you're not selling that pup for $35 are you?" She queried, "Don't you think he's good enough?" My response was, "Good enough—I think he's just about the best Miniature Schnauzer puppy I've ever seen!" Her reply was, "All right, I'll send you another puppy, and keep this one." She kept him and named him after me.

Ch. T.M.G. of Marienhof was the leading sire of this period, producing 20 champions, a record which held until DISPLAY. Ten of T.M.G.'s 11 champion sons produced champions—five sired four or more. His greatest influence, however, was through two breedings to Wild Honey of Sharvogue, from which 14 puppies were produced. Eight became champions, and six of them left champion descendants.

The Sharvogue dogs, bred by Dr. and Mrs. Briggs, dominated the show ring between 1934 and the War years. In addition to lines from Cuno and Amsel, the Sharvogue dogs carried lines to Flieger and Friefrau, and incorporated others based on the German imports, Ch. Don v. Dornbusch of Hitofa and his son, Ch. Viktor v. Dornbusch.

Two of the champion males from the T.M.G. - Wild Honey breedings offer interesting comparisons. Ch. Stylobate of Sharvogue, owned by Mrs. Charles Gleason, was considered the best by many fanciers. Unfortunately, he was accidentally killed when less than three years old, shortly after going Best of Breed at Westminster in 1941. With limited use, he left five champions. The most successful mating was to Ch. Dorem Dubonnet, and included Ch. Dorem Searchlight, the dam of DISPLAY.

Ch. Sandman of Sharvogue, on the other hand, had a long career, living past 14 years. Sandman was twice Best of Breed at Westminster, and in 1946 became the first Miniature Schnauzer to place in the Group at this prestigious show. Sandman's five champions included four sons, the most successful being Ch. Tweed Packet of Wilkern (out of the DISPLAY daughter Ch. Debutante of Ledahof), the sire of 15 champions. The Sandman son, Ch. Dorem Elect, out of a Dubonnet daughter, gains fame as the paternal grandsire of DISPLAY. As the sire of Ch. Dorem Liberty, Sandman gains a top position in one of the strongest tail-female families of this period. Liberty is the dam of Ch. Enchantress, who rivals Wild Honey as the dam of eight champions. The Enchantress daughter, Am. and Can. Ch. Sorceress of Ledahof, was the first to match the longstanding producing record made by Lotte, actually surpassing it with a 13th champion, albeit Canadian.

From these beginnings emerged the basis for Dorothy Williams' dominant Dorem strain, responsible not only for the great DISPLAY, but over 40 homebred champions. Miss Williams purchased the bitch, Jill of Wollaton II, from the successful breeder and judge, Richard A. Kern, Jr. of the Wollaton Kennel. Although never finished, Jill was Best of Winners in good company at the Associated Terrier Specialties in 1936. First bred to Ch. Jeff of Wollaton, Jill produced Dorem Diva and Dorothy's first homebred champion, Dorem Dilletante. Two years later, put to Ch. Flieger of Edgeover, Jill produced Ch. Dorem Dubonnet. Both Diva and Dubonnet were bred to Ch. Timothy of Sharvogue, strong in Flieger-Freifrau blood. Diva produced Ch. Dorem Escapade, DISPLAY's paternal granddam through her son Dorem Cockade. Dubonnet produced Elect, dam of Cockade's sire, Ch. Dorem Parade.

Intensifying the Cuno-Flieger cross, Dubonnet was then bred to Stylobate, from which came the famous "light" litter of six, including Ch. Dorem Searchlight, the dam of DISPLAY and his influential sister, Ch. Dorem Shady Lady, foundation matron for Marguerite Wolff's prolific Phil-Mar strain.

5

The Dorem and
Phil-Mar Kennels

AMERICAN MINIATURE SCHNAUZERS are 99 percent pure—pure CH. DOREM DISPLAY. The breed has recorded nearly 4,000 American champions since the first, the imported German Siegerin, Ch. Lenchen v. Dornbusch, whelped October 17, 1920. Three-quarters of these champions have finished since the early fifties, and all but two or three have from one to several hundred lines to DISPLAY. Few breeds can claim such a recent singular influence.

The breed's history since 1950, for all intents and purposes, can be traced exclusively through sons and daughters of DISPLAY. It is impossible to find in America an outcross to his completely dominant line.

The singular importance of DISPLAY was the result of many factors, not the least of which was the broad exposure he received at a time, after World War II, in which interest in purebred dogs was rapidly increasing. He embodied in type a more streamlined outline comparable to some of his competitors in the Terrier Group. It served him well and brought him more universal acceptance among both breeders and judges than any Miniature Schnauzer before or since.

Dorothy Williams tells much of it best.

> As breeder of DISPLAY I would like to mention some things not generally known. Marie Mehrer of the famous Marienlust Dachshunds whelped the litter and at birth recognized an outstanding puppy. As soon as he could walk, DISPLAY showed tremendous style and always took a perfect stance. He was a balanced little show dog at all stages of puppyhood. In fact, one hardly realized that he was growing. To this day the same is true of all our best dogs. Furthermore they do not coarsen.

CH. DOREM DISPLAY winning the Terrier Group under John Marvin, handled by George Ward.

At three months DISPLAY was Best in Match at the Garden City Hotel, Long Island, New York under Nate Levine, the well known working dog handler. Nate wanted to buy DISPLAY in spite of his feeling that he was too perfect a dog for his age.

DISPLAY was again Best in Match at a large Queensboro show under the top terrier handler, Henry Sayres. His first appearance at a point show was at Westminster 1945 at ten months of age. Harry Lumb, the great terrier judge, put him Best of Winners and then excused all the specials, except one. That one, DISPLAY's grandsire, Ch. Sandman of Sharvogue, was given the breed and went on to be the first Miniature Schnauzer to place in the Group at Westminster. DISPLAY created quite a stir and it was amazing how the news flew. When I came out of the ring the ringside was lined with terrier judges, many of whom had hardly noticed our breed before.

51

CH. DOREM DISPLAY

March 5, 1945 ——————— February 28, 1959

Ch. Marko of Marienhof
Ch. T.M.G. of Marienhof
Tyranena Pansy of Marienhof
Ch. Sandman of Sharvogue
Ch. Bleuboy of Sharvogue
Wild Honey of Sharvogue
Woots of Sharvogue
Ch. Dorem Parade
Falcon of Sharvogue
Ch. Timothy of Sharvogue
Ch. Friefrau of Edgeover
Dorem Elect
Ch. Flieger of Edgeover
Ch. Dorem Dubonnet
Jill of Wollaton II
SIRE: Dorem Cockade
Ch. Flieger of Edgeover
Falcon of Sharvogue
Cairnsmuir Wistful
Ch. Timothy of Sharvogue
Flieger Heinzelmannchen
Ch. Freifrau of Edgeover
Galloper of Marienhof
Ch. Dorem Escapade
Ch. Cuno of Wollaton
Ch. Jeff of Wollaton
Ch. Jean of Wollaton
Dorem Diva
Ch. Virgo of Tassac Hill
Jill of Wollaton II
Jessie of Wollaton

Ch. Marko von Beutenberg
Ch. Mehitabel of Marienhof
Ch. Porgie of Marienhof
Abigail of Marienhof
Falcon of Sharvogue
Ch. Allsworth Gossip
Falcon of Sharvogue
Ch. Freifrau of Edgeover
Cairnsmuir Wistful
Ch. Flieger of Edgeover
Flieger Heinzelmannchen
Galloper of Marienhof
Flieger Heinzelmannchen
Galloper of Marienhof
Ch. Virgo of Tassac Hill
Jessie of Wollaton
Flieger Heinzelmannchen
Galloper of Marienhof
Ch. Medor Strupp
Mira von Burgstadt
Falk Heinzelmannchen
Sgn. Freifrau Heinzelmannchen
Ch. Viktor von Dornbusch
Grey Girl of Marienhof
Ch. Cuno von Burgstadt
Ch. Lotte v.d. Goldbachhohe
Ch. Bodo von Schillerberg
Ch. Jemima of Wollaton
Ch. Don v. Dornbusch of Hitofa
Ch. Halowell Vega
Ch. Marko von Beutenberg
Judy of Wollaton

CH. DOREM DISPLAY

Ch. Marko von Beutenberg
Ch. Marko of Marienhof
Ch. Mehitabel of Marienhof II
Ch. T.M.G. of Marienhof
Ch. Porgie of Marienhof
Tyranena Pansy of Marienhof
Abigail of Marienhof
Ch. Stylobate of Sharvogue
Falcon of Sharvogue
Ch. Bleuboy of Sharvogue
Ch. Allsworth Gossip
Wild Honey of Sharvogue
Falcon of Sharvogue
Woots of Sharvogue
Ch. Freifrau of Edgeover
DAM: Ch. Dorem Searchlight
Falk Heinzelmannchen
Flieger Heinzelmannchen
Sgn. Freifrau Heinzelmannchen
Ch. Flieger of Edgeover
Ch. Viktor von Dornbusch
Galloper of Marienhof
Grey Girl of Marienhof
Ch. Dorem Dubonnet
Ch. Don v. Dornbusch of Hitofa
Ch. Virgo of Tassac Hill
Ch. Halowell Vega
Jill of Wollaton II
Ch. Marko von Beutenberg
Jessie of Wollaton
Judy of Wollaton

Ch. Cuno von Burgstadt
Lotte von Beutenberg
Ch. Bodo von Schillerberg
Ch. Mehitabel of Marienhof
Ch. Bodo von Schillerberg
Fritzie of Marienhof
Ch. Marko von Beutenberg
Fiffi of Marlou
Ch. Flieger of Edgeover
Cairnsmuir Wistful
Jorg von Dornbusch
Ch. Gretel of Marienhof
Ch. Flieger of Edgeover
Cairnsmuir Wistful
Flieger Heinzelmannchen
Galloper of Marienhof
Ass Heinzelmannchen
Grille Heinzelmannchen
Ass Heinzelmannchen
Elektra Heinzelmannchen
Ch. Don v. Dornbusch of Hitofa
Berwel von Dornbusch
Ch. Affe of Oddacre
Lady v.d. Goldbachhohe
Sr. Friedel von Affentor
Ch. Lenchen von Dornbusch
Ch. Viktor von Dornbusch
Sgn. Gaudi Baltischhort
Ch. Cuno von Burgstadt
Lotte von Beutenberg
Arno of Wollaton
Ch. Jemima of Wollaton

I got telephone calls and telegrams from all over the country and of course many offers to buy. Since I was working and living in New York City, I decided to sell to someone who could campaign DISPLAY properly. Mrs. Phil Meldon was chosen because she allowed me free stud services to DISPLAY for life, and agreed to let me keep him until Ch. Dorem Silverette could be mated.

The resulting litter produced Tribute. Ch. Dorem High Test had already breen born from an accidental mating. Having such confidence in the Sharvogue line, I had purchased Ch. Imprudent of Sharvogue, a litter sister to Sandman, at the age of three months. She jumped into DISPLAY's pen and taught him the facts of life when the dog was only seven months. This accidental but successful mating must have been the basis for the mistaken rumor that DISPLAY himself was the result of an accidental breeding.

Mrs. Meldon took her new dog to his first show at Pocono, Pennsylvania. His trim had grown out but Edwin Sayres, Sr. spotted him in the exercise ring and asked to trim and show him. DISPLAY went through to his first of five Bests in Show. He later topped four Specialties.

But DISPLAY's greatest win was his first in the Group at Westminster in 1947, over 800 terriers. George Ward took him in only one hour after he had been engaged as handler. But this was a great showman and asked for it every minute. When gaited individually, DISPLAY went up and down the length of that Garden barking at the gallery. The next year this big little dog went second to the Best-in-Show winning Bedlington, Ch. Rock Ridge Night Rocket.

Mrs. Meldon was responsible for DISPLAY's show career with the able help of Pop Sayres. Later she sold him to Mrs. H. Weldon Angus of the Benrook kennels. Jigger, as he was known and loved, was no longer young and spent the rest of his life under the loving care of Shirley Angus.

DISPLAY, whelped April 5, 1945, came to the end of a full life in 1959 shortly before his fourteenth birthday. He was one of those rare individuals who are preeminent as both show winners and producers. He was not only the breed's first Best in Show winner, but his record went unchallenged for over two decades. His Westminster record is unparalleled.

As an individual, DISPLAY was about 13 inches tall, with a short back, excellent head and neck and first-class temperament. He was a clear salt and pepper with an unusually dark undercoat, which appeared fairly often in his get.

DISPLAY was only ten months old when his first champion son, Dorem High Test, was whelped. Ch. Dorem Tribute followed in July, and the litter brothers Chs. Delegate and Diplomat of Ledahof in October of 1946. This at once established him as a successful sire while he was still making his big wins in the show ring.

In the early 1950s, the great impact that DISPLAY would have on the breed was just beginning to be recognized. At the same time, the force of this same gene-pool was emerging through the descendants of his full sister, Ch. Dorem Shady Lady, CD, the grand matriarch of the prolific Phil-Mar family.

Shady arrived at Phil-Mar on March 14, 1949, already a champion, and at the time in whelp to Dorem Dominant. She was to be the only foundation

Four generations of Phil-Mar champions. (L to R) Ch. Dorem Shady Lady, CD and her daughter, Ch. Phil-Mar Gay Lady, and her son, Ch. Phil-Mar Gay Knight, and her son, Ch. Phil-Mar Bright Knight.

for a breeding program that extended over three decades. There would be 37 champions bearing Marguerite Anspach Wolff's illustrious Phil-Mar prefix, and all would descend from Shady.

Although a relative novice in dogs when Shady arrived, Mrs. Wolff remembers her as being very different from her famous brother.

> Shady did not look like her brother—she was a short, compact and power-ful bitch, excelling in rear movement. Her front was not the most desirable, but with her huge and deep chest, it was understandable that her forehand was not tightly constructed. Her major fault was that she had large, round eyes, although dark enough in color. Besides being beautiful, lovable and a wonderful mother, she was also brilliant. I took her through her CD degree after just six weeks of training—and at five years of age.

Shady's first litter at Phil-Mar contained Ch. Phil-Mar Watta Lady, plus two others that earned obedience degrees. Watta Lady was the first of a long

Ch. Phil-Mar Watta Lady

succession of champions that would be breeder-owner conditioned and handled to their titles.

Bred next to her uncle, Ch. Dorem Tribute, Shady again produced a litter of seven from which two bitches were retained. One of them, Ch. Phil-Mar Gay Lady, became an easy champion, and Peggy described her as:

> Very much the terrier type, with excellent carriage, sound movement and poise plus. . .and with eyes perfect in size and color.

Shady's final breeding was to the DISPLAY grandson, Ch. Dorem Tempo, from which came her third champion, Ch. Phil-Mar Lucky Lady. Tempo, a son of Ch. Delegate of Ledahof, would prove to be the key sire in the Phil-Mar plans for the future. Mrs. Wolfe's admiration for Tempo is made clear by the following:

> I bred Watta Lady to Tempo, who for my money is one of the greatest sires of all-time. He was owned by Muriel and Jack Ainley of Connecticut. He was a terrific coated dog. Jack showed him continuously for three years, always in perfect show coat. According to Muriel, Tempo was used at stud only nine times. He produced a champion in each litter that he sired for me, including my three Best-in-Show dogs.

From the Tempo-Watta Lady breeding came the great show bitch, Ch. Phil-Mar Lucy Lady, described by Peggy as:

> Beautifully balanced and a sound mover. A well-arched, reachy neck held high her gorgeous head with dark, perfectly shaped eyes.

56

Ch. Phil-Mar Lucy Lady   **Ch. Phil-Mar Lady Be Good**

Lucy was the breed's top winner in 1954, and with her second Best in Show win became the first of only four bitches with multiple Bests. Lucy was also one of the few bitches to win Best of Breed at Westminster. As the dam of the outstanding show dog and sire, Ch. Phil-Mar Lugar, her accomplishments are rare indeed.

Each of Shady's three champion daughters became top producers in their own right. Watta Lady produced three champions, including Lucy, who in turn, had three champion get, including Lugar. Gay Lady also produced three champions, including two top producers: Ch. Phil-Mar Gay Knight (by Tempo), sire of nine champions, and Ch. Phil-Mar Lady Be Good, dam of Ch. Perci-Bee's First Impression, a top sire with 15 champion get, including Lugar. Numerically, Shady's best producing daughter was Lucky Lady with five champions, including Ch. Phil-Mar Lady Love (by Tribute), also the dam of five champions.

In summing up nearly 40 years of successful breeding, Peggy wrote:

> I was fortunate to start with a high-class bitch that was a sound mover, with good topline, coat, and above all, showmanship. All of Shady's fine qualities are fused in varying degrees in all the Phil-Mar Miniature Schnauzers.

The quality that was inherent in the Dorem and Phil-Mar strains will be treated more completely as we examine the tail-male branches from DISPLAY. It is the combination of lines from DISPLAY and Shady in which the entire Delegate branch is based.

6

The Tail-Male
Branches from
CH. DOREM DISPLAY

HAVING ESTABLISHED the tight line-breeding that produced DIS-PLAY, let us now examine the background of his nine top producing sons, as each represents a "branch" from this single great oak.

Before considering them as individuals, an analysis of their pedigrees is essential, since each is the result of varying degrees of line-breeding on the original Cuno-Flieger cross.

Tribute, Delegate and Diplomat—this trio of sires are very nearly identical in background, being out of Spotlight daughters, and sharing the Sharvogue dogs with equal intensity.

The pedigree on Ch. Dorem Tribute shows the result of closer than half-brother to half-sister breeding, Spotlight and Searchlight being littermates. Ch. Dorem Silverette produced five champions by five different sires and had a profound effect on the breed, not only as the dam of Tribute, but also of Ch. Dorem Tempo, who so greatly influenced the Phil-Mar family. Tribute carries five lines to Dorem's foundation bitch Jill of Wollaton II, and the same is so with the brothers, Delegate and Diplomat. Out of Ch. Enchantress, they are from Ledahof's most outstanding litter, also including Chs. Destiny and Debutante of Ledahof. In all, Enchantress produced eight champions, including the foundation matron for the Marwyck family, Am. and Can. Ch. Sorceress of Ledahof.

The background on High Test is strictly within the same family, as his dam, Ch. Imprudent of Sharvogue, is a full sister to Stylobate and Sandman, who figure so prominently in the pedigrees of Tribute, Delegate and Diplomat.

The breeding on Ch. Meldon's Merit shows some variation from the Cuno-Flieger cross, as it introduces the import, Sieger and Champion Qualm Heinzelmannchen, the sire of Ch. Rufus of Marienhof. However, this is hardly an outcross, since Merit's dam is a double granddaughter of Ch. Dorem Liberty, making his breeding much the same as that of the Ledahof brothers.

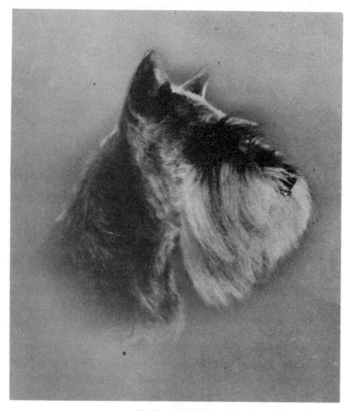

**Ch. Enchantress
and her daughter
Ch. Sorceress of Ledahof**

```
                Ch. Dorem Parade              Ch. Sandman of Sharvogue
        Dorem Cockade                         Dorem Elect
                Ch. Dorem Escapade            Ch. Timothy of Sharvogue
                                              Ch. Dorem Diva

CH. DOREM DISPLAY
                Ch. Stylobate of Sharvogue    Ch. T.M.G. of Marienhof
        Ch. Dorem Searchlight                 Wild Honey of Sharvogue
                Ch. Dorem Dubonnet            Ch. Flieger of Edgeover
                                              Jill of Wollaton II
```

✻ By matching the DISPLAY pedigree above with each of those below and on the next page and a four-generation pedigree emerges for each of his nine top producing sons.

CH. DOREM TRIBUTE

```
                Ch. Stylobate of Sharvogue    Ch. T.M.G. of Marienhof
        Dorem Spotlight                       Wild  Honey  of  Sharvogue
                Ch. Dorem Dubonnet            Ch. Flieger of Edgeover
                                              Jill of Wollaton II

ex CH. DOREM SILVERETTE
                Ch. Timothy of Sharvogue      Falcon of Sharvogue
        Ch. Dorem Escapade                    Ch. Freifrau of Edgeover
                Ch. Dorem Diva                Ch. Jeff of Wollaton
                                              Jill of Wollaton II
```

CH. DELEGATE OF LEDAHOF and CH. DIPLOMAT OF LEDAHOF

```
                Ch. Stylobate of Sharvogue    Ch. T.M.G. of Marienhof
        Dorem Spotlight                       Wild Honey of Sharvogue
                Ch. Dorem Dubonnet            Ch. Flieger of Edgeover
                                              Jill of Wollaton II

ex CH. ENCHANTRESS
                Ch. Sandman of Sharvogue      Ch. T.M.G. of Marienhof
        Ch. Dorem Liberty                     Wild Honey of Sharvogue
                Ch. Dorem Excapade            Ch. Timothy of Sharvogue
                                              Ch. Dorem Diva
```

CH. MELDON'S RUFFIAN

```
                CH. DOREM DISPLAY             Dorem Cockade
        Ch. Dorem Tribute                     Ch. Dorem Searchlight
                Ch. Dorem Silverette          Dorem Spotlight
                                              Ch. Dorem Excapade

ex MELDON'S MEMORIES
                Ch. Dorem High Test           CH. DOREM DISPLAY
        Meldon's Mar Mose                     Ch. Imprudent of Sharvogue
                Ch. Dorem Highlight           Ch. Stylobate of Sharvogue
                                              Ch. Dorem Dubonnet
```

✻ Virtually all of today's winners and producers trace to one or more of the above four DISPLAY sons.

CH. DOREM HIGH TEST
            Ch. Marko of Marienhof   Ch. Marko von Beutenberg
    Ch. T.M.G. of Marienhof   Mehitable of Marienhof II
            Tyranena Pansy of Marienhof   Ch. Porgie of Marienhof
                                                      Abigail of Marienhof

ex CH. IMPRUDENT OF SHARVOGUE
            Ch. Bleuboy of Sharvogue   Falcon of Sharvogue
    Wild Honey of Sharvogue   Ch. Allsworth Gossip
            Woots of Sharvogue   Falcon of Sharvogue
                                                      Ch. Freifrau of Edgeover

CH. MELDON'S MERIT
            Ch. Norcrest Enuff   Ch. Rufus of Marienhof
    Loki of Appletrees   Desire of Marienhof
            Ch. Dorem Liberty   Ch. Sandman of Sharvogue
                                                      Ch. Dorem Escapade

ex EXOTIC OF LEDAHOF
            Dorem Spotlight   Ch. Stylobate of Sharvogue
    Ch. Enchantress   Ch. Dorem Dubonnet
            Ch. Dorem Liberty   Ch. Sandman of Sharvogue
                                                      Ch. Dorem Escapade

AM. & CAN. CH. BENROOK BEAU BRUMMELL
            Ch. Kubla Khan of Marienhof   Ch. T.M.G. of Marienhof
    Ch. Kismet of Marienhof   Ch. Kathleen of Marienhof
            Ch. Neff's Mehr Licht   Eric von Neff
                                                      Mix of Marienhof

ex CH. KAREN OF MARIENHOF II
            Ch. Opal Heinzelmannchen   Balzar v.d. Zwick
    McLuckie's Opal's Gal   Carmen Heinzelmannchen
            Ch. Lucky of Marienhof   Ch. T.M.G. of Marienhof
                                                      Amarantha of Ravenroyd

CH. GENGLER'S DRUM MAJOR
            CH. DOREM DISPLAY   Dorem Cockade
    Ch. Diplomat of Ledahof   Ch. Dorem Searchlight
            Ch. Enchantress   Dorem Spotlight
                                                      Ch. Dorem Liberty

ex SALTY IMP
            Ledahof's Sentry   Falcon of Palawan
    Countess Reta of Ledahof   Neff's Risque
            Ch. Exclusive of Ledahof   Loki of Appletrees
                                                      Ch. Enchantress

CH. BENROOK ZORRA
            Ch. Meldon's Mignon   Ch. Dorem High Test
    Ch. Benrook Basil   Ch. Dorem Highlight
            Ch. Karen of Marienhof II   Ch. Kismet of Marienhof
                                                      McLuckie's Opal's Gal

ex BENROOK BREEZIE
            CH. DOREM DISPLAY   Dorem Cockade
    Benrook Beegee   Ch. Dorem Searchlight
            Ch. Meldon's Manana   Ch. Dorem Tribute
                                                      Meldon's Mar-Mose

Ch. Karen of Marienhof II

The dam of Am. and Can. Ch. Benrook Beau Brummell, the outstanding producer, Ch. Karen of Marienhof II, brings in an additional Heinzelmannchen import through Opal, but as a double grandson of T.M.G., is not an outcross either. Karen was a remarkable producer, serving as foundation for Shirley Angus' successful Benrook Kennels. Each of her four champion offspring were producers of note. Her son, Ch. Benrook Buckaroo (by Tribute) is the sire of 17 champions, from which five more generations of top producing sires descend. Karen's son Ch. Benrook Basil produced Ch. Benrook Banning (9 Chs.). Karen's daughter Ch. Benrook Ben-Gay (4 Chs.) is the dam of Ch. Flirtation Walk Tiara (by DISPLAY), who in turn produced six champions as well as a daughter that produced five.

The remaining three top producing DISPLAY sons came later in his stud career, and were line-bred, already carrying from two to five lines from him.

Ch. Gengler's Drum Major, whelped in 1951, carried two lines to DISPLAY, one from Diplomat. Ch. Meldon's Ruffian, whelped in 1950, was out of Meldon's Memories, who carried a line to both Tribute and High Test. Most intensely line-bred of all, Ch. Benrook Zorra carried five lines to DISPLAY, two from High Test and one from Tribute.

The CH. BENROOK ZORRA branch

Ch. Benrook Zorra sired six champions, all from different dams, and all located in the midwest. None, however, were champion producers, and this "branch" from DISPLAY can be left here.

The CH. GENGLER'S DRUM MAJOR branch

Ch. Gengler's Drum Major sired seven champions, including a son, Ch. High Potentate of Gengl-Aire (out of a Drum Major daughter) with five champions. The tail-male line of top producers, however, ends here.

There are active tail-female lines stemming from Drum Major, the main family connection being through the DISPLAY daughter, Ch. Flirtation Walk Tiara. The Tiara granddaughter, Blikaywin Pixie's Peggy, bred to Potentate, produced the foundation stock for the dozen Kansho champions bred in Texas by Margaret Brown. Among the four champions sired by Mrs. Brown's multiple Group winning Potentate son, Ch. Winposa Arch Rival, was Ch. Kansho's Sugar Time, with four lines from Drum Major.

Sugar was selected by Carol and Gerald Somers to blend with their original family based on the Drum Major granddaughter, Ch. Rosalinde von Brittanhof II. Over two dozen Zomerhof champions have emerged based on the

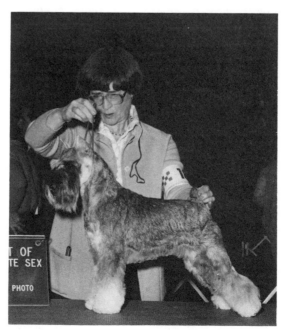

Ch. Zomerhof's Glory B the 25th champion owned by Zomerhof, is pictured with her breeder-owner Carol Somers.

Ch. Kansho's Sugar Time

Ch. Rosalinde von Brittanhof II

combination of Sugar and Rosalinde offspring. The Somers are currently into their ninth generation of homebreds from their Michigan Kennel.

The Somers selected the Diplomat branch to complement their foundation stock, basically breeding to studs tightly line-bred within this branch. Their top producer to date is Am. and Can. Ch. Zomerhof's Ruffy Ringo (7 Chs.). A recent Zomerhof champion, the multiple Group winning Am. and Can. Ch. Zomerhof's Limited Edition, carries 32 lines to Drum Major. He is on his way as a producer, with seven champion get from his first crop of youngsters.

In retrospect, Mrs. Somers remembers both Rosalinde and Sugar as follows:

> Rosalinde was Jerry's dog from the minute she came to live with us. She read the paper with Jerry every night, lying next to him in his big easy chair. Sugar was most appropriately named. She was sweetness personified and loved everyone. I feel her wonderful temperament came right down through Kim and Ringo and all of his offspring. It was a good beginning—from Rosalinde and Sugar our temperaments have been so enjoyable. Kim was just short of 15 when she died of various old age complications, and Ringo lived past 15. We are especially pleased with the longevity within our line.

Drum Major has his broadest extension in modern pedigrees through his son, Ch. Bramble of Quality Hill. The Bramble son, Ch. Wid's Von Kipper, CDX can be found behind many of today's top winners and producers, as the maternal grandsire of the highly influential Ch. Sky Rocket's Uproar (35 Chs.), one of the cornerstone sires of the Ruffian branch.

Ch. Dorem
High Test

The CH. DOREM HIGH TEST branch

Ch. Dorem High Test was from DISPLAY's first litter and became his first champion son. The circumstances were aptly described by Dorothy Williams (Dorem) in an earlier chapter. As the sire of 15 champions, he stands fourth among DISPLAY's nine top producing sons. High Test was purchased as a puppy by Audrey Meldon, who at the time also owned DISPLAY and his son, Tribute.

High Test was an immediate success in the show ring and as a sire. He finished at eight months and produced his first litter at ten months, out of Ch. Dorem Highlight (litter sister to DISPLAY's dam). The High Test-Highlight combination had a great impact on the breed, producing four champions plus five others that produced champions. Foremost among them were Ch. Meldon's Mignon (5 Chs.) and Meldon's Mar Mose (3 Chs.).

The tail-male line of top producers from the High Test branch traces only two generations further, ending with Ch. Benrook Banning, a Mignon son. Banning carries two lines to High Test, the other through his maternal granddam Mar Mose. Although Banning sired nine champions, he leaves few, if any modern descendants.

The current lines to Mignon come primarily through his son, Ch. Dody's Dimitri, and two daughters, Ch. Dorem Inspiration and Ch. Phil-Mar Lady Be Good. Dimitri, inspite of his spectacular breed "first" as Best in Show at Montgomery County from the classes in 1955, was little used at stud and left only two champions. He is one of nine champions bred in Maryland by Dorothy Goldsworthy, all descending from the DISPLAY daughter, Ch. Ben-

(L to R) Leda Martin (Ledahof) with Ch. Sorceress of Ledahof, Marguerite Jones (Minquas) with Minquas Vivacious and Dorothy Goldsworthy (Dody) with Ch. Benrook Bon-Bon of Marienhof at Morris and Essex in 1948.

rook Bon-Bon of Marienhof. Dimitri carries a line to three DISPLAY branches —High Test, Tribute and Merit—and figures prominently in current west coast bloodlines as the sire of Ch. Minquas Alicia.

Marguerite Jones, also in Maryland, began working with Marienhof stock during the 1940s. There were ten homebred Minquas champions, nine of them descendants of the DISPLAY daughter, Minquas Vivacious. Mae Dickenson's Delfin strain was founded on two Minquas bitches, Ch. Minquas Athena, a Vivacious daughter, and Ch. Minquas Merry Elf, a Tweed Packet daughter. There would be 20 homebred Delfin champions, the "star" being Ch. Delfin Janus (34 Chs.).

It was the Dimitri daughter, Ch. Minquas Alicia, that would bring more High Test blood to the west coast, as foundation matron for the Mutiny Kennel. Alicia gave them five champions, including Ch. Mutiny Coquette, foundation matron for the California-based Windy Hills (see DIPLOMAT branch).

Ch. Meldon Mignon's daughter, Ch. Dorem Inspiration is the key behind all the top producing Helarry dogs (see RUFFIAN branch), through the Inspiration son, Ch. Dorem Choice Play. The foundation matron at Helarry, Helarry's Delsey, is a Choice Play granddaughter. He is also the great-grandsire of yet another Helarry matron, Ch. Dorem Symphony II. Choice Play's litter sister, Dorem My Play, can be found in the Michigan-based Budhof, Multi-Lakes and Miown families (see BEAU BRUMMEL branch).

Mignon sired two early Phil-Mar champions, including Ch. Phil-Mar Lady Be Good, the dam of Ch. Perci-Bee's First Impression (15 Chs.) from which so many top producers descend.

66

In addition to Mignon, the High Test-Highlight combination produced three non-champion Meldon bitches of note: Meldon's Mar Mose, Marie and Shirley A. The broadest impact came through Mar Mose. Her granddaughter Ch. Benrook Bona (by DISPLAY) has a family of her own, based on her nine Handful champions. The Mar Mose son, Ch. Meldon's Sea Biscuit, is behind Barclay Square's foundation bitch, Trayhom Truly Fair, CD. Most importantly, Mar Mose's daughter, Meldon's Memories, bred back to DISPLAY, produced Ruffian, who has a branch of his own.

Also from the High Test-Highlight combination, Meldon's Shirley A became foundation for the Orchardlawn Kennel in Indiana, giving them five champions. Meldon's Marie produced Benrook Vogue (by DISPLAY), foundation for the Elflands.

Florence Bradburn's Elfland Kennel was well established in Southern California when DISPLAY emerged on the scene. Miss Bradburn bred several champions during the forties based on her original foundation bitch, Vanessa Anfiger, bred by Anne Eskrigge. In the summer of 1952 Florence met Ben Burwell, a highly regarded professional handler who had come to California to show some dogs from the east coast. According to Florence:

Ch. Fancy Filly of Elfland with Florence Bradburn

Ben put me in touch with Mac Silver, the manager of Benrook Kennel, who sent me Benrook Vogue (DISPLAY-Meldon's Marie) and the beautiful Benrook Jewel II (Ch. Benrook Buckaroo-Benrook Brilliance). Ben was out here at the time of Jewel's first show, and he handled her to a five-point win from the puppy class. I finished her championship very easily myself.

Both Benrook bitches sent to Elfland carried lines to High Test, and eventually were meshed to form the Elfland family, which is still active after four decades. The quality of the Elfland breeding program reached its zenith with the advent of Ch. Samos of Elfland who was Best in Show (entry of 1,850 dogs) at the Santa Anna Kennel Club in 1964.

The story of Elfland and its pioneer breeder Florence Bradburn, also involved important research on eye problems which existed in the breed. It was Florence who first took the initiative to "tell it like it is," which she again does here.

During the late fifties I began to hear rumors of blindness in Miniature Schnauzers, even in some that I had bred, and in 1961 I saw the defect for myself in a litter in my own kennel. My veterinarian, Dr. Raymond Wietkamp, examined the puppies, and we decided that at least four of the six were affected. In an effort to obtain as much help as possible, we telephoned Dr. Robert Cello who headed the Ophthalmology Department at the Veterinary College, Davis, University of California, which is Dr. Weitkamp's school. Dr. Cello said that he would be delighted to help if we would send the puppies to him. They were hand-delivered to him, and were never heard from again.

I decided then that I wanted to satisfy my curiosity as to whether the defect actually was transmitted as simple recessive. But losing that litter meant that I had no breeding stock except probable carriers. I then wasted considerable time breeding a possible carrier dog to his dam (our affected litter was from her) and to his sisters. No cataracts. Discouraged with the whole thing, I allowed the owners of these bitches to breed to other studs, and in a short time we had several affected puppies to raise. Also, at this time an adult bitch of my breeding was made available. I still needed an affected stud dog. Then along came Charlie B, whose third owner, Kay Erwin, made him an active part of our program, and we could do as much breeding as we wished.

There were others aware of the problem at the same time, or even before, I was. Dr. Robert Huber visited my kennel to see if we were talking about the same defect, and he sent out a young affected male which died before we could use him. Joan Huber was actively interested, and shortly thereafter, Jeanette Schulz, M.D., a geneticist, joined the battle to make breeders face the facts. In my area many people were interested and helpful, particularly Dorothy and Ivan Mayberry of Dorovan Kennel.

Dr. Weitkamp was my ally throughout, and when in early 1968 there had been eight litters which seemed to demonstrate the mode of inheritance, he wrote Dr. Richard Donovan at the Retinal Foundation in Boston. He told him that we knew of his interest in cataract research, and that if the results of the breeding that I had been doing were of sufficient interest to him, we would appreciate hearing from him. Dr. Weitkamp also vouched for the accuracy of my records, and as a result several of my affected animals went to Dr. Donovan, and I learned how to do genetic pedigrees.

It was through these early efforts that the American Miniature Schnauzer Club formed the Committee on Eye Problems, initially headed most effectively by Dr. Schulz. Currently there are hundreds of Miniature Schnauzers that have successfully been test-bred for congenital juvenile cataracts (CJC), and the program is ongoing. If the large base of tested stock continues to dominate, this defect can be completely eradicated.

Although lines to the DISPLAY son, Ch. Dorem High Test, can be found in current show stock throughout the country, it was in California that this branch came forward with the greatest impact.

The Elfland family developed by Florence Bradburn was the first to bring High Test blood to the west. The success of this branch was greatly enhanced by the efforts of Ruth Ziegler's Allaruths. In the early 1950s, Mrs. Ziegler acquired Doman Mehitabel, CDX from Frederick von Huly, a breeder of some years both in the east and west. Blinken of Mandeville was selected as the sire for the first litter raised by Ruth. He was a litter brother to the top winning bitch of that period, Ch. Forest Nod of Mandeville, a two-time Best in Show winner. Blinken and Nod were sired by High Test, and out of a High Test granddaughter. The Blinken-Mehitabel breeding produced Ch. Frevohly's Best Bon-Bon, UD, the breed's first Champion - Utility Dog. Bon-Bon was described by Ruth as a bitch with both beauty and brains.

> She was unfailingly gay and inquisitive, affectionate and companionable. The fact that she was of good heavy bone with a lovely head meant little to me in my total inexperience. The fact that she was a good clear salt and pepper meant less. It was only that personality-wise we were in accord. "Shatzie" and I had an understanding that trancends words or actions and is simply implicit in our relationship.
>
> When she was six months old her obedience training began. Schatzie was a bright, quick learner and never resented discipline, but she was enamored of the world and all its interests and it was difficult to maintain her attention. When it was time to enter her in competition, a problem developed. I showed her three times in Novice and three times she gave a brilliant performance—and flunked. After being left on the Recall, she could not wait to be called but would bound down the ring to me before she ever heard "Schatzie come." And so we failed to qualify although we were going for 199 and 198 scores. A change of handlers seemed indicated, so June Williams took over and together they gained the CD degree.
>
> In the meantime, Schatzie also began her show career. At 11 months she was Best of Winners and Best Opposite Sex at the Golden Gate K.C. in January 1955 and finished by going Best of Breed at Del Monte in May. She was handled at all times by Ric Chashoudian, who also finished all five of Schatzie's champion kids as well as several grandchildren.

Ch. Frevohly's Best Bon-Bon, UD

Over the years Schatzie was bred to four different dogs of rather different type. I found it interesting to experiment with bloodlines and outcrossed her on three occasions. But in every case, she has produced what I call "Schatzie puppies." They are exceptionally strong in bone, coat, head and substance.

Bon-Bon was the first western-bred bitch to produce five champions, and for her entire lifetime held the record as the west's top producing bitch. It was her breeding to Ch. Marwyck Pitt-Penn Pirate that proved most significant. From it came Allaruth's Jolly Anne (3 Chs.), plus Chs. Allaruth's Jorgette and Joshua. The latter, as the sire of Ch. Allaruth's Jericho (ex Cookie v Elfland) has brought this family forward to the present.

Jericho was shown extensively in the early 1960s, and was twice Best of Breed at the Northern California Specialty. He sired seven champions, all from line breedings. When bred back to the Bon-Bon daughter, Ch. Allaruth's Miss Dinah Mite, he produced Ch. Allaruth's Jasmine, the dam of the cornerstone sire, Ch. Landmark's Masterpiece.

The Jericho daughter, Ch. Allaruth's Jemima, out of Fran Cazier's foundation bitch, Minchette Maier (6 Chs.), became the foundation for Dr. Jeanette Schulz's Janhofs, giving her two champions, including Ch. Janhof's Bon-Bon of Adford, who numbers among her four champion get, Ch. Orbit's Lift Off, CDX, foundation for Carol Parker's very successful Skyline family.

The Allaruths, Orbits and Skylines are treated more fully in the chapter on the Diplomat branch.

Minchette
Maier

Ch. Allaruth's
Jemima

The CH. MELDON'S MERIT branch

Ch. Meldon's Merit sired nine champions, five sons and four daughters. The current lines of descent from this branch were brought forward primarily through the Merit sons, Ch. Handful's Me Too of Marienhof (see DIPLOMAT branch) and Ch. Kenhoff's I'm It. The major family from the Merit branch comes through his daughter, Ch. Dody's Rhapsody, the granddam of Ch. Dody's Dimitri, discussed earlier in relation to the High Test branch.

The tail-male line of top producers from Merit extend only three generations, beginning with his son, Ch. Kenhoff's I'm It (8 Chs.) and ending with the I'm It grandson, Ch. Glenshaw's Gadget (7 Chs.).

In the late 1940s and early 1950s, activities in the northern Pennsylvania and Ohio areas hosted by members of the Penn-Ohio club, played a major role in the breed's advancement. Marion Evashwick's Marwyck family based on Sorceress provided a number of breeders with foundation stock. Much of the remainder came from Grace and Herb Kaltoff's already well-developed Kenhoff family.

Built from lines to T.M.G., and brought forward by their Ch. Gracon Canis of Kenhoff (5 Chs.), the Kenhoffs were in good stead when DISPLAY emerged. The Tribute-Canis daughter, Kenhoff's Handsome Annie, bred to DISPLAY produced the sisters, Chs. Kenhoff's Katy Did Too and That's Me. Annie's sister, Belinda of Kenhoff, bred to Merit, produced I'm It. Their sons and daughters, blended with the Tribute branch, formed the foundation for the Glenshaw Schnauzers bred by Chris and Robert Snowdon.

I was a frequent visitor to the Spruce Knoll farm in Alison, Pennsylvania as a youngster, Chris and Bob playing a major role in my development. When in 1959 it came time to plan the first issue of *Schnauzer Shorts,* the cover dog was their Ch. Glenshaw's Gadget. The Snowdons had initially achieved great success in Cocker Spaniels with a breeding program begun in 1934. Many Glenshaw homebreds earned Specialty, Group and Best in Show awards, and several were leaving a lasting imprint on the breed. Backed by the practical knowledge gained in those early years, the Snowdons were to enjoy immediate success with their very first Miniature Schnauzer. Chris remembers it well:

The first young gentleman to come to our home was a five month-old puppy who later became Ch. Kenhoff's I'm It. He was the winner of the American Miniature Schnauzer Club trophy for having won the most Group placements in 1953. That year he was Best of Breed at Morris & Essex in the east and Harbor Cities in the west, as well as the Chicago International. When bred to Ch. Kenhoff's Katy Did Too, owned by Norman Austin, he produced Chs. Salt 'n Pepper Sampler and Salesman, as well as Salt 'n Pepper Scintillation, the latter purchased by Richard Matheny. She produced four champions for him, including his record-setting Ch. Fancy Free Fancy Package, the first of the breed to win over 100 Bests of Breed.

Ch. Kenhof's I'm It

Ch. Salt 'n Pepper Sampler

Ch. Glenshaw's Top O'The Mark winning the Terrier Group under Judge Maxwell Riddle, handled by breeder-owner Chris Snowdon.

I was extremely fortunate to make the acquaintance of Audrey Meldon while she owned DISPLAY and his two sons, Tribute and High Test (oh, that gorgeous, long, exaggerated head). I used to visit her, sit in her kennel and just watch all the many offspring of these dogs. I would ask who sired this one and that one—and always got an answer. I finally came to the conclusion that the way to do this was to line-breed closely to DISPLAY through his best producing sons —Tribute, High Test and Diplomat. It seemed to me that in most instances DISPLAY potency came through his sons, while that of Tribute was most evident in the bitches. So that is what we did, and for 23 years we never went out of this line.

There would be 18 Glenshaw champions, culminating in the Group and Specialty winning Ch. Glenshaw's Top O'The Mark, who carries seven lines to DISPLAY. Mark was the breed's No. 1 dog in 1962, the year the Knight System ratings were initiated. Glenshaw was disbanded a few years later. The Snowdons can presently be found enjoying life with a few dogs in the hills of Arkansas.

The AM. & CAN. CH. BENROOK BEAU BRUMMELL branch

The DISPLAY son, Am. & Can. Ch. Benrook Beau Brummell, sired 13 American champions, based principally on the Canadian connection provided by Ethel and William Gottschalk in Ontario. They purchased Beau Brummell in 1951, and he was Best of Breed at the first Specialty offered by the newly formed Miniature Schnauzer Club of Canada. He is behind all 14 Champions bred at the Gottschalk's Cosburn Kennel—five American, eight Canadian and one in South Africa.

The tail-male line of top producers from the Beau Brummell branch extends five generations, ending with Ch. Travelmor's Witchcraft (5 Chs.). The Beau Brummell grandson, Ch. Cosburn's Esquire, would be instrumental in bringing the tail-male line forward.

Esquire was a leading winner in the 1950s, beginning his show career as Winners Dog at the AMSC Specialty in February 1954, and finishing in six shows with five majors (RWD at Westminster). He won his 26th Best of Breed in November 1958, doing most of his winning while owned by Priscilla Deaver. Esquire sired Ch. Sparks Exotic (3 Chs.) for Mrs. Deaver (now Kelly) before going to the Yankee Kennel of Edward Boehm, and eventually to head William and Olive Moore's Travelmor Kennel in New Jersey.

The story of Esquire and that of Travelmor go hand in hand. It began in 1957, and as the Moores tell it:

Wish we could say that we knew Esquire from the beginning, but that beginning, like so many others, came in the form of Ollie's Christmas gift to Bill—Yankee's Dark Drama, known to us as "Melody," and our top bitch.

The dominant person behind all of what quickly followed was Ed Boehm, who sold us Melody. Edward Marshall Boehm, widely known as the world's most famed bird sculptor, was also a top dog breeder and judge. He could "put

74

Ch. Cosburn's
Esquire

Ch. Travelmor's Fantazio and Ch. Travelmor's Rango as youngsters with William Moore.

down" a Schnauzer as well as any handler. Because of him, and with his help, we learned a great deal about the breed in a comparatively short time.

It was together at Tom Gately's kennel that we first met Esquire. Ed felt, probed, posed and moved him—and was obviously impressed. He decided to buy him, and offered us a half interest. Tom showed Esquire for us all in November 1958, and at his last three shows, was pitted against one of the country's best known winners, Ch. Phil-Mar Lugar. We are mighty proud to say that Esquire won two out of three, retiring from the ring in this final burst of glory at nearly six years of age.

The Moores became the sole owners of Esquire in 1960, also acquiring much of the late Edward Boehm's breeding stock when his kennel was dispersed. All the early Travelmor champions, owner conditioned and handled, were based on their blend of Tribute bitches to the Beau Brummell branch through Esquire.

Do-it-yourselfers, the Moores took great pride in one dog in particular, achieving an outstanding record with Ch. Travelmor's Witchcraft, who had three lines to Esquire. The Moores remembered him as something special, right from the beginning, although a broken leg at five months of age might have ended it:

> "Crafty" had his leg in a cast for three weeks, hobbling around as we worried about his future. It turned out quite well, thanks to our terrific veterinarian friend, Dr. Armour Wood, and in no time the leg was normal.
>
> Shyly and slowly he came on, until before us stood the animal we had planned. We could see he had an impeccable topline, high tail-set, good front with excellent shoulder placement and a refined head. He had balance, and his movement both coming and going proved to be superior.
>
> Having bred and shown many Travelmor dogs to their titles, we would be kidding ourselves if we said that Crafty was other than a mighty fine Miniature Schnauzer. He would have to prove it . . . *the hard way*!

The hard way, of course, is owner prepared and handled, but Witchcraft had one remarkable advantage. He was one of those rare individuals that retained a superior double coat, reminiscent of the early Marienhof dogs. The Moores with judicious care were able to show him over a three-year span, never once being completely stripped. In all he won 64 Bests of Breed and 25 Group placements. Among several Specialty Bests was the AMSC at Montgomery County under the famed all-rounder Percy Roberts.

Witchcraft sired five champions, plus the good producer, Travelmor's Tattle Tale (3 Chs.). Most importantly, his son, Ch. Travelmor's Fantazio, exported to England, sired Eng. Ch. Buffel's All American Boy of Deansgate, England's all-time top producing sire, with nine champions (see BRITISH chapter).

An important addition to the family was made on March 16, 1971, when Jennifer Allen came to manage Travelmor. The Moores had advertised for a kennel maid in Dog World, and it was Jenny, then 19 years of age, who

Charles Marck awarding Ch. Travelmor's Witchcraft a Group placement in 1967, breeder-owner handled by Olive Moore.

Jennifer Moore with Ch. Travelmor's Turned On.

---

answered their needs. They are truly a family, now, as Jenny became their adopted daughter.

The Moores took a different tack in the mid-1970s, adding first-class members of the Delegate and Ruffian branches to their family, and with great success, both here and abroad.

Yet another line from the Beau Brummell branch through Esquire was developed by Elinor and Andrew Czapski in Connecticut. Andrel was founded in the late 1950s with the purchase of the Esquire son, Ch. Andrel's Viceroy. He sired seven champions, all with the Andrel prefix, and is behind seven more champions that would come from this breeding program through the mid-1970s. The Viceroy son, Ch. Andrel's Importance, became a Best in Show winner in 1965, and together with his sire, they won Best Brace in Show two years later.

Ch. Miown Exotic Poppy with Kathy Laughter.

Ch. Benrook Beau Brummell exerted much of his influence in the state of Michigan. More than half of his champion get came from the Multi-Lakes Kennel near Detroit. Most important of these was his son, Ch. Budhof's Stylist of Multi-Lakes, out of the line-bred DISPLAY daughter, Dorem My Play. This line was brought forward by the Stylist son, Miown Erich Von Brach (4 Chs.).

Harry and Patsy Laughter, along with their talented children, bred, conditioned and handled over 20 champions bearing their Miown prefix. The star was clearly Ch. Miown Exotic Poppy. Her tragic death as a yearling left quite a void. I saw Poppy on her second coat, as a puppy champion at the February 1969 AMSC Specialty in New York. Even at that age she was displaying talents that quickly made her one of the breed's all-time top winning bitches.

A champion at eight months, handled by Kathy Laughter, then a teenager, Poppy then went to professional handler Joanne Trubee for a 1969 campaign that netted her two all-breed Bests in Show, 13 Group placements and her second Michigan Specialty Best. That year has to go down in the record books as one of the best ever. In addition to Poppy's pair of Bests, 1969 saw Ch. Mankit's Alex of Dunbar win five Bests in Show, Ch. Abingdon Authority, four and Ch. Mankit's To The Moon, two.

There were five generations of Miown champions through the mid-1970s, and several current Michigan-based breeders carry Miown breeding in their foundation stock.

The Beau Brummell branch has its greatest effect to the present through yet another Cosburn export, Can. Ch. Cosburn's Deborah, founding matron at Brittanhof in Illinois. Mr. and Mrs. Charles Brittan purchased Deborah in 1951, and finished five champions from her three litters by Ch. Applause of Abingdon, CD.

There was an immediate spread resulting from these breedings. A daughter, Ch. Fricka von Brittanhof, produced five champions at Helen and Harry Wiedenbeck's Helarry Kennel in Illinois. Fricka was one of the first bitches to go to Ruffian. Their son, Ch. Helarry's Dynamite, headed Jinx Gunville's Merry Makers Kennel, and as the grandsire of Ch. Merry Makers Dyna-Mite (15 Chs.) brings forward this aspect of the Beau Brummell branch.

The Applause-Deborah son, Ch. Johannes von Brittanhof, provided a strong base for the Dansel and Alpine families. Johannes was owned by Donald Doessel, and is behind all his nine homebred Dansel champions, eight of them bitches.

This family was brought forward by Seme and Louis Auslander, also Illinois-based. Their purchase of Ch. Dansel Dutch Treat in 1965 began a breeding program that produced 14 Alpine champions, including the Best in Show winning bitch, Ch. Alpine Baby Ruth. The Auslanders chose to breed into the Tribute branch and came up with the top producing brace, Ch. Alpine Cyrus The Great (8 Chs.) and his son, Ch. Alpine Great Scott (7 Chs.). Two Alpine bitches were well placed, and have brought their bloodlines to the present. Ch. Alpine Double Dutch went to Dorothy and Edward Harvey in New Jersey, giving them four champions, plus two more generations of Deeanee homebreds. Alpine Ultra Violet went to Shirley and Robert Rains in California, giving them four champions, including the Best in Show winner, Ch. Rainbou's Tornado.

By the early 1960s another top producing Brittanhof bitch emerged in the double Deborah great-granddaughter, Typhoon von Brittanhof. Never bred to the same dog twice, Typhoon produced a champion in every litter save one, and that contained a dog with 12 points. Among her five champions was the Best in Show winner Ch. Rojo's Buster von Brittanhof.

Typhoon has an extraordinary line of champion descendants, numbering in the hundreds. These champions come mainly through her daughters, Ch. Thumbelina von Brittanhof and the sisters, Regatta and Ch. Salty von Brittanhof. Thumbelina stayed in Illinois with Hope and Charles Meland, and line-bred within the Tribute branch, gave them four Melandorf champions. Salty also stayed in Illinois to found the Iles Kennel of Mr. and Mrs. Jerauld Iles. They chose to outcross her, selecting Ch. Helarry's Harmony, from the Ruffian branch. This combination produced Ch. Harga's Covington (3 Chs.) and the bitches, Ch. Iles Heidi and Ch. Tasse Kuchen.

Ch. Dansel Dutch Treat

Typhoon von Brittanhof

Two Salty granddaughters have had a major influence on current top winning and producing lines. One of these, Ch. Harga's Terri (by Covington), served as foundation matron for Carl and Carol Beiles' Carolane Kennel in New York.

The other Salty granddaughter, Heather's Windy Weather (ex Kuchen), exerted her influence in the west, as foundation for Judy and Donald Smith's Jadee Kennel, now in Iowa.

Perhaps Typhoon's greatest impact came through her tightly line-bred granddaughter, Ch. Miranda von Brittanhof (ex Regatta). Purchased as a puppy by Mr. and Mrs. Charles Congdon, Miranda founded the Marcheim Kennel in 1967, along with Ch. Alpine Patent Pending, both of which they finished. All eight Marcheim champions trace to them. Line-bred within the Tribute branch, Miranda produced the multiple Group and Specialty winner, Ch. Marcheim Poppin' Fresh (26 Chs.). At Marcheim, he sired Ch. Marcheim Helzapoppin (ex Patent Pending), the sire of seven champions, but Poppin' Fresh's best effort came in the form of record-setting Ch. Hughcrest Hugh Hefner.

Bred by Rosemary and Harv Morehouse, Hugh Hefner's youthful career was managed by Judy and Chris Hughes of Hughcrest Kennel in Illinois. He served notice as a puppy, finishing at 11 months of age with a Group 1st. In six weeks of showing as a champion in 1972, he won two more Groups and a pair of Specialty Bests. Purchased in the spring of 1973 by Kelly Hoskins, he was turned over to Clay Coady who professionally managed his brilliant career thereafter. He finished 1973 as the No. 2 Schnauzer (Knight System).

Hugh Hefner was far and away the No. 1 Schnauzer for the next two years, and in 1974 established several new "one-year" records: the most Specialty wins (7), the most Breed wins (56), the most Group placements (36) and the most Knight points (1,354). In a career which spanned five years, Hugh Hefner was for a time the leading Specialty winner (14) and Breed winner (131). He still holds these records: Group wins (29), Group placements (92) and Knight points accumulated (2,413). His record of five Bests in Show is surpassed by only three others: Ch. Hi-Charge of Hansenhaus (10), Ch. Abingdon Authority (9) and Ch. Mankit's Alex of Dunbar (7); his Specialty record, only by Ch. Blythewood National Acclaim (17) and Ch. Penlan Peter Gunn (15).

Ch. Hughcrest Hugh Hefner sired 15 champions, including Ch. Hughcrest Harvey Wallbanger (8 Chs.), a double Poppin' Fresh grandson, whose get include Best in Show winning Ch. Glendee's Jose Floorbanger. Another Hugh Hefner son, Ch. Bokay Dandy Lion, has champion get here and in Japan, where he was exported in 1980.

The most important family being developed from Poppin' Fresh comes through his daughter, Jana PD, the dam of seven Regency champions, all sired by Ch. Skyline's Blue Spruce. The Regency successes are given further attention in the chapter on Ch. Meldon's Ruffian.

We have attempted in this chapter to examine the four branches from DISPLAY which have not progressed in tail-male, but have female lines still active. Although virtually all current show stock carry lines to Ch. Gengler's Drum Major, Ch. Dorem High Test, Ch. Meldon's Merit and Ch. Cosburn's Beau Brummell, they have been meshed with tail-male lines from the four stronger branches—those of Tribute, the brothers Delegate and Diplomat, and most emphatically, Ruffian.

**Ch. Marcheim
Poppin' Fresh**

**Ch. Hughcrest
Hugh Hefner
with Clay Coady**

7

The
Ch. Dorem Tribute
Branch

**Ch. Dorem
Tribute**

CH DOREM TRIBUTE, whelped July 2, 1946, was far and away the leader among DISPLAY's nine top producing sons. His record of 41 champion get is just one short of the numbers achieved by his illustrious sire.

Tribute was sold to Audrey Meldon as a three-month old puppy, and made an auspicious ring debut just four months later, going Best of Winners at the AMSC Specialty in New York. He was Reserve the next day at Westminster, where DISPLAY won the breed, and was Winners or better in five of the next seven shows, twice going Reserve to Ch. Dorem Delegate. Tribute's first appearance as a champion was exactly one year after his debut, defeated again at the AMSC Specialty and Westminster by DISPLAY. Then he took four straight breed wins, going on to two Group Seconds, and was not shown again by Mrs. Meldon.

How he returned to Dorem is explained by Dorothy Williams:

> After repeated efforts, I finally persuaded Mrs. Meldon to sell Tribute. Nicholas Daks and I bought him in December 1949, and I bought him outright a year later. He took Best of Breed every time shown by me except at the AMSC Specialty 1950, where he went Best Opposite Sex to my Ch. Dorem Inspiration, and at Westminster and the 1952 Specialty where he never made the grade. I consider his top win to be the Best of Breed award gained at the AMSC Specialty in February 1951, at almost five years of age.
>
> Tribute had only sired four champions when he came back to Dorem. Mrs. Meldon had pushed DISPLAY and High Test in preference to him. However, for us he sired 75 litters and had 37 more champions before his retirement at age 12. He died on July 17, 1959.

Whereas the breed since the 1950s is 99 percent DISPLAY, it is also 98 percent Tribute. There are few, if any American champions of the last three decades that do not carry hundreds of lines to Tribute. The Tribute branch also claims the largest number of top producing sires, nearly 60 of them tracing to him in direct tail-male line. In our examination of each of the other branches from DISPLAY, the name of Tribute will appear almost as a constant, and his influence is inestimable.

Tribute sired three top producing sons: Ch. Meldon's Seabiscuit (5 Chs.), Ch. Benrook Buckaroo (17 Chs.), and most importantly, Ch. Dorem Favorite (16 Chs.). The line from Seabiscuit extends only through his daughter, Ch. Minquas Athena, while there are six generations of top sires descending from Buckaroo and ten from Favorite.

The CH. BENROOK BUCKAROO line

Ch. Benrook Buckaroo had enjoyed considerable success as a young show dog before being purchased by John and Claire Specht to head their Jonaire Kennel in Mt. Pocono, Pennsylvania. Claire tells the story:

> John bought "Bucky" for my birthday in November 1952. He was already two years old, having finished his championship taking four Bests of Breed and four majors. He was specialed, but not extensively, in 1952, acquiring ten more Breed wins and several Group placements. Probably the finest win was at the AMSC Specialty in February where he went Best of Breed at just 18 months of age.

Her description of Buckaroo in his tenth year gives us some insight as to his type:

> "Bucky" looks just the same today at ten as he did at two—always making the most of himself with natural action and poise, showing his beautiful head, arched neck, excellent topline, deep chest and well-developed body. He still carries a hard coat and thick furnishings with a decided spring to them. He has always had a very sweet, "eager to please" nature.

55 Sires of 5 or more A.K.C. Champions trace in direct tail-male lines to Ch. Dorem Tribute

*Sires that are in *italics* produced fewer than 5 Champions, Eager (4) and Trademark (4) missing the mark by one.

A1 **Ch. Meldon's Seabiscuit (5)**

A2 **Ch. Benrook Buckaroo (17)**

    B1 *Ch. Jonaire Pocono High Life**

        C1 **Ch. Jonaire Pocono Rock 'N Roll (11)**

    B2 **Ch. Benrook Randy (10)**

        C2 **Ch. Melmar's Random Rain (5)**

            D1 **Ch. Melmar's Jack Frost (18)**

                E1 **Ch. Adford's Bob White (6)**

                E2 **Ch. Orbit's A-OK of Adford (5)**

                    F1 **Ch. Orbit's Time Traveler (5)**

                        G1 **Ch. Gandalf of Arador (5)**

A3 **Ch. Dorem Favorite (16)**

    B3 **Fanciful of Marienhof (10)**

        C3 **Ch. Yankee Pride Colonel Stump (15)**

    B4 **Ch. Dorem Original (13)**

        C4 *Ch. Geelong Playboy**

            D2 **Ch. Geelong Little Sargent (11)**

    B5 **Ch. Mankit's Adam (10)**

        C5 **Ch. Trayhom Tramp-A-Bout (7)**

        D3 **Mankit's Hector (6)**

        D4 **Ch. Winsomor Critique (5)**

            E3 **Ch. Fancway's Tom Terrific (6)**

    B6 **Ch. Perci-Bee's First Impression (15)**

        C6 **Ch. Phil-Mar Emmett (9)**

        C7 **Ch. Phil-Mar Thunderbolt (6)**

        C8 **Ch. Dorem Vanguard (6)**

        C9 **Ch. Phil-Mar Lugar (26)**

            D5 **Ch. Dorem Denominator (7)**

            D6 **Ch. Blythewood Main Gazebo (31)**

                E4 **Ch. Blythewood Chief Bosun (11)**

                E5 **Ch. Blythewood His Majesty (11)**

                E6 **Ch. Swinheim Salutation (6)**

Buckaroo sired 17 champions, ten for Jonaire, and half of these out of their foundation bitch, Ch. Winsome High Style, including Ch. Jonaire Pocono High Life, the sire of Ch. Jonaire Pocono Rock 'N Roll (11 Chs.). Buckaroo had left four champions at Benrook, and it is from these breedings that the tail-male and female lines progressed. Ch. Benrook Jewel II went to California to give a new start for the Elflands. Ch. Benrook Randy went to Maryann Vann to head her Belvedere Kennel in Illinois.

Randy was a leading winner in his day, with a record of two Bests in Show, and over two dozen Group placements from 40 Bests of Breed. He sired ten champions, most importantly a trio out of the Ruffian daughter Ch. Melmar's Rain Song, bred in Seattle by Mel and Virginia Schultz. These included the Best in Show winner Ch. Melmar's Random Rain (5 Chs.), who in turn produced the influential sire, Ch. Melmar's Jack Frost (18 Chs.).

Jack Frost was owned by Adele and William Staniford (Adford). With two lines to Ruffian, he was a departure from the lines and families developing in Southern California, and served as an outcross for the tightly bred Diplomat bitches of Allaruth, Fancway and Orbit breeding. He also carried the black and silver gene, and sired two champions of this then rare color variety, including the Group winner, Ch. Tiger Bo Von Riptide. Jack Frost produced a Best in Show winner in Ch. Samos of Elfland, but most importantly, two top producing sons and a top producing daughter.

The Jack Frost sons, Ch. Adford's Bob White (6 Chs.) and Ch. Orbit's A-OK of Adford (5 Chs.) both appear in modern pedigrees, the latter principally through his son Ch. Orbit's Time Traveler (5 Chs.), and his son, Ch. Gandalf of Arador (5 Chs.).

The Jack Frost daughter, Ch. Janhof's Bon-Bon of Adford, bred by Dr. Jeanette Schultz, has had the broadest impact on contemporary lines and families through her daughter (by Time Traveler) Ch. Orbit's Lift Off, CDX, foundation for all the Skyline top producers.

The CH. DOREM FAVORITE line

More than three-quarters of the top producing sires that descend from the Tribute branch came through his son (and maternal great-grandson) Ch. Dorem Favorite. He was obviously a "favorite" at Dorem, as Miss Williams describes:

> Ch. Dorem Favorite and his sister Fashion are probably the most similar pair of champions we ever bred. They are both pure silver. The dog is very masculine, taking after his sire, Tribute, and the bitch very feminine, as was her dam, Dorem Flair. Both parents were silver, although Tribute darkened with age.

Favorite, like so many of his predecessors from Dorem, enjoyed instant success in the show ring. He earned four points and a Group 3rd at his first show at nine months. At his next show a month later, he was Best of Breed at the AMSC Specialty for five points. The next day at Westminster he was

Ch. Benrook Buckaroo

Ch. Benrook Randy

Ch. Melmar's Jack Frost

Reserve, but his sister Fashion was Winners Bitch. Favorite won the breed in his next three outings, twice more gaining Group 3rds. Lightly shown in 1953, he added nine Bests of Breed out of 13 times shown.

Favorite's first litter produced Ch. Dorem Original (13 Chs.), out of the DISPLAY daughter, Ch. Dorem Choice Play. Original's career as a stud dog was sporatic, having been sold at the age of two years, and reacquired in January 1958. According to Dorothy Williams' records he sired 38 males and 50 females, from which emerged 13 champions as well as 16 others with champion descendants. Ch. Geelong Playboy came from his first litter and is behind ten Geelong champions bred by Randolph Higgins, including the top producing sire, Ch. Geelong Little Sargent (11 Chs.).

Original is best known for his outstanding daughters. Ch. Dorem Originality (ex Dorem Fame) is the dam of Ch. Dorem Denominator (7 Chs.) and Helarry's foundation bitch, Ch. Dorem Symphony II (4 Chs.). The Original daughter Ch. Allaruth's Miss Dinah Mite is the maternal granddam of Ch. Landmark's Masterpiece (32 Chs.). All the Winsomors and Barclay Squares carry lines to the Original daughter, Ch. Gunlad Meg. Robert Moore's foundation bitch, Ch. Benrook Bethel, by DISPLAY out of a Tribute daughter, produced Ch. Bethel's Original Ember (5 Chs.) by Original. Three Ember daughters, all by Ch. Helarry's Harmony from the Ruffian branch, advanced the Bethel family, producing foundation stock for Shorlaine, Shadowmark and eventually Carolane.

Ch. Dorem Favorite was used by Mrs. Slattery early in his stud career, giving her Fanciful and Ch. Fashion of Marienhof. Fanciful, although well over the size limit, was purchased by Mr. and Mrs. Peter Babisch to head their Yankee Pride Kennel in Michigan. Fanciful sired ten champions, including one of the top show dogs of the late 1950s and early 1960s, Ch. Yankee Pride Colonel Stump. Whelped July 13, 1956, he began his show career in January 1957, finishing with six Bests of Breed, a Group 1st, and Group 3rd at the last of the great Morris & Essex shows. He was then sold to Mrs. Joseph Sailer and turned over to professional handlers, Tom and Kay Gately, with whom he lived out his entire life. Shown a total of 95 times over a period of six years and ten months, he earned 80 Bests of Breed, 13 Group 1sts, 30 additional placements, and three Bests in Show. His Specialty record is equally impressive, including three consecutive AMSC and Mount Vernon Specialty wins, the last from the veterans class, October 13, 1963. Add to this his three consecutive breed wins at Westminster, along with a Group 2nd and 3rd, and we have a most extraordinary record.

Colonel Stump lived past 15 years, and left 15 champion get. Current lines to him can be found principally through the Dansel and Alpine families. Early on he was used by Andrel, Blythewood, Pfulhans and Sparks, but lines to these breedings seem not to have progressed.

The strongest tail-male lines from Ch. Dorem Favorite were brought forward by a breeding program begun in the 1960s, based on DISPLAY's last, and most important champion daughter, Ch. Gladding's Bie Bie (10 Chs.). Bred

Ch. Dorem Favorite

Ch. Dorem Original

Ch. Yankee Pride Colonel Stump

by Mary Seamans of New Hampshire, Bie Bie was purchased as a puppy by Mr. and Mrs. Emanuel Miller of Indiana. Their initiation into the breed was clearly the beginning of a love affair that has lasted to the present, although breeding and showing at Mankit ceased in 1971. Kitty Miller describes those beginning years so well:

> In December 1957, when we learned from our good friends, Ben Burwell and Wendell Sammett, well known handlers in the east, that a daughter of DISPLAY was available, we decided that she would be our Christmas present to each other that year.
>
> We met a plane in the middle of the night during a snow storm. This gift had no gala wrappings, but was a shipping crate marked *Live Dog*. We could hardly wait to set it down in the kitchen and open it. When we did, out walked Gladding's Bie Bie into our arms and into our hearts.
>
> Soon afterwards we attended the Westminster show and made arrangements with Julayne Kirk, a then teenage girl interested in dogs from Junior Showmanship days, to keep her while we were gone. Julayne asked if she might show Bie Bie at Marion, Indiana, and there she won her first two points. Next Bie Bie was shown at the Chicago International where she went from American-Bred to Best of Winners and BOS for five points. Three weeks later after three shows in Ohio, she completed her championship with four majors.

The Millers selected the Tribute son, Favorite, for Bie Bie's first breeding, and from it came their first four champions. The lone male, Ch. Mankit's Adam, was the first to finish, followed closely by Chs. Mankit's Ada, Alfreda and Augusta.

Rarely does a first homebred champion from an unestablished breeding program receive much recognition from the fancy. Adam was an exception and sired ten champions, including a pair for Blythewood and Winsomor. His most important son for several reasons was Ch. Trayhom Tramp-A-Bout (ex Handful's Snow Flurry). The Mankit and Trayhom families, both human and canine, were as one throughout the 1960s. Wayne and Twylla Miller (Trayhom) were not only successful breeders, but as professional handlers, almost exclusively of Mankit stock, brought both prefixes into national prominence.

Tramp-A-Bout was not the first Trayhom champion, but surely one of the best. He was given a grand reception as a youngster. Tramp came to the AMSC Specialty in February 1961 as an 11-months puppy, already with both majors. Judge William Kendrick carried him through Best of Breed, and his comments were glowing:

> Bred-by-Exhibitors had four present. First to Trayhom Tramp-A-Bout. Stood out. A highly satisfying Schnauzer if he does not grow any more. His head is of rare quality with a good flat skull and good depth of foreface of balanced length. His neck fits nicely into well laid shoulders. A level topped one with good depth, the ribbing carries well back. Thus, with his broad loin the so desired right kind of underline is achieved. He has wide quarters with well let down hocks with

Ch. Gladding's Bie Bie (below) with her first four champions from her first litter. (L to R) Chs. Mankit's Adam, Alfreda, Ada and Augusta.

Ch. Mankit's Yo Ho

Ch. Mankit's Xerxes

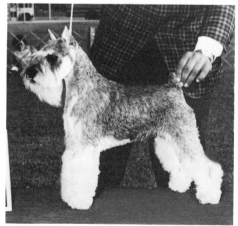

93

good length of stifles. Owns ample bone and good feet. His movement at both ends is what is wanted.

Tramp completed his title with five Bests of Breed and a Group 1st, and added two more Group wins on his first specials coat before his untimely death at just 15 months of age. His few litters were born at Trayhom, Mankit or at Mildred and Howard Amato's Winsomor Kennel in Ohio. Tramp's blood flows most prominently in west coast lines through his son, Ch. Winsomor Critique (5 Chs.) and his son, Ch. Fancway's Tom Terrific (6 Chs.). Most importantly, Tramp can be found in the pedigrees of two record-holding bitches. He is the paternal grandsire of the breed's top dam, Ch. Faerwynd of Arador, and the paternal great-grandsire of the breed's top winning bitch, Ch. Winsomor Miss Kitty. Shown 32 times as a champion, from January through October 1966, Miss Kitty's record stands at 29 Bests of Breed, including two Specialties, 15 Group 1sts and three Bests in Show.

The three champion sisters of Ch. Mankit's Adam were like peas in a pod, their heads almost identical. How Augusta became a favorite is best told by Kitty:

> As inexperienced as we were, we seemed to realize almost from the beginning that "Gussie" was very special. It is ironic that she is the one who was with us from the first to the last, as she died in our family room of smoke inhalation the night of the fire. "Gussie" wasn't bossy or aggressive—she didn't have to be, as the others just naturally seemed to defer to her and she accepted the role. She was always kind and protective to the others. I remember once when two others had litters about the same time she did, and was the self-appointed supervisor of the maternity ward, not only watching her own, but from time to time, even at night, checking and inspecting the others, too.
>
> "Gussie" was a good-sized bitch—13¾ inches, which is probably one of the reasons she was such a good brood bitch. I'll never forget her beautiful head, as it could be seen again and again in her descendents. One year she was not only the top producing Miniature Schnauzer dam, but also tops among all the terriers.

Although Augusta's record of nine champion get fell one short of her dam's, she is behind 22 of the 32 champions bred at Mankit. Their choice of Ch. Phil-Mar Lugar as Augusta's first mate added more blood from the Tribute branch, and worked remarkably well. Ch. Mankit's Eager was the result. Although falling one short of the five champions designating a top producer, Eager leaves an extensive tail-male line, not only of top producers, but top winners as well.

As the Millers began line-breeding on Bie Bie, the results were a succession of multiple Best in Show winners. Ch. Mankit's Signal Go, by an Eager son, out of Augusta, was the trend-setter. He was a champion by ten months of age, and in a specials career which spanned five years (1964-1968), earned three Bests in Show, a "record" eight Specialty Bests, 24 Group 1sts and 48 additional placements, handled throughout his career by Wayne Miller.

Ch. Trayhom Tramp-A-Bout scores Best of Breed at the AMSC Specialty, February 1971, from the Bred-by-Exhibitor class under William Kendrick, shown by Twylla Miller.

Ch. Mankit's Signal Go

The Miller combination brought forth a sixth generation Mankit in 1968. The new youngster carried nine lines to Bie Bie, and an incredible 171 lines to DISPLAY. On the Montgomery County weekend that year, Mankit's To The Moon came to these events with one major and some single points. At the Devon Show he scored a five-pointer as Winners Dog, the breed going to his uncle, Ch. Mankit's Xerxes. At the AMSC Specialty To The Moon cleared the breed and later was selected Best in Show. A year later he returned to win an unprecedented *Second* Best in Show at Montgomery County, topping over 700 terriers.

To The Moon set several records before he and his handler, Wayne Miller, retired. This team accounted for 12 Specialty Bests, seven of these in 1969, the year in which he led the breed (Knight System) with the largest point total (877) to date, as well as earning two Bests in Show. These records are even more remarkable when one recalls that To The Moon was sharing the show circuit with kennel mate, Ch. Mankit's Alex of Dunbar, who was himself a record-setter, with seven Bests in Show.

With the retirement of their handlers and mentors in 1970, the Mankit breeding program tapered off, but not before 32 Mankit champions had been made up. The most important part of the Mankit influence is seen through the broad effects of their many outstanding stud dogs. Over 30 top producing sires trace from Ch. Mankit's Eager, representing more than half of those descending from the Tribute branch. Two Eager grandsons shared equally in this broad extension. Signal Go claims five top producing sons among his 21 champion get, including Ch. Mankit's Dashing Dennis (8 Chs.), the sire of To The Moon (11 Chs.) and Alex (5 Chs.).

Signal Go's younger brother, Ch. Mankit's Yo Ho (7 Chs.) claims fewer top producing sons, but has had a far greater impact on current lines and families. The Yo Ho sons, Ch. Marcheim Poppin' Fresh (26 Chs.) and Ch. Moore's Max Derkleiner (7 Chs.) have left a host of champion descendants, principally at Valharra, but also in the background of the Alpine, Hughcrest, Marcheim and Shirley's Schnauzers, and the many current families descending from them.

Shirley and Dick Willey were the first to bring Mankit bloodlines to the west coast. Their involvement with the breed began much sooner, having bred their first litter in 1968, sired by their first Miniature Schnauzer, Shirley's New Beau, CDX, and out of their second, Shirley's Sugar 'N' Spice, CD. The champions and obedience titlists from this combination were just the beginning. In the next two decades, and over six generations later, the Willeys could claim 24 homebred champions and almost an equal number of obedience winners descending from their initial blend.

In January 1970 Ch. Mankit's Bang Bang of Dunbar was acquired as an unshown yearling by the Willeys and successfully incorporated into their family. He sired seven AKC and two Japanese champions, as well as four obedience winners, two of them also conformation champions. Bang's best producing son is their Ch. Shirley's Show Time (7 Chs.) out of Ch. Shirley's Show Off, CD (4

Ch. Mankit's To The Moon
Best in Show at the Montgomery County Kennel Club All-Terrier classic in
1968 under James Farrell, Jr. (above) and again in 1969 under John Marvin
(below).

Ch. Mankit's Bang Bang of Dunbar

Chs.), and this family with both beauty and brains continues to flourish in California.

The tail-female aspect of the Mankit-Trayhom combination had as its principal torch bearer a bitch line-bred within the Diplomat branch. Trayhom Truly Fair, CD had produced a champion at Trayhom before being sold to Dale and William Miller to found their Barclay Square breeding program now well into their third decade.

Dale Miller describes those early years:

Trayhom Truly Fair, CD was the lady left behind in the dispersal of Trayhom Kennel, apparently because she was not quite a champion (she had 11 points with both majors). Twyla Miller gave me more truth than sales pitch when she said "Woody" would out-produce some of their champion girls. At 3½ years she came to Barclay Square. "Woody" is remembered by me mostly as a best buddy, but to others she is known mainly as the dam of Barclay Square Brick Silver, the only puppy retained from the two litters she produced for me.

Brick Silver is light years away from being a show specimen. To turn a phrase, where she is good she is very very good, and where she is bad she is horrid. I think it was Dorothy Williams (Dorem) who theorized that a breeder's bitch would most likely be one who might probably have glaring faults but must certainly be long in special virtues, rather than being one neither grim nor glorious anywhere. I chose to believe her and kept "Little John."

Trayhom Truly Fair, CD

Barclay Square Brick Silver

"John" is a huge, strong (but nowhere coarse), heavy boned, very dark-coated animal, superb and exaggerated in head and neck, with an unhindered working-dog like gait . . . all of which wouldn't be worth feeding were it not coupled with a gorgeous temperament. She has had her surprises and her consistencies. Her six litters numbered 1, 9, 9, 7, 8 and 1. Being prepotent in the extreme, her stamp is stronger than any other single dog of our stock. She, herself, was the image of her sire Ch. Winsomor Dubbl Y Money (a Tramp son, and double Adam grandson). The great majority of her puppies are distinctly HER. The most interesting exception is her best producing daughter, Ch. Barclay Square Becky Sharp, who is just as distinctly an outward reflection of her sire, Ch. Mankit's Signal Go. In contrast to "John," among Becky's 19 offspring, all full brothers and sisters, one is hard pressed to find two alike.

Brick Silver produced three champions and four top producers. Ch. Barclay Square Brickbat, a brother to Becky, sired nine champions, eight of them bearing Barbara Vohsen's Archway prefix. Two non-champion Brick Silver daughters also carried on, Barclay Square Bid To Fame producing four champions for Zomerhof in Michigan, and Barclay Square Bold Type, three at home. Becky proved to be the most influential of the Brick Silver offspring, and Dale recalls how it might never have been:

Ch. Barclay Square Becky Sharp wasn't meant to be! A funny thing happened on the way to the airport, and "Little John" was sent, through a

A litter of nine by Ch. Mankit's Signal Go out of Barclay Square Brick Silver. The two puppies at the left became Ch. Barclay Square Brickbat and Ch. Barclay Square Becky Sharp.

comedy of errors too involved to relate and too stupid to admit, to Ch. Mankit's Signal Go. Though Signal Go was then barely more than a pup, he was already one of my all-time favorites, and I can't say we were the least bit disappointed with the turn of events. "Little John" outdid herself with nine kiddies. We figured out of all those pretty pups there ought to be a winner (there were two). We kept Becky, and she was a champion at eight months, conditioned and handled by Wayne and Twyla Miller.

We do honestly believe in and endorse meticulously planned long-range breeding programs, and let there be no mistake about our intention to have Ch. Mankit's Xerxes sire Becky's first litter. Becky and Xerxes complemented each other in every detail, and their combined pedigree is an interesting web of inbreeding and line-breeding. What we hoped for from this first breeding and what we got are miraculously the same.

The first breeding produced an all-champion litter of four, including the Best in Show winning Ch. Barclay Square Be Grand, owned by Jeannette and Allen Stark of St. Louis. Be Grand sired three champions, but more importantly is the sire of Ted and Betty Bierman's foundation bitch, Ballwin Bonnie Bedelia, dam of five Ballwin champions in Texas, and Grace Church's Cinder von Kirche, CDX, dam of three Kazels champions in Missouri.

The Xerxes-Becky Sharp combination was repeated three more times, resulting in 19 puppies, 12 of them champions. It was Becky's last champion daughter, Bugle Ann, that brought the Barclay Square breeding program forward. Their bloodlines are well dispersed throughout the states, as well as in the Rosehill dogs of Canada. They have had an extraordinary influence on continental bloodlines through the seventh-generation Barclay Square littermates, Midas and Minx.

In the late 1970s, long-time Swedish breeders Benny and Ulla Blid (Maximin) imported Barclay Square Maximin Midas and Minx, out of the

100

**Ch. Barclay Square Brickbat and
Ch. Barclay Square Becky Sharp**

Bugle Ann daughter, Ch. Barclay Square Bugle Call Rag, and sired by Ch. Sky Rocket's Uproar. Dale's enthusiasm over their impact is clear:

> The Scandinavian connection did not die on the vine. I sent Midas and Minx when they were six months old to Benny, a friend not a stranger. He lives outside of Stockholm, and is well known as a breeder and judge. The two dogs are having an unbelievable impact on the breed there and in England.

Their continental influence is covered in the chapters on England and the Scandinavian countries.

The broadest extension of the Xerxes-Becky Sharp combination is found in Anne Lockney's Ruedesheim family in Oklahoma, where Xerxes lived out his retirement years. Two bitches from this family, Ruedesheim's Runzel and Ruedesheim's Splendor served as foundation for over a dozen Ruedesheim champions to date.

Mrs. Lockney chose the Delegate and Diplomat branches for her particular blend. From the Delegate side she chose Peter Gunn's best producing son, breeding Splendor to Ch. Penlan Peter's Son. Three champions emerged, including Ch. Ruedesheim's Entrepeneur (15 Chs.) who claims four top producing sons to date: Chs. Ruedesheim's Landmark, Momentummm and Encore of Wil-O-Be, and Ch. Aachen Sling Shot. Yet another current top winner and producer, Ch. Tomei Super Star, is out of a Splendor granddaughter.

Runzel was bred into the Diplomat branch, producing Ch. Ruedesheim's Free Spirit by Ch. Landmark's Masterpiece. Spirit, in turn, produced Landmark and Momentummm.

Returning to Tribute's most influential son, Ch. Dorem Favorite, we find that more than half of the top producing sires descending from Tribute carry

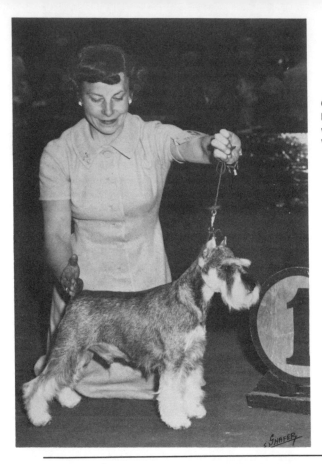

Ch. Perci-Bee's
First Impression
with Marguerite
Wolfe.

Ch. Phil-Mar Lugar

lines to the Favorite son, Ch. Perci-Bee's First Impression (15 Chs.). His handler, Marguerite Wolfe (Phil-Mar) remembered him with enthusiasm:

> Perci-Bee was a small dog that did a lot of winning. He was bred and owned by Claire T. Shelley of Huntington, New York. Claire bought Ch. Phil Mar Lady Be Good from me and bred her to Ch. Dorem Favorite, a gorgeous exaggerated dog. They produced Perci-Bee, at 13¼ inches, one of the greatest small terriers I have ever seen. He was perfectly balanced, with a long neck and beautiful head and expression. A showing fool, he actually asked for all his wins. He did not have the most desirable front. Because of his depth of chest and huge ribbing, his front legs were not closely placed. But could he move! He outshowed every terrier in the ring. He was not only beautiful, but had showmanship-plus.

Of further note is the enviable show record that Perci-Bee made in his relatively short career in the ring. His record includes 53 Bests of Breed and 26 Group placements. He led the breed in 1956, won four Specialties in a day which saw many fine champions being shown, and also was a Westminster breed winner. His early death at age 6½ cut short the full measure of a remarkable and valuable sire.

Although Perci-Bee left four top producing sons, the lines from Ch. Dorem Vanguard (6 Chs.), Ch. Phil-Mar Emmett (9 Chs.) and Ch. Phil-Mar Thunderbolt (6 Chs.) have not progressed. Perci-Bee's son, Ch. Phil-Mar Lugar (26 Chs.), however, has brought the line forward. An impressive list of over 35 top sires trace in direct tail-male to Lugar. He was unquestionably one of Peggy's favorites:

> My most beloved Ch. Phil-Mar Lugar, twice Best in Show, is a most remarkable dog—almost perfect, he was so well balanced. Lugar was one of the best moving dogs that I bred. He had gorgeous layback of shoulder, a level topline and beautiful length of neck with an arch. Lugar showed like he owned the world—head held high, with movement like he was floating on a cloud.

His quality was well rewarded. The breed's leading winner in 1959-60, Lugar won an all-breed Best each year and retired with a record of 70 Bests of Breed, including two Specialties. In Group competition he was placed 40 times, including a dozen Group 1sts. He was viewed positively by an ever-widening group of fanciers, and used extensively. Lugar sired 26 AKC champions, plus titlists around the globe. He produced six champions for Blythewood, including the outstanding sire, Ch. Blythewood Main Gazebo (31 Chs.).

Ch. Blythewood Merry Melody

Joan Huber of the Blythewood Kennel in Pennsylvania, became involved with the Tribute branch early on in a breeding program which began in the early 1950s and has produced over 100 champions. It was yet another instance in which one good bitch started it all. Mrs. Huber recalled it as follows:

> My first homebred, Ch. Blythewood Merry Melody was one of a litter of seven whelped on March 22, 1956, out of Minquas Blythe Spirit, CD and by Ch. Delfin Janus. She was my choice in the litter from the time she was born. Melody did well in the show ring, and her lovely, hard, steel-colored coat with her white furnishings and whiskers made her a crowd pleaser. Despite my novice, incompetent handling, she finished with three majors in stiff eastern competition. When I think back on those early shows now, I can count hundreds of mistakes I made in handling and grooming. I guess everyone's first show dog, which is owner-handled suffers the same way. However, you can never again have the good feeling that comes with finishing your first dog.

Melody founded an extraordinary family, bred exclusively within the Tribute branch, first with three champion daughters by Favorite, three more, along with a son, by Lugar, and her eighth champion, a daughter, by Perci-Bee. Ch. Blythewood Sweet Talk (Favorite-Melody) was chosen to bring this family forward, and did so with remarkable success, producing seven champions,

Ch. Blythewood Main Gazebo

including Gazebo, who leaves three top producing sons: Ch. Blythewood Chief Bosun (11 Chs.), Ch. Blythewood His Majesty (11 Chs.) and Ch. Swinheim Salutation (6 Chs.).

Blythewood has been a breeding kennel for over three decades and is a constant supplier of first-class foundation stock throughout the world.

Henrietta Tare in New Jersey has bred two dozen champions based on one bitch—Blythewood Shady Lady. She produced the first five Tare champions, four by Ch. Blythewood Ricochet of LaMay. Foremost among them was Ch. Tare Misty Morning, serving as foundation for Barbara Mazgiel's Contempras, giving her four champions. This family continues forward through Misty's son, Ch. Contempra Foolish Pleasure (7 Chs.), and daughter, Ch. Contempra Belle Starr. The latter, owned by Martin Marks (Markworth), gave him the good producer, Markworth Contempra Collage (4 Chs.), dam of the Top Bitch of 1985, Best in Show winning Ch. Markworth Lovers Lane.

Three other Tare bitches tracing to Shady Lady have become top producers: Tare Bruiser Barbie (3 Chs.), Ch. Tare Twenty-Four Karat (3 Chs.) and Tare-Royalcourt Happy Hooker (3 Chs.), the latter as foundation for Gloria Lewis' Royalcourts, also in New Jersey.

Homer and Isabel Graf round out the group in New Jersey who have based breeding programs on Blythewood stock. Ch. Blythewood Maid Marion

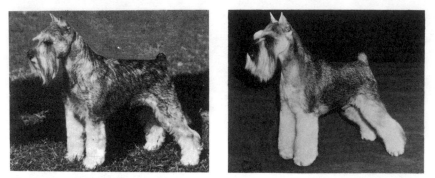

Ch. Blythewood Chief Bosun

Ch. Blythewood His Majesty

(3 Chs.), a daughter of Ch. Mankit's Adam, was the foundation bitch at Reflections, and two top producing bitches have since emerged. Ch. Reflections Refreshin' Image (3 Chs.) numbers among her get Ch. Reflections Lively Image (7 Chs.), who brought new life into the Travelmors.

In the west, Blythewood lines were brought forward by Jean Heath (Black Watch), with Blythewood Morning Star (6 Chs.), and by Earl and Marietta Hungerford (Hanalea). Three generations later, Hanalea's Pele's Pride (4 Chs.) would provide Jay and Janet Balch (Island) with a fine beginning.

Ch. Blythewood Honey Bun (Perci-Bee-Melody) may well have had the broadest impact on current winners and producers. She served as foundation for the Bon-Ell family developed in California by Jack and Dori Prosen. Honey Bun is the great-granddam of Ch. Landmark's Masterpiece (32 Chs.), as well as Can. Ch. Landmark's Spy of Rosehill, who leaves dozens of Canadian champion descendants.

Top dogs and top wins have been a tradition at Blythewood, starting with Ch. Blythewood Merry Maker (Favorite-Melody), one of the few bitches to win an AMSC Specialty. Chief Bosun was the No. 1 dog (Knight System) in 1966, after setting a record as a puppy. Joan remembers it with pride:

> We showed him exactly four weekends and each Sunday he was Winners Dog for a major. Sunday seemed to be "Sunny's" day to win! He went Reserve on the only three Saturdays shown. So in seven shows, still seven months of age, he had finished his champiionship. We are particularly proud of these wins since three of the majors were at three consecutive Specialties, including the AMSC, Montgomery County. We are told that this unusual career in the classes set a record for the breed.

As one of our leading professional handlers for over twenty years, Joan Huber has piloted many others to the No. 1 spot—her own Ch. Mutiny Uproar in 1970 and Homer and Isabelle Graf's Best in Show winning Ch. Sky Rocket's Bound To Win in 1973. She has had the pleasure of showing three

Blythewoods to Best in Show: Ch. Blythewood His Majesty, Ch. Blythewood Shooting Sparks and Ch. Blythewood National Acclaim, the latter a record-holder with 17 Specialty Bests.

Joan has been a trend-setter in grooming and presentation, and there has always been a "Blythewood style." When asked about her secrets, she replied:

> There really are no deep secrets, as such. Knowing your breed inside and out is a must. This knowledge is supposed to allow you to decide what visual appearance the breed should have in every detail of conformation. Once you have a mental picture of what the breed should look like, trimming is done to achieve the ideal. I'm a perfectionist! I devote a lot of time to "detail," starting with the health and conditioning of the animal.
>
> It is attention to detail that is of ultimate importance. A top groomer must have an eye for line and form, but the majority of breeders can achieve remarkable results if enough attention is given to basics, like the proper initial stripping, where attention is given to each animal's individual skeletal and muscular structure.
>
> I work hard toward clearly defining lines. I do not like a fuzzy look, with brows running into stop and side-lines. I like a "stylized" sharp look, neat in every detail.

A crusader on several levels, Joan had her way concerning one of the most important problems faced by Miniature Schnauzer breeders to this day. Her story bears repeating:

> A college education aimed at a teaching career found me highly motivated in the area of biology in general, and genetics in particular. However, it was not until 1961 and my marriage to Bob Huber that my interest was specifically directed to "modes of inheritance" of genetic problems. Being married to a veterinarian who was an associate of Dr. Lionel Rubin, one of the top canine ophthalmologists in the country, brought me in direct contact with up-to-date theories concerning inherited defects. Bob and I initiated a test-breeding program with Dr. Rubin's help, and came to accept the hypothesis concerning the mode of inheritance of congenital juvenile cataracts (CJC). We found it followed a very definite pattern and was a simple autosomal recessive gene. We made blind-to-blind breedings and got all blind; we bred carrier-to-carrier and got the simple Mendelian percentages. For over a year, we sold no puppies with papers for breeding or show, because all were the results of test breeding.
>
> As an "active" member of the AMSC board, I made a presentation on this medical problem. The results were "horrendous!" Word soon flashed across the nation, and back, that "all Blythewood dogs are blind!" But, I got what I wanted. The board did agree to appoint a committee to look into health problems. A small beginning, but "a beginning."

Her efforts, along with those of others (see the *Elfland story* in the DIPLOMAT chapter), have reaped rewards beyond measure. The problem of CJC is in a position to be completely eradicated, as long as tested animals continue to dominate in current breeding programs.

8

The

Ch. Diplomat of Ledahof

Branch

**Ch. Diplomat
of Ledahof**

SECOND RANKED among DISPLAY's top producing sons, Ch. Diplomat of Ledahof was the sire of 29 champions, the last of them whelped in 1956. Diplomat was undoubtedly a "favorite son" at Ledahof, where he enjoyed over 14 years as companion to his breeder, Leda Martin and her daughter Joan Dalton. He was the culmination of a breeding program that was launched in the late 1920s and highlighted by the "D Litter," containing Chs. Diplomat, Delegate, Destiny and Debutante of Ledahof.

Diplomat served notice as a prepotent sire early on, when line-bred to Mrs. Evashwick's great foundation bitch, Ch. Sorceress of Ledahof. The initial breeding produced four champion sons, one of which died at the age of two, while the others became top producers: Ch. Marwyck Scenery Road (9 Chs.), Ch. Marwyck Brush Cliff (7 Chs.) and Ch. Marwyck Penn Hurst (5 Chs.). Contemporary lines to this breeding trace principally through the Brush Cliff daughter, Doman Mehitabel, CDX, who is behind all the Allaruth dogs.

34 Sires of 5 or more A.K.C. Champions trace in direct tail-male lines to Ch. Diplomat of Ledahof

*Sires that are in *italics* produced fewer than 5 Champions, Master Spy (4), Eager Beaver (4) and Winsome Lad (4) missing the mark by one.

A1   Ch. Marwyck Scenery Road (9)
    B1   Ch. Applause of Abingdon, CD (6)
A2   Ch. Marwyck Brush Cliff (7)
A3   Ch. Marwyck Penn Hurst (5)
A4   Ch. Diplomat of Marienhof (11)
    B2   Ch. Handful's Bantam (10)
    B3   *Ch. Handful's Blue-Winged Teal**
        C1   Ch. Handful's Pop Up (8)
A5   Ch. Asset of Ledahof (10)
    B4   Ch. Marwyck Pitt-Penn Pirate (44)
        C2   Ch. Fancway's Pirate Jr. of LaMay (25)
            D1   Ch. Caradin Fancy That (9)
            D2   Ch. Blythewood Ricochet of LaMay (22)
                E1   Ch. Boomerang of Marienhof (10)
                    F1   Ch. Allaruth's Daniel (8)
                        G1   Ch. Valharra's Dionysos (28)
                            H1   Ch. Valharra's Big Sir (5)
                            H2   *Ch. Valharra's Studley Dudley**
                                I1   *Ch. Zomerhof's Archipelago**
                                    J1   Ch. Zomerhof's Limited Edition (7)
                    F2   *Allaruth's Hang-Up**
                        G2   Ch. Allaruth's Mama's Boy (5)
                            H3   Ch. Country Squire Soot N Cinder (5)
        C3   *Ch. Allaruth's Joshua**
        D8   Ch. Allaruth's Jericho (7)
A6   Ch. Delfin Janus (34)
    B5   Ch. Windy Hill Defiance (12)
    B6   Ch. Mutiny I'm Grumpy Too (17)
        C4   *Ch. Mutiny Master Spy**
            D4   Ch. Landmark's Masterpiece (32)
                E2   Ch. Skibo's Fancy Clancy (14)
                    F3   Ch. Far Hills Midnight Angel (5)
                    F4   *Ch. Glory's Eager Beaver**
                        G3   Ch. Sercatep's Strut N Proud (9)
                E3   Ch. Lanmark's Playboy (10)
                    F5   Ch. Playboy's Block Buster (22)
                        G4   Ch. Hi-Charge of Hansenhaus (11)
                        G5   Ch. Baws Strait Shot of Hansenhaus (5)
                    F6   Ch. Playboy's Special Edition (7)
                E4   *Ch. Walters' Irish Coffee **
                    F7   *Walters' Dapper Dan**
                        G6   Ch. Walters' Tradewinds (5)
                E5   *Ch. Blythewood Winsome Lad**
                    F8   *Ch. Cobby Land Rising Son**
                        G7   Ch. Eclipse Shadow of the Son (5)

Ch. Marwyck S.D. Comet   **Ch. Marwyck S.D. Cupid**

Lines to Scenery Road and his top producing son, Ch. Abingdon's Applause, CD (6 Chs.) can be found in current show stock carrying Brittanhof and Helarry breeding. This tail-male line had extraordinary success in obedience. Applause was for over two decades the leading sire of obedience titleholders with eight, including two CDXs and one UD. He heads one of only two lines with three generations of both bench and obedience titlists: Applause is the sire of Ch. Kundry von Brittanhof, CD, the dam of Ch. Pfauenbeck's Butcher Boy, CD. Second to Applause among sires of obedience titlists was until 1985, his uncle, Brush Cliff with seven, including three with CDX degrees.

Bred back to Diplomat, Sorceress produced the S.D. Comet, Cupid, Blitzen trio of champions, with Ch. Marwyck S.D. Comet by far the most important. As the dam of Ch. Marwyck Pitt-Penn Pirate (44 Chs.), her tail-male influence is enormous.

Mrs. Slattery (Marienhof) also used Diplomat early on in his stud career, getting his top producing namesake, Ch. Diplomat of Marienhof (11 Chs.) from which came in successive generations virtually all of the Handful champions bred by Gene Simmonds. Miss Simmonds has neatly condensed the "Handful Story" as follows:

> In 1951 my last two housepets and stud dogs had passed away, Ch. Hosea of Marienhof, the last uncropped champion, age 17, and Am. & Can. Ch.

Ch. Benrook Bona

Handful of Marienhof, age 16. I had two new puppy males who became Ch. Handful's Me Too of Marienhof and Ch. Diplomat of Marienhof, but I needed a bitch to start Handful again.

After a talk with Shirley Angus of Benrook, I was to obtain the choice of two bitches, Benrook Bellona and Benrook Bona, from a litter of six by CH. DOREM DISPLAY out of Ch. Meldon's Manana, whelped April 16, 1950. The pair, along with the male pups, were to be exhibited at the Specialty in New York and Westminster, where I was to make my selection. Seeing all six in a playpen, one quick look separated the two bitches from their four brothers, and an even quicker look told me Bona was mine! She was far more Schnauzery, lower and cobbier than her sister, with a quality head, beautiful neck and lay-back of shoulder, a good spring of rib and enough loin to allow perfect movement, front and rear. Yes, I definitely wanted Bona.

The Specialty was being judged by old "Pop" Sayres, as fine a terrier man as the States will ever know—the handler who carried DISPLAY to Best in Show honors. He did not take long to choose Bona for his winner. However, Shirley still said she thought Bellona better, and to wait until the "Garden" was judged on Monday before I made a final choice. I knew Bona was to be mine, and so when Bellona won at Westminster, I was thrilled to hear Shirley say, "Now are you sure you still want Bona?" and even more thrilled to know she was glad to hear me say, "Yes, I still want her."

Due to illness and emergencies, Bona was forced to wait until May to come to Handful, and the life she took to as the Queen, making everyone her

Ch. Diplomat
of Marienhof
surrounded by his
first two champion
daughters, Ch. Handful's
Ruddy Duck and Ch.
Handful's Teal.

loving slave, two and four-footed. She loved to show and finished easily. It was not possible to start breeding her until May 1952. Since she was always guarded by Me Too and Diplomat, neither dared to breed her. Finally, we took all three into the vets, tried both, and with no luck, drove them back to Handful, threw all three over the garden fence, and by the time we went through the house, Bona and Me Too were tied, while Diplomat sat on the terrace looking very sad and lonely.

The first litter contained two males, never shown or bred, and four bitches. All four bitches were shown, and Chs. Handful's Ruddy Duck and Teal finished. The other two, nearly finished, were bred and produced champions.

Top wins, top pups for the next year or so finally made it necessary to thin out a bit. The first to go were Ch. Handful's Bantam and Ch. Handful's Wren, to California, and sister, Ch. Handful's Quail, to Florida, starting those regions on their way. The long-standing Handful policy began at this point. When a new region wanted a Handful Schnauzer, it meant that they must take the best we had to be their house pet, their show dog and their start in producing the best possible in their area.

In 1956, illness suddenly put Handful on sale, and from this the midwest got Handful's Snow Flurry and Ch. Handful's Pop Up, which did well for Trayhom, and combined, started the Winsomors and Mankits in Ohio and Indiana. Ch. Handful's Popper and Handful's Doll founded Andrel in Connecticut. Crown Post was started by Handful's Periwinkle and Petunia in New Jersey. Handful's Buff Cochin, Snowstorm, Ragula and Raguletta went to Virginia to start the Pfulhans. Ch. Handful's Corbo, with Bantam, Fashion and Wren, started Windy Hill in California, and Belleve in Denver. Ch. Handful's Tanter went to Salt Lake City, while the LaMays in Reno and the Fancways in California all completed the Bona line.

The magic that was Handful occurred in the 1950s, with 25 homebred champions emerging in short order. Several families were developed from sons

**Ch. Handful's
Bantam**

and daughters of the Diplomat-Bona cross. Their best producing son, Ch. Handful's Bantam (10 Chs.) owned by Marjorie Walters, exerted his influence on the west coast. He is the sire of Best in Show winning Ch. Brausestadt's Terri Dee, but most importantly, he is the maternal grandsire of Ch. Windy Hill Defiance (12 Chs.). The most significant of the Diplomat-Bona offspring turned out to be the non-champion sisters, Handful's Snow Flurry and Snow Flake. Both went to the midwest, Snow Flurry to found Trayhom and Snow Flake for Ursafell.

Snow Flake, line-bred within the Diplomat branch, produced Ursafell Niblet. Inbred to her sire, Ursafell Sandpiper, Niblet produced Miss Little Guys. Crossed to the Ruffian branch, Miss Little Guys is the matriarchal head of a tail-male line of current top producers second to none. Through her only champion son, Ch. Sky Rocket's First Stage (8 Chs.), has emerged no fewer than two dozen more top producers (see RUFFIAN branch).

Snow Flurry, as the foundation for Twylla and Wayne Miller's Trayhom Kennel, produced three champion sons, each an outstanding winner and producer. Twice bred into the Diplomat branch, she produced Ch. Trayhom Talleyrand (by Ch. Handful's Pop Up) and Ch. Trayhom Tatters (by Pirate). Her most important breeding, into the Tribute branch, produced Ch. Trayhom Tramp-A-Bout.

The most profound influence Diplomat would have on the breed was through his sons, Ch. Asset of Ledahof (10 Chs.) and Ch. Delfin Janus (34 Chs.). Asset, out of the Diplomat daughter Annabelle of Ledahof (3 Chs.), enjoyed considerable success as a show dog in the early 1950s under the ownership of Dorothy and Allen Hauck of Ohio, winning several Groups. He proved quite an asset as a sire. Among his ten champion get was the leading sire of the 1960s and 1970s, the great Pirate, from which trace in tail-male line, nine more top-producing sires.

Handful's Best Team in Show at Westminster Kennel Club, February 8-9, 1954 consisted of Ch. Handful's Bantam, Ch. Handful's Pheasant, Ch. Handful's Quail and their dam, Ch. Benrook Bona. They were owner-handled by Gene Simmonds.

```
                      Ch. Dorem Display
              Ch. Diplomat of Ledahof
                      Ch. Enchantress
       Ch. Asset of Ledahof
              Ch. Diplomat of Ledahof
       Annabelle of Ledahof
       Stardust of Ledahof
CH. MARWYCK PITT-PENN PIRATE
                      Ch. Dorem Display
              Ch. Diplomat of Ledahof
                      Ch. Enchantress
       Ch. Marwyck S.D. Comet
              Ledahof Sentry
       Ch. Sorceress of Ledahof
                      Ch. Enchantress
```

The CH. MARWYCK PITT-PENN PIRATE line

The line-breeding wisdom instilled by her mentor Leda Martin was brought to fruition in 1954 by Marion Evashwick. On February 15th that year was born the record-setting cornerstone sire, Am. Can. and Mex. Ch. Marwyck Pitt-Penn Pirate (44 Chs.). His breeding offers a lesson in successful mixing and matching based on a single individual—Ch. Enchantress (8 Chs.). Pirate is intensely line-bred to the Enchantress son, Diplomat, who was not only his double grandsire, but one of his paternal great-grandsires. A fourth line to Enchantress in this extremely tight pedigree comes through Pirate's maternal granddam, the Enchantress daughter, Ch. Sorceress of Ledahof.

Pirate's dam, Ch. Marwyck S.D. Comet, was sold as a young bitch to Dorothy Whitton of Buffalo, New York. When it came time to choose a mate for Comet, Marion suggested her half-brother, Ch. Asset of Ledahof, and the result was a single puppy—Pirate. He was raised in Pittsburgh by Cathryn and Walter Francis, the "Pitt-Penn" part of the Marwyck prefix. Pirate was started on his show career by Mrs. Evashwick, achieving his first big win at the tender age of seven months—Best of Breed from the puppy class at the Michigan Specialty. He finished at 11 months with four majors, after which he was sold to Dr. Rod King. In the hands of professional handler Thomas Lenfesty, Pirate enjoyed further success as a yearling champion.

Eventually Jean and Glenn Fancy (Fancway) of California acquired half-ownership of Pirate, showing him throughout the west, as well as in Mexico and Canada, earning both additional titles. His show career spanned five years, during which he won 75 Bests of Breed, his last at six years of age. In addition, he earned 38 Group placements, ten of them firsts, and was Best in Show at the Sequoia Kennel Club's first all-breed show.

At some point Pirate became solely owned by the Fancys and lived out the last eight years of his illustrious life as their cherished housepet and the ardent companion to their two young sons and baby daughter. I was introduced to Pirate in their home in 1962. At eight years of age he was still in his prime,

115

Ch. Fancway's Pirate Jr. of LaMay

looking very competitive. He was obviously intelligent and possessed extraordinary dignity and serenity, but was not without this breed's typical sense of humor. As to type, Pirate was racy in outline, well up on leg, but without exaggeration. He had a neat head with no suggestion of coarseness, small eyes and well-set ears. Only moderately angulated at both ends, his movement, coming and going was good.

Given every advantage, Pirate in short order became the leading producer throughout the early 1960s. By 1966 he had passed the long-time record established by DISPLAY, and before his death, September 23, 1965, had produced 44 champions, plus others that gained titles in Canada and Mexico.

It was very late in Pirate's stud career when he produced his most important son. Aptly named, Ch. Fancway's Pirate Jr. of LaMay became his forty-second champion as well as his top winning and producing offspring. Bred by Virginia LaMay of Reno, Nevada, Pirate Jr. went to the Fancys as a four-month-old puppy and immediately began to follow the pattern established by his sire. Pirate Jr. scored his first important win at seven months at the Chicago Specialty in April 1965, winning the Sweepstakes under Helen Wiedenbeck (Helarry) and going Reserve to the ultimate Best of Breed winner in the regular classes under Marguerite Wolff (Phil-Mar). The next day at Chicago Inter-

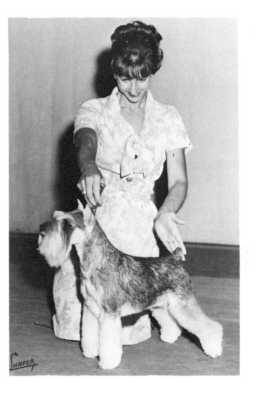

**Ch. Blythewood
Ricochet
of LaMay
with Joan Huber.**

national he won his first five points. Thereafter, his career was extraordinary. With all but one win from puppy class, his title quest included six Bests of Breed and five Group placements.

Pirate Jr. enjoyed continued success as a yearling, returning to the Chicago Specialty in 1966 to go Best of Breed under Leda Martin (Ledahof), and added another Specialty Best in Denver under yet another breed pioneer, Gene Simmonds (Handful). He continued to win well for the next two years, topping the AMSC Regional Specialty in 1967 and the Southern California Specialty in 1968. Pirate Jr. also went north and south of the borders to gain titles in Canada and Mexico. He was eventually sold to Jane and Charles Post (Postillion) for whom he sired three champions, including their Best in Show winner, Ch. Postillion's Riviera Pirate.

As an individual, the Fancys described Pirate Jr.:

> Beautifully balanced Schnauzer type, with a hard coat and very short back. He moves to perfection and shows like a terrier should. Perhaps his best feature is his heavily-loined, well-angulated rear, producing that strong driving movement so essential in the breed. He is truly a great dog in a small package, being only 12¾ inches tall.

Although he may not have achieved in numbers the record of his famous sire, Pirate Jr. left an indelible mark of his own with four top producers, two sons and two daughters, including the breed's all-time top dam, Ch. Faerwynd of Arador (16 Chs.).

Virginia LaMay, who bred Pirate Jr., also bred his first champion and best producing son, Ch. Blythewood Ricochet of LaMay. Sold as a puppy to Joan Huber (Blythewood), Ricochet finished his championship in just seven days on the 1967 Florida circuit, earning two five-pointers, one of these with Best of Breed. Shown sparingly as a yearling champion, his wins included the New York Specialty, and he returned to Florida the next year to dominate that circuit, including Best at the South Florida Specialty.

Bred primarily to eastern bitches, Ricochet sired 22 champions, including eight at Blythewood. Among his get are two top producers—a son, Ch. Boomerang of Marienhof (10 Chs.) and a daughter, Ch. Tare Misty Morning (4 Chs.).

Lisa Grames, formerly of Florida and now in New Hampshire, has based her Jilmar breeding program on Ricochet, getting her first homebred champion from him, as well as Jilmar's Star Image. Bred to Ch. Moore's Max Derkleiner, Image produced two bitches, both retained, and the dams of Jilmar's next generation of champions. Ch. Jilmar's Stardust produced two champions, while her sister, Jilmar's Starlet produced four. Most noteworthy is Starlet's son, Ch. Jilmar's Allstar, by Acclaim. He became the youngest male to achieve an AKC title, finishing on the day he turned seven months. Jilmar has averaged a champion each year since 1975, all owner handled. The latest, Ch. Jilmar's Barbarella, is a double great-granddaughter of Star Image.

Pirate Jr.'s other top producing son was Ch. Caradin Fancy That with nine champions, including a top producing daughter, Ch. Bokay Angelic Wisteria (4 Chs.).

In addition to a strong tail-male line of top producers based on Ch. Marwyck Pitt-Penn Pirate, several important families were founded on Jean and Glenn Fancy's limited breeding program throughout the 1960s. Seldom housing more than three or four adults, through judicious placement of homebreds and occasional stud puppies, over three dozen Fancway champions were produced, all tightly line-bred to Pirate.

The most significant litter bred by the Fancys was whelped in May 1964, and carried five lines to Pirate. From it came the top producing sisters Ch. Fancway's Vampira (6 Chs.) and Ch. Fancway's Voodoo Doll (3 Chs.), the former foundation for Margaret Haley's Aradors and the latter, Carole Hansen's Hansenhaus Kennel, both in the Los Angeles area.

The importance of starting with a good bitch is clearly illustrated in both cases. Mrs. Haley waited three years to get Vampira, and Mrs. Hansen secured Voodoo Doll as a proven producer.

Like so many successful breeders, Mrs. Haley's first experience with Miniature Schnauzers was an oversized "pet shop" male. What he lacked in type he

Ch. Jilmar's Allstar winning the Sweepstakes at the New York Specialty, June 1980, under David Owen Williams (Dow), breeder-owner handled by Lisa Grames (Jilmar).

Ch. Fancway's Voodoo Doll
with Cindy Fancy.

Ch. Fancway's Vampira

made up for in brains, earning two obedience degrees, and serving as Margaret's introduction to the Southern California Club.

Mrs. Haley writes about what followed:

> I decided I wanted to get a puppy bitch and try to do the whole "show bit" myself. As luck would have it, it was Jean Fancy that I contacted, and she said if I would stick with her, she would see that I got a good one. It took almost three years to get Vampira. Jean eventually had two litters, and let me have my pick of the bitches. I brought Vampira home when she was nine weeks old. Jean kept Voodoo Doll.
>
> Vampira was a good-sized bitch—13½ inches, well balanced, good body, solid topline, beautiful shoulders and front, lovely, dark, hard coat, and effortless movement. She needed a stronger rear, more eyefill, smaller eye and more furnishings.

Vampira was entirely owner conditioned and shown, and became the first bitch to win a California Terrier Group. Her six champion offspring were a result of tight line-breeding within the Diplomat branch. Mrs. Haley explained her choice of studs:

> I line-bred her, trying to keep what I liked of Pirate, while trying to improve her faults. Pirate Jr. added bone, rear and furnishings, Boomerang gave me beautiful head and eye, Time Traveler ideal outline and super temperament.

Had Vampira produced only one litter, her importance would have been assured, as the Pirate Jr. daughter, Ch. Faerwynd of Arador claims the title as the breed's all-time top producing dam. Faerwynd produced two litters at Arador resulting in six champions, and then she was acquired by Enid Quick in Illinois, founding her Valharra family.

Mrs. Quick used her Ch. Allaruth's Daniel for Faerwynd's first Valharra litter, and hit the jackpot! Ch. Valharra's Dionysos was a standout puppy, the first to top both AMSC Sweepstakes, first at Montgomery County and then in New York. His Breed win from the classes at Westminster also was achieved under a year of age. Dionysos enjoyed two full years of showing, handled professionally by Robert Condon. His record included a Best in Show, six Specialty Bests, eight Group wins and 23 additional placements.

As a sire, his accomplishments are equally noteworthy with 28 champions, the large majority bred at Valharra. His line of descent is brought forward several generations, principally through daughters. His best producing daughter, Valharra Prize of Blythewood, is the dam of ten Blythewood champions bred by Joan Huber.

Valharra's Victoria, by Dionysos out of a Daniel daughter, is the dam of six Paxon champions bred by Aileen and Richard Santo of New York. Paxon, using Valharra stock, has bred over a dozen champions, including two top producing Victoria sons, Ch. Paxon's Re-Play (6 Chs.) and Ch. Paxon's Magic Factor (5 Chs.).

120

Ch. Allaruth's Daniel

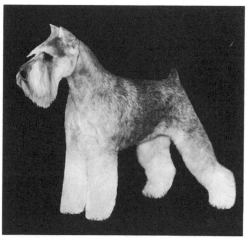

Ch. Faerwynd of Arador

Ch. Valharra's Dionysos with Robert Condon.

KE SHORE
ENNEL
CLUB
PRIL 16 1972

BEST
IN
SHOW

Ch. Valharra's Max Pax winning the Sweepstakes at the AMSC Montgomery County Specialty, October 1973, under Judie Ferguson (Sky Rocket) handled by Clay Coady.

After a second Daniel litter, which produced two more champions, Enid decided on outcross breedings for Faerwynd, using her Ch. Moore's Max Derkleiner twice, and Ch. Penlan Paperboy once. From the first Max litter, three finished and another had 13 points—all were males. The first to finish was Ch. Valharra's Max Factor, winning three Sweepstakes and a Group as a puppy. His untimely death as a yearling was a great blow. His brother, Ch. Valharra's Max Pax followed through with equally impressive wins, including Best in Sweepstakes at AMSC Montgomery County as well as at the Chicago Specialty. He finished with three five-pointers, two earned at AMSC and Southern California Specialties. Max Pax also was short-lived, but did sire seven champions, including Magic Factor.

Faerwynd's litter by Paperboy also had three male champions, including Ch. Valharra's Prize of Penlan (8 Chs.). Her final litter, by Max, produced a single puppy, Ch. Valharra's Melba Moore, CD (3 Chs.).

The ongoing breeding program at Valharra has produced nearly 40 champions. Perhaps their crowning achievement was Ch. Valharra's Extra, an outstanding dog on all counts. As of 1985, he had sired ten champions, including three active sons: Ch. Sunshine Sounder (10 Chs.), Ch. Valharra's

122

Ch. Valharra's Melba Moore, CD winning the Sweepstakes at the Chicago Specialty, June 1975, under Richard Smith (Richlene) breeder-owner handled by Enid Quick (Valharra).

Double Extra (9 Chs.) and Ch. Valharra's Extra Allaruth (5 Chs.), the latter, No. 1 (tie) Miniature Schnauzer of 1982 (Knight System).

At the February 1985 Southern California Specialty Ch. Valharra's Double Extra came from the veterans class to win Best of Breed at seven years of age. Like his sire, he is full of virtues, and his condition was a credit to owners, Violet and Robert Baws. Double Extra already has a top producing daughter in Ch. Skyline's Everlasting (5 Chs.), and it is through the Double Extra son, Ch. Valharra's Jaxson (4 Chs.), that we find the longest extension of the Arador-Valharra family in the littermates, Chs. Fannon and Faro of Arador. They carry lines to Vampira in all quarters of their pedigree, three descending from Faerwynd. It is clear that this family continues in good hands.

Vampira's litter sister Ch. Fancway's Voodoo Doll had already produced Ch. Caradin Fancy That (9 Chs.) before she was acquired by the Hansens. The line from Fancy That continues to the present through another Fancway bitch, Ch. Fancway's Carrousel, foundation for the Bokay breeding program of Dr. & Mrs. Kay Kawahara. Carrousel bred to Fancy That produced Ch. Bokay Angelic Wisteria (4 Chs.) from which two more generations of Bokay champions have emerged.

Judge Jack Prosen (Bon-Ell) awards Winners Bitch and Reserve, respectively, to Ch. Playboy's Talk of the Town, breeder-owner handled by Carole Hansen, and Ch. Playboy's Shady Lady, co-owner handled by Betty Hancock (Arbet).

The Hansens took a slightly different path in their choice of studs for Voodoo Doll, going into the Ch. Delfin Janus line from the Diplomat branch. They had already successfully campaigned the Masterpiece son, Ch. Lanmark's Playboy (10 Chs.) to some top-class wins including Specialty Bests, and he gave them the two good producing bitches, Ch. Playboy's Talk of the Town (3 Chs.) and Ch. Playboy's Shady Lady (2 Chs.).

Playboy is behind virtually all the Hansenhaus Schnauzers, half of his champion get being their top producers. The most recent, Ch. Love-A-Lot of Hansenhaus (5 Chs.), carries three lines to Playboy, and three of her champion get carry yet another.

Hansenhaus has always been a co-operative effort. Voodoo Doll's two champion daughters have champion descendents bearing several prefixes. You will find Shady Lady behind champions bred by Arbet, Belgar, Fotinakes, and St. Roque. Talk of the Town has even more—Arbet, Baws, Belgar, B-Majer, Fairfield, Kelvercrest and Hi-Crest.

The large majority of recent Hawaiian-bred champions carry lines to Talk of the Town principally through her son, Ch. Hi-Charge of Hansenhaus (11 Chs.), co-owned with Arnold Hirahara (Hi-Crest). Hi-Charge, with ten Bests in Show, is the record-holder in this department and is Hawaii's all-time Top Dog,

All-breeds. His best producing son to date is Ch. Fairfield Flyer of Hansenhaus (4 Chs.), sire of Ch. B-Majer Bolero v Kelvercrest, a recent top producer with four champions from her first two litters.

There were several Voodoo Doll descendants retained at Hansenhaus, now being worked into a sixth generation, continuing to breed primarily within the Masterpiece line of the Diplomat branch. The Hansenhaus champions from Voodoo Doll differ from those bred at Arador from Vampira in one basic way. Vampira was bred within the Pirate line, while Voodoo Doll was bred into the Janus line through Masterpiece.

The most successful sires at Hansenhaus carry no lines to Voodoo Doll. Playboy, and his two top producing sons, Ch. Playboy's Block Buster (22 Chs.) and Ch. Playboy's Special Edition (7 Chs.), were selected as the outcrosses for her descendants. They will be considered further, as a part of the Janus line.

Ch. Hi-Charge of Hansenhaus winning a record-setting 10th Best in Show under Australian judge Graham Head, handled by Bergit Coady for co-owners, Carole Hansen (Hansenhaus) and Arnold Hirahara (Hi-Crest).

Fancway's Carefree

Yet another Fancway bitch would serve as foundation for a breeding program in Texas. Fancway's Carefree was purchased by Margaret Smith of Dallas, and produced three champions bearing her Skibo prefix. Carefree is intensely line-bred to Diplomat, carrying four lines to Pirate. She is a grand-daughter of two of the west's leading sires, Pirate Jr. and Masterpiece.

Carefree went to live with Shirley and Dale Reynolds at three years of age, and over a decade later still shared their bed. The Reynolds whelped her second and third litters, retaining Ch. Skibo's Just Call Me Angel (7 Chs.) from the second and Ch. Skibo's Fancy Clancy (14 Chs.) from the third. This pair formed the foundation for the Reynolds' Far Hills breeding program which is now into the fifth generation and has produced over two dozen champions based on the Clancy-Angel combination.

126

Ch. Skibo's Fancy Clancy
with Dennis Kniola.

Ch. Far Hills Flamin' Fandango
with Shirley Reynolds.

Ch. Skibo's Just Call Me Angel
with Dora Lee Wilson.

Some exciting wins came their way, beginning with Clancy, a Best in Show winner both here and in Canada, where he was the No. 1 Miniature Schnauzer in 1977. His son, Ch. Far Hills Midnight Angel (5 Chs.) earned over 50 Bests of Breed and 37 Group placements, including five 1sts. Another son, Ch. Far Hills Night Flyer (4 Chs.) is producing well, and yet another, Ch. Glory's Eager Beaver (4 Chs.) is the sire of the breed's leading black and silver sire, Ch. Sercatep's Strut N Proud (9 Chs.).

The Clancy-Angel granddaughter, Ch. Far Hills Flamin' Fandango (3 Chs.) was the top bitch in the breed for 1981, with 25 Bests of Breed, 37 Best Opposite Sex awards and 11 Group placements, including two 1sts. These wins were accomplished breeder-owner conditioned and handled by Mrs. Reynolds. Fandango's third champion, Ch. Far Hills Go For The Gold, was born in our Olympic Year 1984, and is a fourth-generation homebred for Far Hills.

```
                                    Dorem Cockade
                          Ch. Dorem Display
                                    Ch. Dorem Searchlight
                   Ch. Diplomat of Ledahof
                                    Dorem Spotlight
                          Ch. Enchantress
                                    Ch. Dorem Liberty
CH. DELFIN JANUS
                                    Ch. Sandman of Sharvogue
                          Ch. Tweed Packet of Wilkern
                                    Ch. Debutante of Ledahof
                   Ch. Minquas Merry Elf
                                    Ch. Meldon's Merit
                          Minquas Melita
                                    Minquas Vivacious
```

The CH. DELFIN JANUS line

Ch. Delfin Janus (34 Chs.) is far and away the top producing Diplomat son. He was the jewel in the Delfin crown, and his impact on the breed was profound. Whelped July 6, 1952, Janus was bred by Mae Dickenson, out of her Ch. Minquas Merry Elf, a triple great-granddaughter of DISPLAY.

Janus was a champion at nine months of age. Shown nine times, he was Winners Dog or better at six shows, going on to earn five Bests of Breed and two Group placements. He continued his career as a yearling champion adding 20 Bests of Breed and 11 more Group placements, failing, however, to win a Group.

Janus lived for over 16 years as Mrs. Dickenson's companion, producing 12 of her 20 homebred Delfin champions. Six of these were out of Delfin's other foundation bitch, Ch. Minquas Athena, and include Ch. Delfin Victoria. Bred back to her sire, Victoria produced three champions, and produced three more by other sires.

Ch. Delfin Janus with Mae Dickenson.

The last Delfin champion finished in 1966. Am. and Can. Ch. Delfin Do Dona, owned by the LaBountys, and later by Dr. and Mrs. Patrick Baymiller, carries three lines to Janus, and is one of the few bitches to win Best of Breed at Westminster. As the dam of multiple Group winning Ch. Mutiny Uproar (4 Chs.), this line continues to the present.

As one of the youngest sires of the early 1950s which carried several lines to DISPLAY, Janus was broadly used by eastern breeders. In addition to champions produced at Delfin, others came from Blythewood, Mai-Laur, Mel-Mar, Minquas, Mutiny, Rik-Rak, Travelmor and Windy Hill.

An extraordinary family of champion-obedience titlists was developed by Nancy Ackerman, beginning with the Janus daughter, Ch. Brenhof Katrinka, CD. She became the first champion Miniature Schnauzer to earn CD degrees here and in Canada. Her daughter, Am. and Can. Ch. Rik-Rak Rebel's Banner, CD also owns a "first," earning bench and obedience titles in two countries. Banner continued this unusual line by producing Ch. Rik-Rak Regina, CD, the dam of two champions. Yet another first came to Rik-Rak when the Janus daughter, Ch. Delfin Echo produced Am. Can. and Mex. Ch. Rik-Rak Ramie, the first of the breed with titles in three countries. Her Mexican title was earned in 1961 by winning three consecutive Group 1sts, breeder-owner handled.

The major families based on Janus were developed by Mrs. Huber at Blythewood, the Prosens at Bon-Ell, the La Bountys at Mutiny and the Goulds at Windy Hill. The Janus daughter, Ch. Blythewood Merry Melody (8 Chs.) is behind a host of top winning and producing Blythewood champions (see TRIBUTE chapter), while the Janus sons, Ch. Delfin Paion and Ch. Mutiny I'm Grumpy Too, exerted an equally profound influence in the west.

129

**Ch. Windy Hill
Defiance**

Barbara and Robert LaBounty came to California in the early 1960s, bringing Paion and Ch. Minquas Alicia with them. Combined, they produced Ch. Mutiny Coquette who went to San Francisco, giving a new start to Thelma Gould's Windy Hill Kennel.

Coquette is the dam of three Windy Hill champions, including Ch. Windy Hill Wishing Star. Bred back to Janus, Wishing Star produced her own "star" in the top producing Ch. Windy Hill Defiance (12 Chs.). I had the distinct pleasure of showing Defiance in his very first outing, taking him to Reserve at seven months of age in a five-point entry at the Northern California Specialty in 1961. I showed him on one other occasion in which he was selected by Glenn Fancy (Fancway) as Best of Breed over champions in another five-point entry. His record in the classes included three more Bests of Breed and two Group placements. Defiance earned further success as a champion, including Best at the Northern California Specialty in 1962.

A favorite son at Windy Hill for nearly 15 years, Mrs. Gould remembered him with pride:

> As an individual, Defiance is an excellent specimen, standing 13½ inches tall and possessing many of the qualities which we have been striving for and are only recently obtaining. He has a superb head piece with desired length of foreface, and still full and square in muzzle. This lovely head holds a dark eye and well set ears, always giving an expression of keen alertness. Perhaps his most distinguishing quality is his well angulated and strong driving rearquarters, which he uses correctly in movement. Particularly lovely is his clear coat coloring, darkly pigmented and well distributed. He is heavy in bone with excellent arched feet, thick in pads and up on toes. Most important is the picture of over-all balance which he presents, both in and out of the show ring, always making the most of himself.

**Ch. Mutiny
I'm Grumpy Too**

A dozen more Mutiny champions emerged during the 1960s, highlighted by Ch. Mutiny Pandemonium who established a record in 1967, topping the largest entry for a Miniature Schnauzer bitch to date with her Best in Show in California, from the classes to finish at 13 months of age. Amateur handled by Barbara LaBounty, this was also a breed first for bitches. Pandemonium was an inbred daughter of Mutiny's kingpin stud, Ch. Mutiny I'm Grumpy Too (17 Chs.).

Grumpy was clearly the heir apparent in the Janus line, and Jack and Dori Prosen were among the first to recognize this. Their Bon-Ell breeding program based on the Janus granddaughter, Ch. Blythewood Honey Bun, stayed within the Janus line to produce most of their dozen or so Bon-Ell champions, but first brought in the Tribute branch by breeding Honey Bun to Ch. Melmar's Jack Frost. Bon-Ell Bit O'Honey (4 Chs.) from this breeding, produced two top producing bitches when bred to Grumpy: Ch. Bon-Ell Mighty Fine (3 Chs.) and Ch. Bon-Ell Sand Storm (3 Chs.). Bit O'Honey bred to Ch. Landmark's Masterpiece, produced Ch. Bon-Ell Dust Storm, the dam of Ch. Bon-Ell Moonglow (4 Chs.).

The Prosens can claim much of the credit for progress being made in England. They sent over the inbred Grumpy son, Eng. Ch. Risepark Bon-Ell Taurus (5 Chs.) to Peter Newman (see BRITISH chapter) with remarkable long-term results. The Bon-Ell breeding program here has its greatest spread through Bon-Ell Ulla, the dam of Ch. Mutiny Master Spy, Grumpy's best producing son.

Gloria Weidlein's Ch. Mutiny Master Spy (4 Chs.) falls one short of the mark designating a top producer. However, his son, Ch. Landmark's Masterpiece (32 Chs.) also owned by Mrs. Weidlein, has a dynasty of his own, leaving a dozen top producers to date in direct tail-male line.

Ch. Landmark's Masterpiece from a painting by the author.

Ch. Mutiny I'm Grumpy Too	Ch. Delfin Janus
Ch. Mutiny Master Spy	Ch. Minquas Alicia
Bon-Ell Ulla	Ch. Delfin Apollo
	Ch. Blythewood Honey Bun
CH. LANDMARK'S MASTERPIECE	
Ch. Allaruth's Jericho	Ch. Allaruth's Joshua
Ch. Allaruth's Jasmine	Cooki v Elfland
Ch. Allaruth's Miss Dinah Mite	Ch. Dorem Original
	Ch. Frevohly's Best Bon-Bon, UD

The CH. LANDMARK'S MASTERPIECE line

Masterpiece caused quite a sensation on his first show weekend. After going Reserve at Ventura, July 30, 1966, he scored Best of Breed at Santa Barbara the next day—at age six months and one day. Shown in the classes by Ric Chashoudian, he was then piloted to Group Second (to the BIS winning Scottie) by Barbara LaBounty. His record thereafter was a fitting tribute to his quality.

Barbara LaBounty (now Rhinehart) relates her personal feelings about Masterpiece:

> The very fact that Gloria, the epitome of low key, named him "Masterpiece" says an awfully lot. From the very first he was truly special—and so good

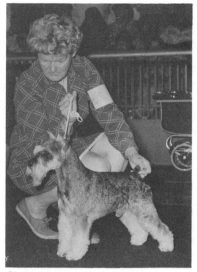

**Ch. Landmark's Masterpiece
with Gloria Weidlein.**

**Ch. Landmark's Masterpiece
with Ric Chashoudian.**

it was scary. Those of us who watched him grow had the uneasy feeling something was bound to go wrong—he was just too good.

And he was truly different. He was like a whole step forward for the breed in several respects. "Lumpy" had very heavy bone that ran clear into his feet—tight feet with thick pads. He had a foreface we'd only read about in the standard—length with real eye fill, and a mouth full of strong, large teeth, square across the end. Ours is one of the few terrier standards that doesn't call for strong teeth, and it should.

His great substance gave rise to early comment among some fanciers. They said, "He'll coarsen with age" or "He's too big." He never coarsened—just developed more rib spring—and on his toes he measured 13½ inches.

Conformation-wise he was the dog I'd always dreamed of. Prior to "Lump," while Gloria and I were travelling to shows, we'd spend many long hours in the car discussing structure. I remember trying to describe my ideal—"a short topline with long underline." It's a horsey term, but applies equally to dogs. It means that both the neck and tail come off the top of the dog, while a well-laid shoulder and correspondingly angled rear quarters stand the legs over a lot of ground. It means a short back (not short body) with room underneath to reach and really cover ground like a working dog. I thought this ideal was only a wishful dream until little "Lumpy" arrived and began to grow. Then there it was!

I said he was a whole step forward for the breed, but in one respect he brought the past with him. He had a coat of iron. His was truly a terrier jacket. He had adequate furnishings, but a real old-fashioned coat. And what a value this turned out to be in his producing years.

133

Ch. Lanmark's Playboy

Masterpiece finished by going Best of Winners at the Montgomery County AMSC Specialty, again handled by Barbara. As a champion, handled by Ric, he earned over 30 Bests of Breed, including two at Westminster. Perhaps his best win was Best of Breed at the February 1967 AMSC Specialty, topping 74 entries, including ten champions under Marguerite Wolfe (Phil-Mar). Masterpiece was shown one last time as a veteran, winning Best of Breed at the Southern California Specialty in 1972.

Masterpiece was a much admired dog, and by his owner Mrs. Weidlein, much loved:

> ·   If he were a person, you would definitely call him a gentleman—and it was this—his gentle presence that now makes our home so terribly empty. Happy, healthy, well adjusted, he could take care of any situation that arose—a perfect companion, and a perfect house dog. "Lump" never started a fight, but handled all the young males that came along. He put them in their place with a lot of loud conversation, and made them believers.
>
> He loved to travel, loved dog shows and always came out of his crate raring to go. A judge once made the remark on seeing him going around the ring, neck arched, "He looks like fire should be coming out of his nose!" Ric always said, "A stubborn little s.o.b., but when I ask him to give, he gives." He was always on his toes and looked larger than life.

Although Masterpiece's top producing son was Ch. Skibo's Fancy Clancy (14 Chs.), his strongest tail-male line comes through his son, Ch. Lanmark's Playboy (10 Chs.), and broadens considerably through the Playboy sons, Chs. Playboy's Block Buster (22 Chs.) and Special Edition (7 Chs.).

Block Buster served notice as a seven-month-old puppy when he topped 49 class entries as Best of Winners at the Northern California Specialty in September 1972, owner-handled by Carole Hansen. He went east in February

Ch. Playboy's
Block Buster

and was Best of Winners at Westminster. In his debut as a yearling champion Buster was Best of Breed at the AMSC Specialty in California, handled by Ric Chashoudian, and went from success to success. He was No. 3 (Knight System) in 1974 and his total record includes two Specialty Bests, 35 other Bests of Breed, and 21 Group placements including three 1sts.

As a sire, Buster proved equally outstanding, producing almost all of his champions for local Southern California breeders. He sired six Rainbou champions, three at Baws, including the top producer Ch. Baws Strait Shot v. Hansenhaus (5 Chs.), and left four at Hansenhaus. Buster's best-producing son and daughter had a broad influence on Hawaiian breeding. Ch. Hi-Charge of Hansenhaus (11 Chs.) and Ch. Sugar Ruff Scruff (6 Chs.) are behind most of the recent island champions.

The tail-female line from Buster is most strongly extended by his daughter, B-Majer Mazurka, dam of four B-Majer champions bred by Peggy and Jerry Blakley. The Mazurka daughter, Ch. B-Majer Bolero v. Kelvercrest, co-owned with Vera Potiker (Kelvercrest) produced two champions in each of her first two litters by Ch. Regency's Right On Target. Another non-champion Buster daughter, Hillock Happy Heart, produced three littermate champions for Sharon Piette (Hillock).

Dolores Walters used Masterpiece as a cornerstone for her breeding program which enjoyed success in all color varieties. Best known for her blacks (see BLACK chapter), it is a salt and pepper double Masterpiece great-grandson, Ch. Walters' Tradewinds (5 Chs.) which carries the tail-male line of top producers to the present. Tradewinds, located in the Pacific northwest, leaves champion descendants at Abiqua, Linalee and Mi-Sher. Tradewinds has a top producing daughter in Ch. Linalee's EZ Love'n of Mi Sher (3 Chs.). One of her get, Ch. Mi-Sher's One And Only, is the result of a breeding back to Tradewinds.

135

Masterpiece has had a broad influence on all color varieties, particularly in the black and silvers derived from his son Ch. Blythewood Winsome Lad (4 Chs.). The black and silver Ch. Eclipse Shadow of the Son (5 Chs.) is doubly bred on Winsome Lad, and brings in other lines from Janus through the Defiance daughter, Ch. Sparks Maidel of Defiance. More black and silver champions descend from the Lad son, Ch. Tammashann's Town Strutter. The Masterpiece son, Ch. Aljamar P.M. Lightning Bug, is the sire of Aljamar Fanny May (4 Chs.), foundation for another strong black and silver family (see BLACK AND SILVER chapter).

The Masterpiece son Ch. Starfire Criterion Landmark only sired a few litters before he was sold to the continent, where his impact is extraordinary. His influence here comes from a single litter out of Jean and Glenn Fancy's Specialty winning Ch. Walters' Country Girl. Four good producers emerged, including Ch. Fancway's Carrousel, foundation for Bokay, and Fancway's Carefree, foundation for Far Hills.

The male from this breeding, Fancway's Daktari, only sired a few litters, but is a principal factor in the Sole Baye breeding program. Yvonne Phelps took her Masterpiece daughter and first champion, Ch. Sisterce of Sole Baye, to Daktari and got Ch. Manta of Sole Baye, dam of the top producer Ch. Sole Baye's Miss Musket (7 Chs.). Miss Musket sons have been very successful, and include the Brazilian multiple Best in Show winner, Ch. Sole Baye's Sound-Off. Sole Baye is now into a fourth generation of homebred champions.

Masterpiece has several top producing daughters from which strong families have developed. Palmyra's Peridot (6 Chs.) is the dam of Ch. Blythewood Palmyra I'm Amy (3 Chs.) and Ch. Reflections Winning Image. Image is the dam of Ch. Reflections Refreshin' Image (3 Chs.), who in turn produced Ch. Reflections Lively Image (7 Chs.). The Masterpiece daughter Ch. Ruedesheim's Free Spirit (3 Chs.) has two top producer sons: Ch. Ruedesheim's Landmark (5 Chs.) and Ch. Ruedesheim's Momentummm (8 Chs.). A dozen Fotinakes champions stem from the Masterpiece daughter Fotinakes Heide (3 Chs.) and Ch. Shirley's String of Pearls has produced three champions for the Shirley's Schnauzers.

Ch. Landmark's Masterpiece appears in the pedigrees of many dozens of champions as the maternal grandsire of Ch. Allaruth's Daniel (8 Chs.), most of them through the Daniel son Ch. Valharra's Dionysos (28 Chs.).

The Diplomat branch from DISPLAY continues to be a strong force in current lines and families. It is clear that two distinct lines have developed, one through Pirate and the other through Masterpiece. Many successful winners and producers have resulted from a blend of these two lines, while others have come from outcrosses to the other branches—Tribute, Delegate and particularly Ruffian.

Ch. Sole Baye's
Miss Musket
with Yvonne Phelps.

The Miss Musket
grandson
Ch. Sole Baye's
T. J. Esquire
with Maripi Wooldridge.

137

9

The

Ch. Delegate of Ledahof

Branch

**Ch. Delegate
of Ledahof**

CH. DELEGATE OF LEDAHOF, as one of DISPLAY's early champions, might have enjoyed a far more impressive stud career had he been as widely publicized and as centrally located as his litter brother, Ch. Diplomat of Ledahof. Delegate's five champions seem to compare poorly with the 29 champions produced by his more broadly used brother. However, among the five was Ch. Dorem Tempo, who so impressed the mistress of Phil-Mar that

138

28 Sires of 5 or more A.K.C. Champions trace in direct tail-male lines to Ch. Delegate of Ledahof

*Sires that are in *italics* produced fewer than 5 Champions

A1   **Ch. Dorem Tempo (6)**

    B1 *Belvedere Andy**

       C1 **Ch. Belvedere Gay Boy (5)**

    B2 **Ch. Phil-Mar Gay Knight (9)**

       C2 **Ch. Phil-Mar Dark Knight (18)**

          D1 **Ch. Penlan Paragon (11)**

             E1 **Ch. Penlan Paragon's Pride (30)**

                F1 **Ch. Merry Makers Dyna-Mite (15)**

                F2 **Ch. Penlan Paperboy (45)**

                   G1 **Ch. Richlene's Big Time (16)**

                      H1 **Ch. Falling Timbers Country Boy (8)**

                   G2 **Ch. Charmar Copy Cat (19)**

                      H2 **Ch. Maroch Master Charge (7)**

                   G3 **Ch. Valharra's Prize of Penlan (8)**

                F3 **Ch. Penlan Pride's Promise (7)**

                   G4 **Ch. Penlan Promissory (5)**

              E2 *Ch. Penlan Paragon's Fanfare**

                F4 **Ch. Penlan Checkmate (34)**

                   G5 **Ch. Dardane Wagonmaster (6)**

                   G6 **Ch. Bardon Bounty Hunter (9)**

                   G7 **Ch. Penlan Peter Gunn (61)**

                      H3 **Ch. Carolane's Fancy That (7)**

                      H4 **Ch. Penlan Pistol Packer (7)**

                      H5 **Ch. Tomei Super Star (10)**

                      H6 **Ch. Penlan Peter's Son (19)**

                         I1 **Ch. Ruedesheim's Entrepeneur (16)**

                           J1 **Ch. Ruedesheim's Momentummm (8)**

                           J2 **Ch. Ruedesheim's Encore of Wil-O-Be (6)**

                           J3 **Ch. Aachen Sling Shot (6)**

                           J4 **Ch. Ruedesheim's Landmark (7)**

Mrs. Wolfe bred DISPLAY's sister, Ch. Dorem Shady Lady, as well as a Shady daughter and granddaughter to him. Tempo produced a champion in each litter, including three Best in Show winners.

Like his sire, Tempo was lightly used at stud, producing six champions from only nine breedings. Virtually all modern descendants from the Delegate branch trace through Tempo's best producing son, Ch. Phil-Mar Gay Knight, although an unfinished son, Belvedere's Andy, sired a top producer in Ch. Belvedere's Gay Boy (5 Chs.). There are current lines which trace to Gay Boy, principally through the Zomerhof family.

The Delegate son, Ch. Rannoch's Rampion, sired Eng. Ch. Rannoch-Dune Randolph of Appeline, who was exported to England and left many champion descendants (see BRITISH chapter).

The main tail-male line of descent from the Delegate branch comes through the Tempo son, Gay Knight. Five of his nine champion get came out of the Phil-Mar Kennel. The Gay Knight son, Ch. Haldeen's Allegro, not of Phil-Mar breeding, figures prominently in many current lines and families, as he appears twice in the pedigree of the influential sire, Ch. Sky Rocket's Uproar (35 Chs.) from the Ruffian branch.

By far the most important of the Gay Knight offspring was Ch. Phil-Mar Dark Knight, who brought with him three lines to Tribute. Well received by eastern breeders, Dark Knight sired 18 champions. His blood flows currently and most prominently in the midwest, however, through the efforts of Mr. and Mrs. Landis Hirstein, whose Penlan breeding program through 1985 has produced over 70 champions.

The Delegate branch *is* Penlan, with over two dozen top producing sires tracing in direct tail-male to their Dark Knight son, Ch. Penlan Paragon. Penlan, like so many successful ventures, was based on good advice:

Invest in the best bitch you can find.

This was the advice followed by Penny and Lanny Hirstein 25 years ago, and the bitch was Helarry's Lolly. Of Lolly, Penny once wrote:

> Words cannot express the joy Lolly has brought us, nor the gratitude we feel towards her breeder, Helen Wiedenbeck of Helarry Kennel. Lolly's show career, although productive, was cut short because of the expected arrival of our first daughter, but to watch her children and grandchildren carry on her royal heritage in the ring and in the whelping box is more than we ever hoped for. The foundation was cast and we were fortunate to build upon it.

Lolly, whelped January 28, 1961, was tightly line-bred within the Tribute and Ruffian branches, carrying five lines to the former and two to the latter; in addition, she carries one line to High Test. Initially Lolly was bred back closely into the Tribute-Ruffian side of her pedigree, giving the Hirsteins their first champions, as well as their principal producing bitch, Penlan Cadet Too. Never shown, as she was over 14 inches, Cadet was retained none the less, and as Penny once said, "Her exaggerated quality has paid off in the whelping box."

**Ch. Dorem Tempo
with Stephen Shaw.**

**Penlan
Cadet Too**

Ch. Penlan
Paragon

Ch. Penlan Paperboy
with Landis Hirstein.

Ch. Penlan Paragon's Pride
with Landis Hirstein.

Cadet produced a champion in every litter, and each was a Best of Breed winner from the classes and/or a Specialty-point winner. She seemed to produce consistent quality whether inbred to her own sons or loosely line-bred. Penny wrote the following about Cadet:

> We attribute Cadet's success as a producer to two things; her line-bred pedigree based on top producing dogs and bitches, and the exaggeration of Cadet herself. Being genetically clean, with a tightly-bred pedigree and exaggeration in every physical aspect, she proved to be dominant in her offspring, with only subtle influences from her mates. Each was selected for specific reasons, such as the desire for a wider-moving rear and a shorter back. The resulting offspring are the proof of her success.

The first few Penlan champions were shown professionally by Richard and Joanne Trubee. They handled Ch. Penlan Proud Knight, Penlan's first Specialty winner, and showed the littermates, Chs. Penlan Paragon and Paramour. Paragon was Penlan's first Group winner, and Cadet's most significant son.

In an effort to back-track a bit, to not only get a closer line to DISPLAY, but also lines to his sister, Shady, the Hirsteins selected Ch. Phil-Mar Dark Knight for Cadet's third breeding. Paragon was the result, and became Penlan's cornerstone sire, giving them 11 champions, all out of Penlan bitches, including a trio of champions when bred back to his dam. One of these, Ch. Penlan Paragon's Pride, was definitely a "keeper," and Penny's description of Pride explains why:

> As an individual Pride stands 13⅝ inches tall, with an elegant clean head, tremendous reach of neck, and a short, compact body. His topline is firm, tail set high and he has well-angulated, wide-moving hindquarters.

Pride, like his sire, finished with a Group 1st from the classes as a puppy. He was the first Penlan stud to receive the attention of other breeders, and sired 30 champions, including three top producing sons. The Pride son, Ch. Penlan Paperboy, was the obvious heir apparent.

I first saw Paperboy at the New York AMSC Specialty in February 1972. Shown as a 6-9 months puppy, he was Best in Sweepstakes under Patsy Laughter (Miown) and Best of Winners under the famed all-rounder, Alva Rosenberg. Compact and stylish, he excelled in all areas and out-moved the competition with ease.

The Hirsteins decided to go back to the Ruffian branch for Cadet's next breeding, to Ch. Helarry's Dark Victory. Only one pup emerged, but a real flyer, and eventually a significant producer. The singleton was Ch. Penlan Prelude To Victory, another puppy champion, finishing with two five-point majors, including the 1969 AMSC Specialty at Montgomery County, where Robert Moore (Bethel) awarded her WB, BW and BOS. Prelude produced four

Ch. Penlan Paragon
 Ch. Penlan Paragon's Fanfare
  Penlan Prissy Cindy

Ch. Phil-Mar Dark Knight
Penlan Cadet Too
Tiger Bo's Black Bart
Penlan Ekta Lu

Ch. Penlan Checkmate
 Orlane's Tom Agin
  Orlane's Middle Maid
  Orlane's Little Maid

Ch. Swinheim Salutation
Orlane's Lucky Lady of Glen-Sed
Orlane's Taylor Made
Orlane's Flash of Wit

CH. PENLAN PETER GUNN
 Ch. Penlan Paragon
 Ch. Penlan Paragon's Pride
  Penlan Cadet Too

Ch. Phil-Mar Dark Knight
Penlan Cadet Too
Ch. Helarry's Danny Boy
Helarry's Lolly

Ch. Penlan Proud Of Me
 Ch. Helarry's Dark Victory
 Ch. Penlan Prelude To Victory
  Penlan Cadet Too

Ch. Meldon's Ruffian
Helarry's Delsey
Ch. Helarry's Danny Boy
Helarry's Lolly

champions, including Ch. Penlan Proud Of Me (by Pride), the dam of the breed's all-time top sire, Ch. Penlan Peter Gunn.

Lanny and Penny brought Peter Gunn to the New York AMSC Specialty in 1975 as a yearling, along with a homebred puppy bitch, (Ch.) Penlan Pin-Up of Wolffcraft, they had sold to James Wolff and Paul Reycraft (Wolffcraft) of Indiana. Peter Gunn went Best of Winners, repeating the next day at Westminster, while Pin-Up won the Sweepstakes under Marguerite Wolff (Phil-Mar). Both finished quickly, Peter Gunn undefeated in the classes.

The pedigree of Peter Gunn shows the only infusion of "outside" blood brought into the Penlan family, through Checkmate's dam, Orlane's Middle Maid. Ch. Penlan Checkmate came to Penlan in 1971 as payment for stud service, and eventually was sold to Jean and Charles Kriegbaum in Pennsylvania. Checkmate sired 34 champions, including four top producing sons. With the addition of Checkmate was added a strong concentration from the Tribute branch, with over a dozen crosses to the Tribute son, Ch. Dorem Favorite. Checkmate carried additional lines to Diplomat, Merit and Ruffian, so that all the important branches are incorporated in the background of Peter Gunn.

Sold as a yearling champion, Peter Gunn began a spectacular specials career, managed professionally by Claudia Seaberg, with complete support given him by his owners Carol and Dr. Carl Beiles (Carolane). In 1977, Peter Gunn topped all systems with a pair of Bests in Show, eight Group 1sts and six Specialty Bests. . .the same year in which 16 of his get completed their titles! This was the first of several breed "records" set, as he also led the breed in Specialty wins (15) until this record was surpassed. As a sire, however, his record continues to be unequalled, with over 60 champion get, including four top producing sons to date, and the prospects for more.

144

Ch. Penlan Peter Gunn pictured above going Best of Winners at the AMSC Specialty, February 1975, under Anne Rogers Clark handled by his breeder, Landis Hirstein, and below going Best in Show at the Tuscaloosa K.C. in November 1977 under Gene Simmonds (Handful) handled by Claudia Seaberg.

Ch. Penlan Peter's Son winning Best of Breed at the 1976 AMSC Specialty, Montgomery County, under Louis Auslander (Alpine), handled by Landis Hirstein; Club President Margaret Pratt (Wademar) presenting club medallion.

The Hirsteins dominated the top spots in the various rating systems through much of the 1970's. They had become well established as professional handlers, but continued to suppoort their own breeding whenever possible.

In 1973, Ch. Penlan Paperboy missed being No. 1 (Knight System) by 15 points. Three years later, the No. 3 and No. 4 rankings were held by the Penlan duo, Ch. Penlan Peter's Son and his sire, Peter Gunn, both AMSC Specialty winners. In 1977, this pair was joined in the top ten by yet another Penlan— Ch. Penlan Pistol Packer. The Hirsteins piloted the Paperboy son, Ch. Cyngar's Ultimatum to No. 1 in 1978, and two years later another of their charges, Ch. Bardon Bounty Hunter, was No. 1. He is by Checkmate out of a Peter's Son daughter. No. 2 that year was Ch. Penlan Pride's Promise, the last champion produced by Pride, while in the classes, another Penlan was setting his own pace.

Ch. Penlan Pacesetter was purchased as a puppy by Gene Simmonds (Handful) and went out to California with the Hirsteins in June 1980, for the 100th Anniversary Specialty of the American Miniature Schnauzer Club (AMSC), going Best in Sweepstakes under Cynthia Garton (Cyngar). The next

Ch. Penlan Promissory with his breeder-owners Mr. & Mrs. Landis Hirstein.

year he led his nearest competitor in the Knight System ratings by over 350 points. He was an AMSC Specialty winner, and became Penlan's third Best in Show winner. Pacesetter currently resides in Tennessee with David Hallock.

Penlan's fourth Best in Show winner followed in 1982. Ch. Penlan Promissory, sired by my personal Penlan "favorite," Pride's Promise, represents all that is Penlan, and was well rewarded as a show dog. He earned four Bests in Show (two from the classes) and six Specialty Bests. As the sire of five champions by 1985, he is Penlan's fourth generation of top-producing sires.

Penlan since its inception has provided foundation stock for new breeders throughout the midwest and east. From one of the first Penlan litters came Penlan Sally Lyn-Mar, who went to Jeanne Lindell (Liebchen). Sally became the dam of two top producing bitches: Ch. Liebchen Watch It Widget produced four Cyngar champions for Cynthia and Richard Garton; Nishna Holley Gawley gave Ruth and Douglas Dempster (Mariah) their first four champions.

Richard and Arlene Smith (Richlene) of Fort Wayne, Indiana have built a firm foundation based on Penlan bitches. Ch. Penlan Paragon's Exceptional (Paragon-Cadet) turned out to be truly exceptional, giving the Smiths four

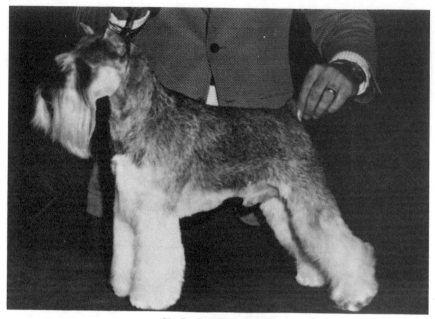

Ch. Penlan Checkmate

champions, plus nearly two dozen more in the next two generations. Exceptional's best producing son, Ch. Richlene's Big Time (16 Chs.), brings the tail-male line from Delegate another generation, through his top producing son Ch. Falling Timbers Country Boy (8 Chs.), out of Ch. Richlene's Sugar Baby (3 Chs.), foundation matron at Joy Hathaway's Falling Timbers Kennel in Florida.

The tail-female line from Exceptional is brought forward by two daughters: Ch. Richlene's Holiday Surprise (3 Chs.), by Peter Gunn, and Richlene's Tweetie Pop (4 Chs.), by Checkmate. The Tweetie Pop daughter, Ch. Richlene's Hearts And Lace, carries this strong family a generation further as the dam of five champions, including Richlene's latest star, Sweepstakes, multiple Group and Specialty winning Ch. Richlene's Marathon II, by Big Time. Exceptional is represented by yet another top producer, her grandson Ch. Richlene's Top Billing, the youthful sire of eight champions to date.

Top Billing was not the first Richlene to go to Sandra and Daniel Nagengast (Angler's) in Connecticut. Like the Hirsteins and the Smiths, the Nagengasts were "do it yourselfers" and finished two other Richlenes before Top Billing was purchased as a six-month old pup, in partnership with Barbara Hall (Wyndwood). After a speedy title quest, handled by Sandy, he provided them with the thrill of winning Best of Breed at AMSC Montgomery County, at just 14 months of age. The Angler's-Wyndwood partnership continues to produce breeder-owner handled champions.

**Ch. Richlene's
Top Billing**

**Ch. Richlene's
Round-Up
with Richard Smith.**

**Ch. Richlene's
Marathon II**

Ch. Bardon Bounty Hunter

In the midwest, Patricia and Richard Roozen founded their Ardicia breeding program on Ch. Penlan Paramour (Dark Knight - Cadet) and Marcia Trent's Trenmars were based on Penlan Pandarella. Each gave their owners three champions, Paramour, in turn producing Ch. Ardicia's Autumn Venture, dam of three more Ardicia champions.

The Hirsteins were chosen as mentors by Barbara and Donald Snobel, and kept them right on the mark beginning with Ch. Penlan Persistance, by Paperboy. She gave them Ch. Bardon Liberated Lady Byrd, who in turn produced Ch. Bardon Borne A Starr. Clearly the "star" of the Bardon breeding program, among her six champion get is Ch. Bardon Bounty Hunter, winner of 12 Specialties and the sire of nine champions to date.

In the east, Joseph Williams (Charmar) and Marie Voss (Ayre Acres) have done well, the former with Penlan Prim 'N Proper (by Pride) and Mrs. Voss with Penlan Paragon's Encore (Paragon-Cadet). Each gave their new owners three champions. Prim 'N Proper, bred to Checkmate, produced Ch. Charmar Checkerberry, dam of Ch. Charmar Copy Cat (by Paperboy). Copy Cat was tied for top sire in 1983, with seven champions, and has added

Carolane's Annie Get Your Gun

substantially to this record with 19 champions to date. Six of these were out of Lynda Lucast's Peter Gunn daughter, Carolane's Annie Get Your Gun, including the Best in Show winner, Ch. Tel-Mo's Top Cat.

The Tel-Mo Kennel in Minnesota was founded in 1960 by Leslie Maudsley, and is presently being maintained by her daughter Lynda Lucast. Originally founded on Blythewood and Mutiny stock from the Ch. Delfin Janus line, a new tack was taken with the purchase of Annie. Her son, Top Cat is owned in partnership with William Arnold (Bark) of Connecticut, who has bred a pair of champion littermates from him.

There are many other current breeders who are indebted to the Hirsteins for their foundation stock. So many more breeders will have progressed by using Penlan studs—ten of which, between them have sired over 200 champions.

Although the Penlan successes have been charted within the Delegate branch from DISPLAY, one must consider that this family owes as much, even more, to the Ruffian branch, as is emphasized in that chapter.

151

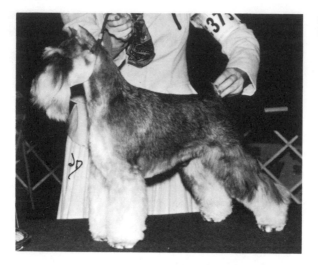

Ch. Ruedesheim's
Entrepeneur

Ch. Aachen Sling Shot winning Best in Sweepstakes at the Lone Star Specialty, March 26, 1982, under Judy Smith (Jadee), handled by his breeder Priscilla Wells (Aachen).

Ch. Ruedesheim's
Momentummm

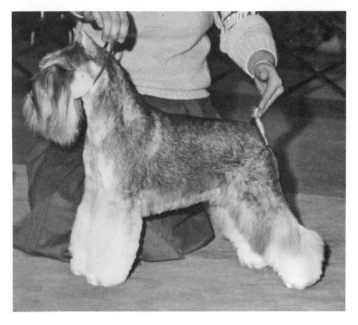

Ch. Tomei Super Star winning Best in Sweepstakes at the New York AMSC Specialty,
February 7, 1982, under Janice Rue (Suelen), handled by Clay Coady.

10

The

Ch. Meldon's Ruffian

Branch

**Ch. Meldon's
Ruffian**

CH. MELDON'S RUFFIAN, whelped December 23, 1950, heads a branch from DISPLAY noted not only for its Best in Show winners, but also as a line of top producing sires that covers a broader spectrum currently than any other branch from DISPLAY.

Ruffian was sold as a young puppy by Mrs. Meldon, and through a set of circumstances found his way to the kennel of professional handlers Larry and Alice Downey in Illinois. They were able to buy him for their clients, Mr. and Mrs. George Hendrickson, although he remained with the Downeys until his death November 2, 1965.

Ruffian's show career began as a puppy, but his big winning came as a yearling in February 1952, taking two Groups and a Best in Show from the

42 Sires of 5 or more A.K.C. Champions trace in direct tail-male lines to Ch. Meldon's Ruffian

*Sires that are in *italics* produced fewer than 5 Champions

A1   Ch. Helarry's Ruff Stuff (7)
A2   *Ch. Helarry's Dynamite**
    B1   Ch. Amigo of Merry Makers (5)
A3   Ch. Helarry's Dark Victory (35)
    B2   Ch. Helarry's Harmony (21)
    B3   Ch. Abingdon Authority (7)
A4   Ch. Helarry's Danny Boy (7)
    B4   Ch. Helarry's Colonel Dan (22)
        C1   *Iles Colonel Smokey Dan**
            D1   Ch. Merwood's Applejack (5)
                E1   Ch. Richlene's Round-Up (8)
                    F 1   Ch. Richlene's Top Billing (8)
A5   *Ch. C-Ton's Bon Fire**
    B5   *Ch. Jay Dee's Sky Rocket**
        C2   Ch. Sky Rocket's First Stage (8)
            D2   Ch. Sky Rocket's Uproar (35)
                E2   Ch. Sky Rocket's Victory Bound (5)
                E3   Ch. Bandsman's Skyrocket In Flite (6)
                E4   Ch. Shorlaine Dynamic Flash (20)
                    F 2   Ch. R-Bo's Victory Flash (13)
                E5   Ch. Jadee's Jump Up (41)
                    F 3   Ch. Sky Rocket's Travel More (9)
                    F 4   Ch. Repitition's Upcharge (5)
                        G1   Ch. Repitition's Bet Beau (6)
                            H1   Ch. Repitition's Rebel Warrior (8)
                E6   Ch. Sky Rocket's Bound To Win (25)
                    F 5   Ch. Postillion's Buccaneer (8)
                    F 6   Ch. Contempra Foolish Pleasure (7)
                    F 7   Ch. Blythewood National Anthem (22)
                      G2   Ch. Blythewood National Acclaim (23)
                      G3   Ch. Blythewood National Newsman (5)
             D3   Ch. Sky Rocket's Upswing (15)
                E7   Ch. Jadee's Hush Up (5)
                E8   Ch. Skyline's Blue Spruce (52)
                    F 8   Ch. Skyline's Sonora (6)
                    F 9   Ch. Dow's Evergreen (8)
                    F10   Ch. Regency's Right On (32)
                    G4   Ch. Regency's Right On Target (50)
                        H2   Ch. Jadee's Royal Supershot (10)
                  F11   Ch. Irrenhaus Blueprint (19)
                    G5   Ch. Imperial Stamp O'Kharasahl (8)
                      H3   Ch. Irrenhaus Stamp of Approval (7)
                    H4   Ch. Irrenhaus Stand Out (14)
                        I1   Ch. Irrenhaus Sensation (8)
                        I2   Ch. Irrenhaus Survivor (9)
                  G6   *Ch. Rampage's Kat Burglar**
                    H5   Ch. Rampage's Waco Kid (12)

classes to finish. Ruffian was not campaigned extensively by current norms. Alice Downey explains why:

> By today's standards Ruffian would not hold up for coat and furnishings. He wasn't shown extensively because of his soft coat, but fortunately his descendants did not have the problem. He was outstanding for head and eye, had an excellent neck and front, and was extremely sound. Above all else, he was elegant and showy, as were so many of his descendants.

Ruffian's record bears noting, as he placed in the Group 27 out of the 29 times he won Best of Breed, and became the breed's second multiple BIS winner. His record, following in the footsteps of his illustrious sire, was the basis for a string of BIS wining descendants second to none.

Ruffian sired 26 champions, half of them for Harry and Helen Wiedenbeck's Helarry Kennel, and most of them handled by the Downeys. The Helarry breeding program began shortly after Ruffian came on the scene. Their top producing bitch Helarry's Delsey (6 Chs.) carries a line to Ruffian, as well as two to Tribute and two more directly to DISPLAY. Her first breeding was to Ruffian and produced a bonanza in the Best in Show brothers, Ch. Helarry's Chester and Ch. Helarry's Dark Victory (35 Chs.). Repeat breedings produced four more champions, including the top producing sons, Ch. Helarry's Danny Boy (7 Chs.) and Ch. Helarry's Ruff Stuff (7 Chs.).

No Miniature Schnauzer before or since has enjoyed a more spectacular beginning than that experienced by Ch. Helarry's Dark Victory. Whelped November 19, 1958, he was purchased through the Downeys by Joseph Obsfeldt, but like Ruffian, lived out his entire 15 years with the Downeys. Dark Victory was shown for the first time on the January Florida circuit in 1960, and completed his championship by winning three consecutive Bests in Show. Yet another BIS came his way in November 1961.

```
                                Dorem Cockade
                        Ch. Dorem Display
                                Ch. Dorem Searchlight
                Ch. Meldon's Ruffian
                        Ch. Dorem Tribute
                Meldon's Memories
                        Meldon's Mar Mose
CH. HELARRY'S DARK VICTORY
                        Ch. Dorem Favorite
                Dorem Corsair
                        Ch. Dorem Choice Play
                Helarry's Delsey
                        Ch. Meldon's Ruffian
                C-Ton's Abigail
                        Miss Belvedere
```

Ch. Meldon's Ruffian winning Best of Breed at his first show at 13 months of age, handled by Larry Downey.

Ch. Abingdon's Authority

The BIS legacy continued as Dark Victory sired three multiple BIS winners: Ch. Victoria of Mary-O (2 BIS), Ch. Helarry's Harmony (5 BIS) and the record-setting Ch. Abingdon's Authority (9 BIS).

Authority, bred by Mona Meiners, carries three lines to Delsey, being a Dark Victory son out of a Danny Boy daughter, whose dam is by Chester—a tight line of BIS champions, indeed. Authority was campaigned by the Downeys under the sponsorship of the Hendricksons. He not only surpassed the Best in Show record of DISPLAY, but went on to almost double it, gaining his ninth Best in 1969. His record of 26 Group Firsts was also tops in the breed to that date.

Authority sired seven champions, including a trio of littermates bred by Grace Church. One of these, Ch. Kazels Favorite, is the record holder in numbers of Best of Breed wins with more than 135. He was the No. 1 Schnauzer, all systems, in 1972, handled by Clay Coady to a one-year record of four Bests in Show, 13 Group 1sts and 16 other placements from 37 Bests of Breed. In addition, Favorite won four Specialties in 1972, including two AMSC wins. Owner-handled thereafter, he won another BIS and a record number of Bests of Breed. The fact that he won Bests of Breed in each of his eight years of showing is also a breed record.

Ch. Kazels Favorite winning a Group First under Alva Rosenberg, handled by Clay Coady.

Ch. Helarry's Harmony winning a Best in Show, owner-handled by Ed Bracy.

Dark Victory's BIS heritage was also carried a generation further by his top producing son Ch. Helarry's Harmony (21 Chs.). Purchased as a nine-month-old puppy by Bette and Ed Bracy, professional handlers in Tennessee, Harmony had all the advantages. The Bracys were breed specialists, and knew he was a good one. His show career began at 14 months of age, and he never looked back. Harmony earned 39 Bests of Breed and 17 Group Firsts. Almost one-third of the time he topped the Group he went on to Best in Show—five times in all, equally the record of DISPLAY. Bette described Harmony:

> A Schnauzer of great substance, with a short, hard back, soundness at both ends, and an exceptional front. These qualities along with his tremendous terrier spirit, make for a great deal of Schnauzer in this 13½ inch frame.

Being the fourth generation of Best in Show winners in his tail-male line, it was inevitable that Harmony would continue this heritage. He is the sire of two BIS winners, Ch. Franzels Quicksilver and Ch. Blue Devil Sharpshooter both earning these wins from the classes.

Harmony is best known for his producing daughters. Robert Moore used him to great advantage, getting the good producers, Ch. Bethel's Lacie and Ch. Bethel's Lulu. Lacie, bred to Dark Victory, produced Rita Lawson's foundation bitch, Ch. Shadowmark's Casey of Ayoub's, dam of four champions by the Ruffian grandson, Ch. Helarry's Colonel Dan. There would be a dozen more Shadowmark champions, all bred within the Helarry line.

Ch. Bethel's Lulu was also bred to Colonel Dan and produced Ch. Bethel's News Flash, foundation for Lori Bush's Shorlaine Kennel in Florida. Her crowning achievement came in the form of the Best in Show and Specialty winning News Flash son, Ch. Shorlaine Dynamic Flash, sired by yet another BIS winner, Ch. Sky Rocket's Uproar. Flash continued this heritage as the sire of 20 champions, including Best in Show winning Ch. R-Bo's Victory Flash.

Victory Flash, bred and owned by Mary Ann Ellis (R-Bo) of Georgia, enjoyed an outstanding show career, professionally handled throughout by Claudia Seaberg. During a four-year campaign he won over 90 Bests of Breed and over 50 Group placements, including a dozen 1sts. He enjoyed his best year as No. 1 Schnauzer (Knight System) in 1979, also winning several Specialties including the AMSC Montgomery County. He is the sire of a dozen champions with the prospects for more.

Ch. Bethel's News Flash had a further impact on the breed through Dynamic Flash's sister, Shorlaine Jeanie Jump Up, dam of the top producing bitch Carolane's Heaven Sent (9 Chs.). Line-bred to Carolane's record-holding stud Ch. Penlan Peter Gunn, Heaven Sent produced eight of her champion get, and further generations are winning today. It is interesting to note here that Peter Gunn is out of a Dark Victory granddaughter, Ch. Penlan Proud of Me. Her dam, Ch. Penlan Prelude to Victory, is out of Penlan's foundation bitch, Penlan Cadet Too. This makes Peter Gunn intensely line-bred to Ruffian, although he appears in the tail-male line from the Delegate branch.

160

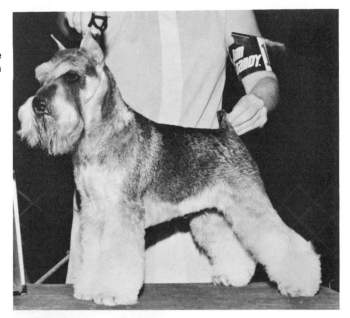

**Ch. Shorlaine
Dynamic Flash**

**Ch. R-Bo's
Victory Flash
with Claudia Seaberg.**

161

**Ch. Harga's
Terri**

Yet another Carolane top producer resulted when the Lacie-Lulu sister, Bethel's Karla, was bred to the Harmony son, Ch. Harga's Covington. Carol and Carl Beiles (Carolane) purchased Ch. Harga's Terri as a puppy, and she has been an extraordinary producer. Bred exclusively to studs from the Delegate branch, she produced seven champions, all but one of which have champion descendants.

Ch. Bo-Turn Greta, bred and owned by Mattie Boyd of Florida, is another top producing Harmony daughter. Bred exclusively to Helarry studs, Greta produced four champions and is behind further generations of Bo-Turn champions.

Of the four top producing Ruffian-Delsey sons, Ch. Helarry's Danny Boy proved most effective in bringing this line forward. Danny Boy had to take a back seat as a show dog in favor of his brothers, Dark Victory and Chester. He did, however, win four Specialties, most importantly the Chicago Specialty in 1961, topping 53 entries under Dorothy Williams (Dorem).

The Danny Boy son, Ch. Helarry's Colonel Dan, is intensely line-bred to Delsey, being out of her double granddaughter, Delsey's Sweet Heidi. Colonel Dan is the sire of 22 champions and is best known as the producer of first-rate bitches. Foremost among them is Ch. Wynmore Summer Song, bred by Josephine Moore (Wynmore). Purchased as a puppy by professional handler Claudia Seaberg, Summer Song was allowed an extraordinary career in the show ring, and was No. 1 bitch for two consecutive years. After one coat as a champion in 1970 which netted her 11 Bests of Breed and ten Group placements, Summer Song really took off the next year, winning two Bests in Show, a Specialty Best and 21 Group placements out of 26 Bests of Breed. She also won nine Group 1sts.

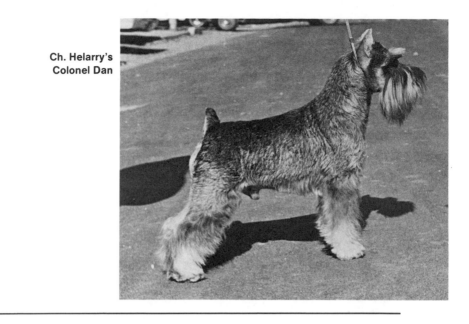

**Ch. Helarry's
Colonel Dan**

Claudia Seaberg has piloted several Best in Show winners, including Peter Gunn, as one of our top professionals. She aptly described some of the specific problems and rewards involved with exhibiting bitches:

> The female Miniature Schnauzer, if she is to be a successful Special must be an animal of superlative quality. She must be outstanding in showmanship, must possess an excess of breed type, substance, soundness and style, otherwise she will usually lose to any mediocre male champion. A bitch Special is rarely appreciated except by the most knowledgeable and experienced judges.
>
> Another factor involved in the decision to Special a bitch is the owner's individual motives and financial circumstances. Specialing requires considerable expense, and if that particular animal's winning is not publicized for the benefit of that particular breeding, or used to draw attention to the quality being produced by that kennel, then the campaign is a useless extravagance.
>
> On the positive side, nothing is more satisfying than to have the beauty and grace of a top-quality female stand out in the show ring. Her qualities will be more subtle than those of the males, but there are some discerning judges who will appreciate and reward them.

The Colonel Dan daughters bred at Bethel, Bo-Turn, Shorlaine and Shadowmark, did much to bring this family forward. A litter sired for Penlan, however, would prove to be the most influential.

The Penlan family, already chronicled in the Delegate chapter, has its roots deeply within the Ruffian branch. Lanny and Penny Hirstein's foundation bitch, Helarry's Lolly, is out of a Ruffian-Delsey daughter, and was bred to a Ruffian-Delsey son to produce Penlan Cadet Too (10 Chs.). The three principal Helarry studs have their broadest impact through the Penlan breeding program.

Ch. Merry Makers Dyna-Mite with Jinx Gunville.

Although the Ruffian son, Ch. Helarry's Dynamite, failed to make the mark as a top producer, he leaves a strong legacy through a son, Ch. Amigo of Merry Makers (5 Chs.), and a maternal grandson, Ch. Merry Makers Dyna-Mite (15 Chs.).

The Merry Makers were established three decades ago by Mabel (Jinx) Gunville in Illinois. Here is where Dynamite spent his autumn years as a cherished housepet. His death occurred the same week in which his namesake was born. Appropriately named, "Topper" was Dyna-Mite in the show ring with a record of three Bests in Show and a dozen Group 1sts, frequently owner-handled, but more often by Robert and Madeline Condon.

The Condons, in addition to their roll as professional handlers, also did a bit of breeding. Their Amigo daughter, Ch. Madeline's Sweet Charity, is the dam of three champions, including Ch. Madeline's Sweet Cyn, by Dark Victory. She, in turn, is the dam of Cyngar's Eliza Doolittle (3 Chs.), by Pride, the dam of Ch. Cyngar's Light Up (3 Chs.).

These top producing bitches are deeply intrenched in the Ruffian branch, Sweet Charity being out of Pickwick's G.W. Dark Angel (3 Chs.), a Ruffian granddaughter and double great-granddaughter. Angel is one of several top producing bitches to emerge from the long-time breeding program at Pickwick Kennel in Michigan, established in the mid-1950s by Ursula Buys and her daughter-in-law Verna Donlea.

164

Helarry's Delsey

If any Ruffian litter should be singled out as most significant it would have to be the one produced by the Tribute daughter, Miss Belvedere. C-Ton's Abigail, from this breeding, gains a strong hold on breed progress as the dam of Helarry's Delsey. Abigail's brother, Ch. C-Ton's Bon Fire, begins a tail-male line of top producers of extraordinary importance. Ch. Jay Dee's Sky Rocket, by Bon Fire out of a Ruffian daughter, brings the line forward as the sire of Best in Show and multiple Group winning Ch. Sky Rocket's First Stage.

Few successful breeding programs begin with the purchase of a male. Such was the case with Judie and Frank Ferguson's Sky Rocket line. First Stage came to live with the Fergusons after a successful show career. Essentially a pet, he was little used at stud. He did, however, produce eight champions, the most important from a breeding to a local "pet" bitch. Mrs. Ferguson describes the events which followed:

> This bitch (Tessie Tigerlily) was quite nice and could have done well in the show ring, but she was just a family pet. The bitch had a litter of four (2 dogs - 2 bitches). Due to whelping problems the litter was delivered by section and had to be hand raised.
>
> When the puppies were six to eight weeks old the owner was anxious to sell. We had not seen the litter but assumed they would be quite nice since the mother and her pedigree were sound. Between the William Hoehns and ourselves we sent two buyers to the breeders. The buyers were helped and advised about

how to pick the best puppy. When the litter was eleven weeks old the breeder called again, now desperate to sell her remaining two puppies before ear cropping. The puppies were so much work and she could not possibly afford any additional expense for their cropping and care. Sight unseen, we bought the remaining puppies, a dog and a bitch, at pet price.

The two rejects—the two puppies no one wanted to buy—were Ch. Sky Rocket's Uproar and Ch. Sky Rocket's Upstart. "Uppity" was the dam of one Best in Show winner and "Bounder" the sire of three. Through their sons and daughters this winning heritage is being continued. Both were the producers of top-ranked winners and producers, but above all else, both were wonderful family pets. Pretty good for two puppies the breeder couldn't sell.

The CH. SKY ROCKET'S UPROAR line

Whelped February 6, 1968, Ch. Sky Rocket's Uproar was an extraordinary individual and enjoyed an extraordinary show career. Finished as a yearling, always conditioned and handled by the Fergusons, he was well received his first year as a Special. He ranked No. 4 in 1970 with a record of 21 Bests of Breed including two at Specialties, going on to earn 13 Group placements, three of them 1sts. The next year was his, earning the largest number of Knight points (970) to that date, and leading all systems. His record that year included a Best in Show and 18 Group placements, seven of them 1sts. Uproar also topped five more Specialties, including the AMSC Montgomery County over a field of 117 under Gene Simmonds (Handful).

Uproar's success as a sire was immediate and dramatic. Within a few years his first and second generation get would be dominating the show rings throughout the country.

Ch. C-Ton's Bonfire	Ch. Meldon's Ruffian
Ch. Jay Dee's Sky Rocket	Miss Belvedere
Oh By Jingo	Ch. Meldon's Ruffian
	Phil-Mar's Glory Lady
Ch. Sky Rocket's First Stage	
Ursafell Sandpiper	Talisman of Ledahof
Miss Little Guys	Ursafell Forest Filligree
Ursafell Niblet	Ursafell Sandpiper
	Handful's Snowflake
CH. SKY ROCKET'S UPROAR	
Ch. Bramble of Quality Hill	Ch. Gengler's Drum Major
Ch. Wid's Von Kipper, CDX	Ch. Dream Girl of Silver Oaks
Mildot's Whiskers Allegresse, CDX	Ch. Haldeen's Allegro
	Haldeen's Miss Whiskers, CD
Tessie Tigerlily	
Ch. Haldeen's Allegro	Ch. Phil-Mar Gay Knight
Martin's Countess von Heidi	Dorem Music
Malmers Miss Tammy	Ch. Trayhom Talleyrand
	Marbert's Tune Topper

Ch. Sky Rocket's Uproar is pictured opposite with Judie Ferguson.

Ch. Sky Rocket's Bound To Win tops 42 puppies as Best in Sweepstakes at the AMSC Specialty 1973 under Sue Baines, handled by Joan Huber (Blythewood).

Ch. Sky Rocket's
Bound To Win

The trend began with his best producing son, Ch. Sky Rocket's Bound To Win (25 Chs.), owned by Isabelle and Homer Graf (Reflections). Joan Huber helped to find this one, and piloted him throughout his career. He was "Bound To Win," and did! Starting as a 6-9 months puppy in the fall of 1972, he won the Sweepstakes at the New York Specialty, won his classes and was Reserve at the AMSC Montgomery County, and capped it the following week with a Best of Breed at the Mount Vernon Specialty. He was brought out again at the February AMSC, where professional handler and breed specialist Sue Baines had her work cut out as the entry of 42 Sweepstakes puppies included some of the best. The 9-12 puppy dog class of eight saw first go to Bound To Win, second to Ch. Jadee's Jump Up and third to Ch. Playboy's Block Buster. All would be breed leaders and top sires. Bound To Win won the Sweepstakes and in 1973 went on to beat by just a few points two of the best—Ch. Hughcrest Hugh Hefner and Ch. Penlan Paperboy—as No. 1 Miniature Schnauzer (Knight System). His record that year included a Best in Show, six Group wins and four Specialty Bests, including the AMSC Montgomery County and his second win at Mount Vernon. He did just as well in 1974, repeating at Montgomery County and winning a third consecutive Mount Vernon Best.

Bound To Win did more than just win, claiming three top-producing sons and four daughters among his 25 champion get. Joan Huber managed the careers of most of his offspring, beginning with her own father-son brace of top producers, Ch. Blythewood National Anthem and Ch. Blythewood National Acclaim. Joan also handled Ch. Postillion's Buccaneer (8 Chs.), Ch. Contempra Foolish Pleasure (7 Chs.) and Ch. Wademar Aagin (4 Chs.).

The Bound To Win grandson, Acclaim, achieved just that—winning the 1978 AMSC Montgomery County from the 9-12 puppy class, topping 111 entries, also winning the Sweepstakes judged by Carol Parker (Skyline). He was a top contender for the next three years, starting as a yearling with a Best in Show, and eventually setting a Specialty record in 1981 with his 17th Best. As a sire his record is still growing.

In addition to Acclaim, Anthem leaves the good producing Ch. Blythewood Rocket Man (3 Chs.), owned by Karen and Gary Clausing (Giminhof) in Kansas. Rocket Man claims two top producing daughters: Ch. Giminhof Ruffle 'N Flourishes (7 Chs.) and Rocket's Ups Shanna (6 Chs.).

Ruffle, out of a black Giminhof bitch, is the foundation for Susan Atherton's Sathgates in Oklahoma. Six of her champions are from two litters sired by Ch. Regency's Right On Target, and include Ch. Sathgate Breakaway who was honored as Best of Breed at AMSC Montgomery County in 1985. His younger sisters, Ch. Sathgate Celestial and Ch. Sathgate Champagne, won Best Brace in Show—all owner conditioned and handled.

Shanna is owned by professional handlers Priscilla and Clarence Wells, also in Oklahoma. Their Aachen Kennel houses mostly client's dogs, but they try to raise a litter or two when time and space permits. Shanna has a top producing son, Ch. Aachen Sling Shot, an active sire with six champions to date.

Ch. Giminhof Ruffle 'N Flourishes

**Ch. Postillion's
Buccaneer**

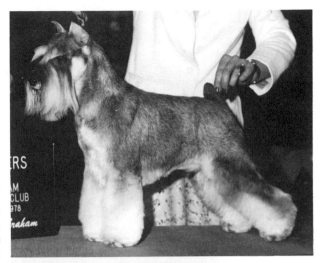

Ch. Blythewood
National Anthem
and his son
(below) Ch. Blythewood
National Acclaim
with Joan Huber.

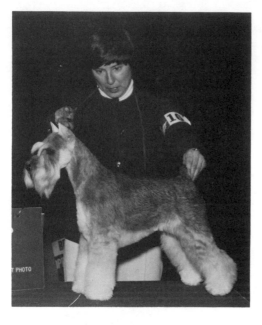

The partnership of Sue Baines and Jacquelyn Hicks (Irrenhaus) was among the first to capitalize on the Bound To Win qualities. He gave them a trio of champion bitches out of their Ch. Winagin Showstopper that included Ch. Irrenhaus Fancy Finish (5 Chs.). Line-breeding Fancy Finish to Ch. Skyline's Blue Spruce gave them two showstoppers in Ch. Irrenhaus Flights of Fancy (8 Chs.) and Ch. Irrenhaus Blueprint (19 Chs.).

Flights of Fancy and Blueprint were shown alternately in 1978 and both accumulated outstanding records. Flights of Fancy was the No. 1 bitch that year, winning 23 Bests of Breed including a Specialty, going on to earn two Groups and nine additional placements. Blueprint almost duplicated her record with 21 Bests of Breed, one at a Specialty, plus 14 Group placements including two 1sts.

Both were even more impressive as producers. Flights of Fancy established a new record as the dam of six champions from a single litter, line-bred to the Blueprint son, Ch. Imperial Stamp O'Kharasahl (8 Chs.). Ch. Irrenhaus Stand Out was clearly the stand out among the sextuplets, and became a Best in Show winner. The youthful sire of over a dozen champions to date, they include the top Schnauzer, all systems, 1984, Ch. Irrenhaus Survivor (9 Chs.), out of the Blueprint daughter, Ch. Irrenhaus Bluet (3 Chs.).

John and Joan Gulbin (Maroch) of Staten Island, New York went to Bound To Win early on, getting Ch. Maroch's Standing Ovation. Line-bred back to Uproar, she gave them their top producer Ch. Maroch's Star Attraction, dam of six champions, including Ch. Maroch Master Charge (7 Chs.).

**Ch. Irrenhaus
Blueprint
with Sue Baines**

**Ch. Irrenhaus
Survivor**

Ch. Jadee's Jump Up

Another solid line of top producers stems from the Uproar son, Ch. Jadee's Jump Up, bred, owned and shown by Judy and Donald Smith (Jadee), and from their first homebred litter. It was far from the best beginning, as Judy tells it:

As everyone does, we waited impatiently for that first important whelping date, and when seven lovely puppies were produced, we were ecstatic! However, all was not to go well, for a few hours later our puppies were gasping and crying ... our beautiful puppies were sick. Over the next three weeks, one by one, six of our seven puppies died. What was left was one scrawny, 2½ ounce boy. Even though his mother had had an infection, I finally decided the only thing I could do was to give him back to her and hope for the best. He soon began to take hold and grow. He just had to be terrific . . . he was all we had.

"Jumper" never failed to give his all in any situation. He was a super pet for our daughters, as they frequently strolled him around in their baby carriage, carefully dressed in doll clothes. He seemed to take it all in stride, as though that was where he belonged.

Later, when we took him into the show ring, "Jumper" showed another side of his personality we had not seen. He was an aggressive show dog . . . always offering his best . . . he seemed to belong there!

174

Over a three-year span, Jump Up won five Specialties and four Groups. His breeding is intensely Ruffian, being out of a Colonel Dan daughter whose dam is by Harmony. Jump Up claims two top producing sons, Ch. Sky Rocket's Travel More (9 Chs.) and Ch. Repitition's Upcharge (5 Chs.), the latter continuing the line with a son, Ch. Repitition's Best Beau (6 Chs.), and his son, Ch. Repitition's Rebel Warrior, with eight champions to date.

Carol and Kurt Garmaker (Repitition), like the Smiths, are currently among our successful professional handlers, specializing in the breed. The Jadees and Repititions have been a dominant factor for the last decade, the latter having a substantial influence in the progress made in black and silvers (see BLACK AND SILVER chapter).

Jump Up is best known for his daughters, including Best in Show winning Ch. Cyngar's Light Up (3 Chs.), the No. 1 bitch in 1977, owned and shown by Ruth and Douglas Dempster (Mariah). The Jump Up get that proved most important came from his breeding to the Garmakers' Jobie (4 Chs.). She produced two of her champions by Jump Up, but more importantly, three non-champion daughters that are top producers: Muffin XXIV (3 Chs.), Repitition's Kyssan Kismett (3 Chs.) and Repitition's Epitome (3 Chs.).

Muffin XXIV, like her dam Jobie, would seem unimpressive in a pedigree, lacking a title and even a prefix. Their producing ability, however, is undeniable. Muffin's champion get, line-bred within this family, include Ch. Repitition's Renaissance, foundation for Carol Weinberger's Bandsman family

---

Ch. Bandman's Celebrity winning Best in Sweepstakes at the 1984 AMSC Montgomery County Specialty judged by the author. The handler is Sue Baines, and Club President Jinx Gunville is presenting the trophy.

**Ch. Repitition's Renaissance
with Carol Garmaker.**

**Ch. Bandsman's Bouquet
with Carol Weinberger.**

in Maryland. A very successful show bitch, Renaissance won over two dozen Breed wins and many Group placements before settling into her more important role as a producer. Her offspring were equally successful, and include Best in Show winning Ch. Bandsman's Legacy. The Renaissance daughter, Ch. Bandsman's Bouquet, by Ch. R-Bo's Victory Flash, produced a first litter in 1984, four of them champions twelve months later. These include the Sweepstakes winner at AMSC Montgomery County, Ch. Bandsman's Talisman. Carol had the distinciton of breeding the Sweeps winner two years in a row, in 1984 with Ch. Bandsman's Celebrity—both Renaissance grandsons.

Repitition's Kyssan Kismett served as foundation for Jerry Oldham's Jerry O's in Oregon, giving her a second-generation top producer in Ch. Jerry O's Kiss 'N Run (5 Chs.), by Hush Up. A nearly finished full sister, Jerry O's Kiss 'N Angel Jadee, is the dam of Ch. Jadee's Royal Supershot, owned by Marge McClung. Handled by his breeder, Judy Smith, he won a dozen Groups in 1985, the same year in which his first five champions crossed the finish line.

Repitition's Epitome has two top producing daughters. Repitition's Midnight Blue, by Blue Spruce, is the dam of three champions, including Ch.

Ch. Jadee's Royal Supershot winning Best of Breed at Westminster under Robert Graham, handled by Judy Smith (Jadee).

Repitition's Best Beau (6 Chs.). Epitome, bred back to her sire, produced Ch. Repitition's Rampage Brand (4 Chs.), foundation for many of the champions from Wisconsin bearing Janice Ramel's Rampage brand. Her champions, all by Ch. Irrenhaus Blueprint, include the good producer, Ch. Rampage's Kat Burglar, sire of the black and silver Ch. Rampage's Waco Kid (12 Chs.). Other top producing bitches at Rampage include the Blue Spruce daughter, Ch. Rampage's Moody Blue (3 Chs.), and her daughter, Ch. Rampage's In The Mood (3 Chs.)

Although best known for his six top producing sons, several families were based on Ch. Sky Rocket's Uproar daughters, six of them top producers. Carolane's Heaven Sent (9 Chs.) heads the list, followed by Ch. Maroch's Star Attraction (6 Chs.). Blythewood Glorious Sky, Ch. Blockley Ms Chief, Ch. Jadee's Juju and Ch. Reflections Refreshin' Image each have produced three champions. Ch. Reflections Lively Image (7 Chs.), a daughter of Refreshin' Image, has had a strong impact on current winners at Travelmor, and most importantly, on the British scene.

177

Ch. Sky Rocket's Victory Bound is Best of Winners at the Chicago Specialty, March 30, 1973 under Olive Moore (Travelmor), handled by his breeder Judie Ferguson (Sky Rocket).

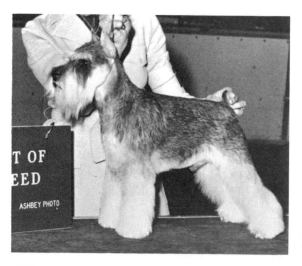

Ch. Sky Rocket's
Travel More

Ch. Repitition's
Rebel Warrior

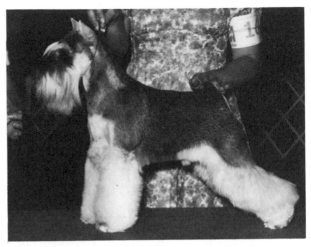

Ch. Daland Dazzling Debut winning Best in Sweepstakes at the New York AMSC
Specialty, February 10, 1980, under the author, handled by her breeder-owner David
Kirkland (Daland.)

Ch. C-Ton's Bon Fire
Ch. Jay Dee's Sky Rocket
Oh By Jingo
Ch. Sky Rocket's First Stage
Ursafell Sandpiper
Miss Little Guys
Ursafell Niblet
CH. SKY ROCKET'S UPSWING
Ch. Jay Dee's Sky Rocket
Ch. Sky Rocket's First Stage
Miss Little Guys
Ch. Sky Rocket's Upstart
Ch. Wid's Von Kipper, CDX
Tessie Tigerlily
Martin's Countess Von Heidi

The CH. SKY ROCKET'S UPSWING line

The Smiths of Jadee had the pleasure of owning Ch. Sky Rocket's Upswing, in addition to Jump Up, continuing to weave their offspring with considerable success. Upswing maintained his Best in Show heritage into a fifth generation, also winning a Specialty Best, shown on only one coat in 1974. He produced well at home, nearly half of his 15 champion get bred at Jadee. Four of these were out of their foundation bitch, Heather's Windy Weather (6 Chs.), and included Ch. Jadee's Jump Up (41 Chs.) and Ch. Jadee's Junebug (7 Chs.); three were out of the Windy daughter, Ch. Jadee's Juju, and include Ch. Jadee's Hush Up (5 Chs.).

Junebug was purchased as a puppy by David Owen Williams (Dow) of New York, and has proven an outstanding foundation for a very prolific family. Among her offspring are three top producing daughters, as well as a son, Ch. Dow's Evergreen (8 Chs.). The star of this family is the Best in Show winning Junebug daughter, Ch. Dow's I Can't Smile Without You, by Peter Gunn. She and her sister, Ch. Dow's Don't Rain On My Parade, have each produced three champions to date, tightly line-bred within the Ruffian branch. Bred to Blue Spruce, Junebug produced Evergreen and Ch. Dow's Lady Sings The Blues (6 Chs.). David was one of the first to combine lines from the breed's two all-time top producing sires—Peter Gunn and Blue Spruce.

Combining efforts with Margo and Joseph Klingler (Dimensions) in Texas, several current winners bear both their prefixes. In 1985, Ch. Dimensions Over The Road, from a Dimensions sire and a Dow dam (all line-bred from Junebug), won one of the largest Best in Shows ever recorded by the breed, topping over 2,500 dogs in Arizona. Two weeks earlier, in February, he won the AMSC Specialty under Nancy Fingerhut (Dana). He had served notice as a puppy, winning the Sweepstakes at Montgomery County under Jean Heath (Black Watch).

Ch. Jadee's Hush Up went to live in the mountains of Idaho to head a breeding program already in progress. Wyoma and Owen Clouse (Wy O's) had

Heather's
Windy Weather

Ch. Dow's Evergreen
and his sister
Ch. Dow's Lady Sings
The Blues
with Margo Klingler.

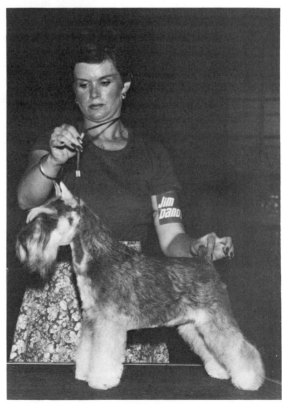

**Ch. Skyline's
Silver Lining**

already finished a pair of bitches when Hush Up joined them. He really hooked Wyoma on showing, as she handled him to several Group placements including two 1sts. The latest Wy O's champions would also be owner-handled.

The greatest impact that Upswing would have came from his litter out of Ch. Skyline's Silver Lining. Foundation bitch—par excellence—Silver Lining, whelped January 12, 1971, is from the first litter bred by Carol Parker (Skyline), originally in California and more recently in Arizona. Seven generations of homebred champions have emerged to date, all based on this one good bitch. And good she was, winning an all-breed Best in Match as a puppy, finishing from the Bred-by-Exhibitor class with several Best of Breeds, and eventually producing six champions from three different sires—all from the Ruffian branch. Five of the six went on to become multiple champion producers themselves, headed by her most famous son, Ch. Skyline's Blue Spruce. Mrs. Parker's formula for success was based entirely on Silver Lining offspring:

> Three of these offspring became the nucleus of our breeding program as it exists today. Ch. Skyline's Blue Spruce (by Ch. Sky Rocket's Upswing), Ch. Skyline's Little Britches (by Ch. Sky Rocket's Uproar) and Ch. Skyline's Summertime (by Ch. Jadee's Jump Up) head the three branches of descendency from Silver Lining which have been meshed and intermeshed in succeeding generations, so that now the name of Ch. Skyline's Silver Lining appears in the pedigrees of our latest youngsters four and five times.
>
> The prepotent influence of balance, substance and movement that "Sparkle" stamped on her offspring has combined with the refinement and elegance of the Sky Rocket bloodlines to create animals of a type we consider exclusively Skyline.

182

Ch. Skyline's Blue Spruce with Carol Parker.

Ch. Jay Dee's Sky Rocket
Ch. Sky Rocket's First Stage
Miss Little Guys
Ch. Sky Rocket's Upswing
Ch. Sky Rocket's First Stage
Ch. Sky Rocket's Upstart
Tessie Tigerlily
CH. SKYLINE'S BLUE SPRUCE
Ch. Gandalf of Arador
Ch. Laddin of Arador
Ch. Faerwynd of Arador
Ch. Skyline's Silver Lining
Ch. Orbit's Time Traveler
Ch. Orbit's Lift Off, CDX
Ch. Janhof's Bon-Bon of Adford

The CH. SKYLINE'S BLUE SPRUCE line

As a breed historian, one hopes to see firsthand those individuals that will have an impact on the future. It was my good fortune to see Ch. Skyline's Blue Spruce in his ring debut at six months and one day old. To say that I was impressed is mildly put, indeed, and so was the judge! Doris Wear carried him through to Best of Breed over one of that year's leading champions. I marveled at her foresight, as the first to recognize his potential.

This was fully realized in short order, from the Pacific to the Atlantic, with stopovers in the midwest. His title quest was on the highest level, earning four Sweepstakes Bests, two of them AMSC. Spruce never took less than Reserve at any Specialty, and twice scored Best of Winners, including Montgomery County in 1974. Two breeder-judges gave their stamp of approval; Dale Miller (Barclay Square) made him Best in Sweepstakes over 46 puppies, and Jinx Gunville (Merry Makers) made him best of the 106 class dogs, bowing for Best of Breed to his cousin, Ch. Sky Rocket's Bound To Win, enjoying a repeat win.

Blue Spruce returned the next year and topped them all at the AMSC under Olive Moore (Travelmor) and the next weekend at Mount Vernon under Gene Simmonds (Handful). He would go on to win four more Specialties over a two-year span, and was No. 1 (Knight System) in 1976. His worth as a sire was just beginning to be realized, his closest competitor that year being his Best in Show winning son Ch. Skyline's Star Spangled Banner, from his first litter.

Ch. Skyline's Blue Spruce was a first-class Miniature Schnauzer—one of the best that ever drew breath! Well off for make and shape, he was square and right, no question about it. He had an exquisite head-piece and a free-flowing way of going, and was well named for his unusual dark "blue" coloring. Carol described him once as having "that added look and attitude of a real stud dog . . . in short, 'sex appeal'!"

Spruce proved not only to be a splendid individual, but an extraordinary sire. In his ten years at stud, he leaves over 50 champions, including six top producing daughters and three sons, with the line continuing to expand.

He figures prominently in the successes achieved at Irrenhaus through his record-setting daughter Ch. Irrenhaus Flights of Fancy (8 Chs.), and equally successful son, Ch. Irrenhaus Blueprint (19 Chs.).

Spruce was a leading factor in the successes at Dow and Dimensions, giving them their best producers, Ch. Dow's Lady Sings The Blues (6 Chs.) and Ch. Dow's Evergreen (8 Chs.).

For Repitition, he sired Repitition's Midnight Blue (3 Chs.), dam of Ch. Repitition's Best Beau (6 Chs.).

Tom and Chris Levy (Abiqua) in Oregon gained two top producing daughters by Spruce. Their foundation bitch, Paddle Wheel's Up Anchor, is his half-sister. Abiqua Dare To Be Different (Blue Spruce - Up Anchor) is the dam of five Abiqua champions, including two Specialty winners. Her sister, Ch. Abiqua's Silk Stockings, is the dam of three Neusky champions, including the Best in Show winner, Am. and Can. Ch. Neusky's Blue Is My World, by half-brother, Blueprint.

Built on superiority, the Skyline breeding program has enjoyed continuing success in succeeding generations. Their superstar was clearly Ch. Skyline's Storm Signal, No. 1 (Knight System) 1983. He virtually skyrocketed to fame,

Ch. Skyline's Storm Signal

gaining his status that year in two short months. He was the first and only Miniature Schnauzer to win the breed four consecutive days on the Montgomery County weekend, earning over 400 Knight points for his efforts. Storm Signal would score well again in 1984, adding two more AMSC Specialties in a row, repeating again at Montgomery County. Mrs. Parker has summed up her entire breeding program in this individual, and describes it appropriately:

> The real purpose of dog shows is not to compile spectacular winning records, but instead to advance the development of a breed by pinpointing those individuals most valuable for breeding purposes. A student of pedigrees will immediately recognize that Storm Signal's background contains the entire history of Skyline. For the first time in six generations of breeding, we were able to combine in one pedigree the three outcross breedings of Silver Lining that formed the foundation of our entire breeding program over the past 15 years. Three crosses go back to Blue Spruce and five to Silver Lining. In addition, the great producing bitch Ch. Faerwynd of Arador appears nine times, and the influential sire Ch. Sky Rocket's First Stage appears ten times. The outstanding DISPLAY son Ch. Meldon's Ruffian is represented well over a hundred times!

Spruce clearly heads the Skyline dynasty, beginning with the successes of Banner in the show ring, and his sister Ch. Skyline's Fern of Winrush as a producer. Fern is the dam of three champions, including Ch. Skyline's Everlasting, who, in turn produced five champions, one bred back to Spruce and a litter of four, bred to the Spruce double grandson—and heir apparent—Ch. Regency's Right On Target.

Regardless of how successful a breeding program may be, unless bitches are advantageously placed in the hands of newcomers, the family will not progress. How fortunate that Beverly Verna (Regency) was able to secure not only foundation stock, but the wisdom that was Skyline in her first years with the breed.

Blue Spruce would figure prominently, as the sire of all seven champions out of Regency's foundation bitch Jana PD. From this breeding came two top producing daughters, Ch. Regency's Reward and Ch. Regency's Rosy Glow, both with four champion get. Their brother, Ch. Regency's Right On, proved to be Spruce's best producing son with over 30 champions to date.

	Ch. Sky Rocket's Upswing		Ch. Sky Rocket's First Stage
Ch. Skyline's Blue Spruce			Ch. Sky Rocket's Upstart
	Ch. Skyline's Silver Lining		Ch. Laddin of Arador
			Ch. Orbit's Lift Off, CDX
CH. REGENCY'S RIGHT ON			
CH. REGENCY'S ROSY GLOW			
	Ch. Marcheim Poppin' Fresh		Ch. Mankit's Yo Ho
Jana PD			Ch. Miranda von Brittanhof
	Jana Paulette		Ch. Howtwo's Hijacker
			Jana Agatha Paulette

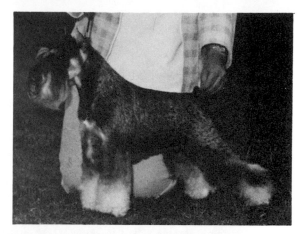

Ch. Regency's
Right On
and below, his son,
Ch. Regency's
Right On Target
with Beverly Verna.

In 1980 Mrs. Verna took a calculated risk when she bred Right On to his litter sister Rosy Glow—and hit the jackpot! Ch. Regency's Right On Target proved not only to be a successful show dog, but an immediate success as a sire.

Target finished with a Group 1st at 9 months of age, in just 23 days, shown entirely from the Bred-by-Exhibitor class. He won the Sweepstakes and was Best of Winners at the June 1981 AMSC Specialty in Los Angeles. For the next four years the name of Target would become a byword, as he was exhibited from coast to coast with great success. His best year was 1982. Although shown but 17 weeks, Target tied for No. 1 Schnauzer (Knight System), earning a Best in Show, three Specialty Bests, 14 Group placements and 30 Bests of Breed. Two years later, he was still winning Specialties and Groups, along with unprecedented recognition as a sire.

Perhaps it was his genetic strength, being from a brother-sister mating; perhaps it was the fact that he nicked so well with the bitches of the time, but whatever it was it seemed as if Target studied the bitch and pulled the appropriate gene out of a hat to improve on her shortcomings. In 1984 he established a new one-year siring record, with 19 champion get, and duplicated the effort as the leading sire again in 1985 with 19 more. Target was on the firing line to prove his worth, and as it turned out, was right on target!

The 1985 show season was uniquely Target's, with the two top contenders his black son and salt and pepper daughter. William and Judy Sousa's Ch. Regency's Shot In The Dark is the first black to earn Top Dog Knight System. Had Martin Mark's homebred Ch. Markworth Lovers Lane (No. 2) achieved the top spot, it would have been a "first" for bitches.

As one looks through current show catalogs, many familiar kennel prefixes catch the eye, along with a host of those yet to be recognized. Some of these will undoubted make their mark on future breed progress. We might well consider at this point the sage advice which concluded a similar section in Mrs. Eskrigge's breed "classic," *The Complete Miniature Schnauzer* (Howell Book House):

A lucky mating or two does not establish a strain, but only lays the foundation for it. All too often a breeder produces a few excellent dogs but does not know how to continue from this beginning and build upon it. Instead of seeking out suitable studs for his good bitches, or suitable bitches for a potentially excellent sire, he is too apt to breed to a big name of the wrong bloodlines or to something easily available. Or he may shy away from the bogey of too much inbreeding and dissipate a valuable line by indiscriminate crosses based on no definite plan instead of holding what he has and building further upon it. The result is likely to be a hodgepodge of bloodlines without specific goal. Luck may produce an individual outstanding litter, but it will not give consistently typical puppies year after year and generation after generation. To establish a successful strain and maintain it over any extended period requires good foundation stock plus careful study of individuals and pedigrees. It involves a lot of hard work, and when it is accomplished is indeed no small achievement.

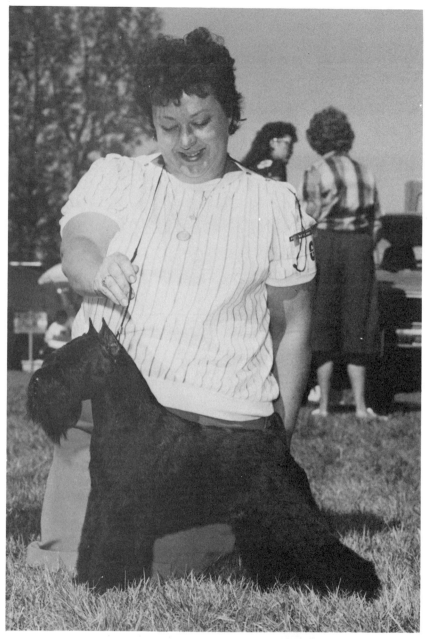

Ch. Regency's Shot In The Dark with Beverly Verna.

11

The History of Black
Miniature Schnauzers

$\mathbf{B}$LACK MINIATURE SCHNAUZERS have been a major factor in the breed since its inception. Peter v. Westerburg, whelped in Germany in 1902, is one of the three main pillars of the breed. Modern blacks (and all other color varieties) trace to Peter thousands of times over.

Blacks were imported into the United States in the mid-1920s, but not nearly on the scale of their salt and pepper cousins. The first American-bred black recorded was Medor Black Lady, but she leaves no champion descendants. Why blacks attracted so little attention in the early days is hard to justify. Their growth and progress in Germany always equalled, and even exceeded that of the salt and peppers. Not until the mid-1930s was a serious attempt made to breed blacks.

Willia Maguire of California took on the task and, after several generations of breeding from original German imports, produced the first black AKC champion. Whelped January 15, 1935, Ch. Cunning Asta of Bambivin started winning as a puppy, and finished in July 1936 with a Group 3rd. She was not a prolific producer and leaves no modern descendants. Longevity was there, however, as Asta lived well over 16 years as Mrs. Maguire's companion.

The next to finish, and first male was the German import, Ch. Hupp von Schonhardt of Crystal in 1942. Although used extensively by his owner William Kuback of the Crystal Kennel in Connecticut, Hupp leaves few, if any, American champion descendants. He left several litters in Germany, however, and there the line still flourishes.

Ch. Cunning Asta of Bambivin, the first black AKC champion.

The third black AKC champion was also from Germany, and would be the last German import of any color to finish. Ch. Dirndl v. Schloss Helmstadt completed her title in 1950. Dirndl leaves champion descendants from her American breedings through Can. Ch. Winsor's Jon Martinique, the first black Canadian champion. Finished in 1972, Jon is a son of Winsor's Johann B and derives his color from a bitch line extending to Dirndl. Jon, who died young, has champion descendants in Ch. Haig's Black Label of Winsor and his son Ch. Brandiwein's Label Me Black. Through her German-bred daughters, Ina and Ida v.d. Burg Heldenstein, Dirndl appears twice in the pedigree of the cornerstone Italian-bred black sire, Eng. Ch. Jovinus Malya Swanee.

It was more than a decade before the next black would finish. This fourth AKC champion would mark a new beginning, as she would be the first to carry lines to the salt and pepper super sire, CH. DOREM DISPLAY. This renaissance would have an international flavor, based principally on imports. The three key dogs, in order of their impact, were Jovinus Rodin of Anfiger, from England, Italian Ch. Malya Gunter from Italy, and Koniglich The Groom from Australia. Rodin and Groom are very similarly bred, from English Jovinus and Italian Malya lines, while Gunter is intensely black-bred from German and Italian lines.

Every post-war black champion carries many lines to DISPLAY, even those descending from Gunter, who has essentially European background. Rodin and Groom trace their lines to DISPLAY through Jovinus Risotto. Her sire was the salt and pepper Eng. Ch. Jovinus Roxburgh, a son of Eng. Ch. Wilkern Tony From America and Eng. Ch. Deltone Delsanta Barbara. Tony has three lines to DISPLAY and Barbara has six, the key branch involved being that of Delegate. These dogs, however, were exclusively salt and pepper. The black color would come from Swanee.

Jovinus Risotto, as the dam of Rodin, brought nine lines from DISPLAY. Groom, doubly bred on Risotto, has 18 lines here, plus another through his maternal great-grandsire, Eng. Ch. Deltone Deldisplay.

```
                        Int.Ch. Ivo v.d. Heinrichsburg (B)
            Frodi v Rekelhof (B)
                        Olga v.d. Heinrichsburg (B)
        Eng.Ch. Jovinus Malya Swanee (B)
                        Ital.Ch. Arno v.d. Walkmuhle (B)
            Ital.Ch. Nixi dei Diavoli Neri (B)
                        Nitty dei Diavoli Neri (B)
JOVINUS RODIN OF ANFIGER (B)
                        Eng.Ch. Wilkern Tony From
                            America (S/P)
            Eng.Ch. Jovinus Roxburgh (S/P)
                        Eng.Ch. Deltone Delsanta
                            Barbara (S/P)
        Jovinus Risotto (B)
                        Amberway Pirate (B)
            Jovinus Ravenna (B)
                        Redenhall Hella (B)
```

The JOVINUS RODIN OF ANFIGER line

In the spring of 1964, Anne Eskrigge (Anfiger) of Massachusetts imported Jovinus Rodin of Anfiger. He enjoyed limited success as a show dog, acquiring five points in the United States during a period when blacks received scant consideration. His principal achievement was as a sire, with over 50 black champion descendants, virtually all of them the result of a single breeding.

In 1965 Alice Gough of Minnesota bred the salt and pepper Gough's Pickwick Silver Belle, CD, bred by Ursula Buys, to Rodin. Intensely line-bred within the Ruffian branch, Belle represented the most modern type in salt and pepper, and was an ideal choice. The Rodin-Belle breeding produced three blacks: a male, Gough's Ebony Royal Guardsman, and two bitches, Gough's Ebony Guardian Angel and Gough's Ebony Gay Gidget, all with champion descendants. Unfortunately, Guardsman was killed by an automobile when only three, leaving just three litters.

The Guardsman daughter, Ch. Johnson's Ebony Kwicksilver, became the first black champion in 20 years, finishing in December 1969. She was the first American-bred to finish since 1936. Her title quest included Winners Bitch at the Paul Revere Specialty—another breed "first." To her advantage was the expert conditioning and presentation given her by handler Joan Huber (Blythe-wood).

**Eng. Ch. Jovinus
Malya Swanee**

Gough's Ebony Royal Guardsman

Ch. Woodhaven's Black Gough Drops

Thereafter, an increasing number of blacks began to appear in the show ring, some of them shown by top professionals.

The next to finish was Ch. Woodhaven's Black Gough Drops, sired by the Guardsman son, Gough's Ebony Knight Longleat, CD, who also sired Ch. Dufferton Mack The Knife.

Although based in Minnesota, Gough Drops was seen from coast to coast. His owners Harry and Helen Smith and their son Dan gave him an extensive show career in which he accumulated several "firsts" for blacks, including two Group 1sts. This exposure served many purposes, opening the door for blacks at a critical period.

Gough Drops was the first to sire four black champions, and is behind at least 40 more, making him, by far, the most influential American-bred black producer.

The principal breeders in the east, midwest and west used Gough Drops, each developing their own families. Alice and Wayne Gough, who really got the ball rolling in 1966, as the breeders of both Kwicksilver and Gough Drops, wisely used him to bring their family forward. They took the Gough Drops daughter, Gough's Ebony Heavens To Betsy (doubly bred on Knight Longleat) back to Knight Longleat to get their star of 1982, Ch. Gough's Ebony Royal Knight, CD. His accomplishments include five Group 1sts, a Specialty Best and the first and only AKC all-breed Best in Show for a black, all wins breeder-owner handled by Alice. A full brother to Royal Knight, Int. Ch. Gough's Ebony Edge of Knight is a Best in Show winner in Sweden. Royal Knight has already distinguished himself as a sire with a Specialty winning son, Ch.

194

Gough's Ebony Thundercloud.

Bob and Nancy Berg, working with Gough's foundation stock, have bred several black, as well as black and silver champions since the early seventies. The black star of the Bo-Nanza breeding program was clearly Am. and Can. Ch. Bo-Nanza's Black Bulletin. He claims the distinction of being the first black to hold both titles, and enjoyed a show career which included Best of Breed wins three years in succession. In all, Bulletin won 20 Bests of Breed and four Group placements, and to date has sired two black champions. The Bo-Nanza breeding program had an even greater impact on black and silvers, as was so with several breeders working with both colors.

Geri and Dick Kelly of Massachusetts have bred champions in all three colors, but are the premier breeders of black champions, with over a dozen homebreds. Most of them are Gough Drops descendants, with Kelly's Fancy Nancy serving as their foundation bitch. Nancy is the maternal granddaughter of the black and silver Ch. Tiger Bo Von Riptide, from which she derives the black and silver gene. Nancy produced Ch. Kelly's Black Onyx (3 Chs.) and Ch. Kelly's Cassandrea Xan (4 Chs.), and the Kellys began to weave their offspring with remarkable success.

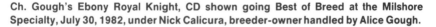

Ch. Gough's Ebony Royal Knight, CD shown going Best of Breed at the Milshore Specialty, July 30, 1982, under Nick Calicura, breeder-owner handled by Alice Gough.

Ch. Kelly's
Black Onyx

The Kelly's blacks claim most of the records for this color variety. Am. and Can. Ch. Kelly's K.E. Ebony Superstar, a Cassandrea daughter, was the first black bitch to gain titles in both countries. Am., Can. and Bermudian Ch. Kelly's K.E. Ebony Show Stopper, an Onyx son, went a step further with titles in three countries. Whelped May 21, 1978, he was a star on several levels, being the first to gain a Canadian Best in Show. His record of eight Group 1sts and 15 additional placements was far and away the best for a black to that date. Most importantly, Show Stopper is a multiple Specialty winner, and the first and only black to win an AMSC Specialty, topping 56 entries including ten champions in New York, February 8, 1981. Before being exported to Japan, he sired two black champion daughters, plus a champion each in salt and pepper and black and silver.

Show Stopper was the maternal grandsire of the Kelly's next star, Ch. Kelly's Flamboyant Black—the top winning black bitch to date. Her one-year record in 1982 netted her No. 4 (Knight System) and top bitch, with 32 Bests of Breed, five Group 1sts and 12 additional Group placements. Like all the Kelly's blacks, she was breeder-owner conditioned and handled by Geri.

Flamboyant went on to set another record when she produced four black champions, three finished in 1984 as puppies. These were sired by the Superstar son, Ch. Kelly's Imperial Black, and include the leading black winner of 1984, Ch. Kelly's Ebony Top of the Line, who outdid her dam with 35 Bests of Breed that year.

Dolores Walters was the first westerner to make use of the Rodin son, Gough Drops. Mrs. Walters' California-based kennel had been producing champions of all three colors for nearly two decades, frequently exporting her best throughout the world with excellent results. Although no champions resulted from the Gough Drops breeding, there are seven Walters champions that are line-bred from him. Most of these descend from Ch. Walters' Black Bonus and his sons, Chs. Walters' Black Topper and Black Bandit.

Even further west, in Hawaii, is another Gough Drops son, Ch. Woodhaven's Black Protege.

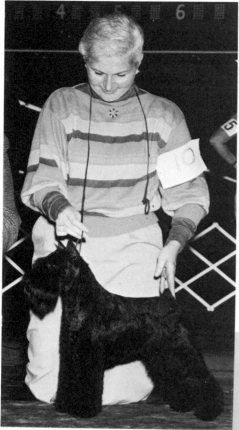

Ch. Kelly's Ebony
Top of the Line
with Geri Kelly.

Ch. Walters'
Black Bonus
with Wood Wornall.

The ITALIAN CH. MALYA GUNTER line

Italian Ch. Malya Gunter was imported from Italy by Janice Rue (Suelen) and Marilyn Laschinski (Aljamar). Gunter was personally selected by Mrs. Rue in 1970, and he immediately left his mark. The Gunter son, Ch. Aljamar Tommy Gun, was the first black to gain points at Westminster, and the Tommy Gun daughter, Ch. Aljamar Honey Bun, the first black bitch to win a Group. Honey Bun is the dam of this color variety's top black sire to date, Ch. Aljamar Rabbit Punch. He is the sire of five black champions, three bred by Galen and Carma Ewer of the Carmel Kennel in Texas. All are out of their salt and pepper Tommy Gun daughter, Aljamar Honey Delite, CD (4 Chs.).

Tommy Gun has also exerted an influence on black and silvers through his black and silver grandson Ch. Aljamar Hot Ice, CD, who has champions in all three colors.

Beverly Pfaff's California-based Jebema Kennel, working along with Robert Heberling and Hilbert Duarte (Robhil), has combined lines from Rodin and Gunter to get Ch. Jebema-Hil Black Jammer, and more recently, Ch. Jebema-Robhil Ebony Marquis, both out of Pfaff-Hils Black Cameo (3 Ch.), a granddaughter of Ch. Kelly's Black Onyx. Beverly is another that conditions and handles her own dogs.

Mary Spring and her daughter Kim of the Spring-along Kennel also have a breeding program involving all three colors. Their 1984 champion, Ch. Spring-along Black Pony, carries lines to both Gunter and Rodin, being by Rabbit Punch out of a daughter of Ch. Dufferton Mack The Knife. The same is true with Cheryl Coffman's 1984 champion, Ch. Jacqueminot's Midnight Guy, sired by Rabbit Punch out of a line-bred Kelly's bitch.

Ch. Aljamar
Rabbit Punch
with Claudia Seaberg.

Ch. Carmel
Crackerjack

199

The KONIGLICH THE GROOM line

Jackie Walsh (now Olsen) of Illinois imported Koniglich The Groom in 1965 from Sylvia Cerini of the Koniglich Kennel in Australia. He is an inbred son of Aust. Ch. Jovinus Rigoletto, a full brother to Rodin, out of one of his daughters. Although Groom sired no champions, he has champion descendants in all three colors, including seven blacks to date.

Sharon Tomanica in Michigan began working with these black lines, producing several pointed blacks, but no champions. Her Groom grandson, Tammashann's Black Jack, out of the imported Rodin sister, Jovinus Rebel Rouser, produced the pointed Tammashann's Black Onyx. He is doubly bred on Groom, being out of his daughter, Walsh's Black Pearl.

The first black champion to emerge from this line was bred by the partnership of Jill Cook and Lucille Kocher. After successive trips to Europe, Miss Cook imported three black bitches in 1968. One of these, the German-bred Helga v.d. Stadtmusikanten, produced Ch. Arbury Gay Uncle Sam when bred to Tammashann's Black Onyx. He would be the most intensely black-bred champion to date, with no salt and pepper and only one black and silver appearing in his three-generation pedigree. As was expected, Sam was a homozygous black, and produced only black get. Because of his German-bred dam, he provided an outcross from those lines already being developed.

There would be a three and four-generation gap before the next black champion would emerge from this line. The Kellys would be responsible for a pair of littermates, Ch. Kelly's K.E. Ebony Son of a Gunn and Ch. Kelly's K.E. Ebony Star Attraction, sired by the salt and pepper super sire, Ch. Penlan Peter Gunn. They were three-quarters salt and pepper breeding, gaining their color from their great-grandsire, Uncle Sam.

The strongest line from Sam is also three-quarters salt and pepper in content, coming through three generations to Sam's great-grandson, Ch. Masterman's Mr. Blackjack, bred by Shirley and Michael Goulet of South Carolina. Blackjack is the sire of one black champion, Ch. Aberdovey Five Card Stud, finished in 1984, and is the grandsire of two: Ch. Aberdovey Ace In the Hole (by Five Card Stud) and Ch. Masterman's Midnight Charisma, both doubly bred on Blackjack.

A new high in black activity was achieved in 1984 when an even dozen champions were finished. By this time a total of 65 black AKC champions had been recorded since the first in 1935. The Rodin branch continues to dominate, with nearly three-quarters of the total carrying from three to 15 lines to Rodin. The majority trace to his grandson, Ch. Woodhaven's Black Gough Drops. The trio of Kelly's littermate champions finished in 1984, as an example, carry five lines to Gough Drops. The Gunter and Groom branches are clearly evident, with a pair of the 1984 champions tracing to each.

There has been far less blending of these three branches than might be expected, and many current breeders are choosing salt and pepper lines to improve type. Salt and peppers figure prominently in five of the 12 champions

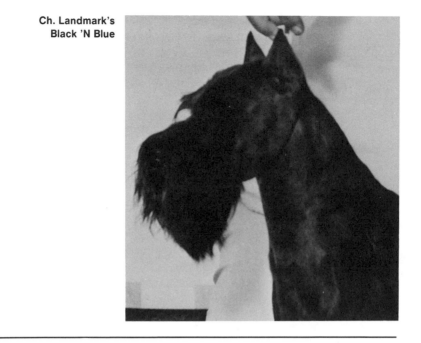

Ch. Landmark's
Black 'N Blue

finished in 1984, and the dominant factor in this respect is Ch. Skyline's Blue Spruce. He is the sire of Ch. Landmark's Black 'N Blue, and the grandsire of Ch. Oak Vue's Blackglama. Three were sired by the inbred double Blue Spruce grandson, Ch. Regency's Right On Target—the first salt and pepper to sire three black champions. All five carry from one to three lines to Ch. Walters' Black Topper from which they derive their color.

These newest black champions were competing on all levels with unusual success. The Target son, Ch. Regency's Shot In The Dark, at just six months of age became the first black to win an AMSC Sweepstakes, topping 20 puppies under breed specialist Sue Baines, and going Reserve in the regular classes under Enid Quick (Valharra). A few months later he finished with back-to-back five-point wins at the June 1984 AMSC and Southern California Specialties —another "first" for blacks. His future looks bright as he finished out the year with 11 Bests of Breed and six Group placements, including two 1sts. In 1985 Shot In The Dark became the first black to achieve Top Schnauzer (Knight System) with a record of 50 Breed Bests. He and his sister, Ch. Regency's Kalea of Jubilee, are owned by Judy and Bill Sousa (Jubilee) and were handled by Beverly Verna (Regency).

Ch. Oak Vue's Blackglama, bred in California by Marianne Douglas (Oak Vue), also enjoyed success at Specialties that summer. Professionally handled by Robert Milano, she was Winners and Best Opposite over three bitch champions at the Chicago Specialty under Barbara Snobel (Bardon), repeating these wins the next day.

Ch. Landmark's Black 'N Blue, bred and owned by Gloria Weidlein (Landmark) was Best in Sweepstakes at the New Orleans Specialty under Mary Ann Ellis (R-Bo), also going Winners Dog and Best Opposite over a champion, handled by Barbara Wysocki (Country Squire).

It will be interesting to see if this recent crop of highly successful black champions, with more than three-quarters salt and pepper breeding, can retain their color in the generations to come.

Breeding Blacks for Color and Type

Anne Eskrigge (Anfiger), who had done so much to promote black progress, gives sage advice in the 1976 edition of *The Complete Miniature Schnauzer* (Howell Book House):

> Why, indeed, try to breed blacks at all? Because one likes their color. Because they add variety to the breed. And because it is a challenge to produce blacks good enough to compete with salt and peppers on even terms. It is the last reason, of course, that demands careful thought and selection.
>
> The first step in planning a color cross is to consider what each color can contribute and how to go about choosing the individuals to be used.
>
> When selecting foundation stock for breeding blacks, the best plan is to choose one or more black bitches. If they are from stock in which some color crossing has already been done, care should be taken to see that such crossing has resulted in improvement of type without serious loss of color quality. It is advisable in most cases to start with black bitches rather than males because there is an almost unlimited choice of top salt and pepper studs available for breeding at a normal stud fee.
>
> As when planning any mating, the male should be chosen for his individual quality, his suitability for the bitch in question (so as to minimize faults and emphasize good points), his record as a producer of quality puppies, if he has one, and his pedigree from a producing angle. Where a mating is of necessity an outcross, it is most important that line-breeding or inbreeding should help to give prepotency to the sire chosen and make the planning of future combinations easier.
>
> It will be easier and quicker to achieve the desired results if you have two or three black bitches available when you start operations, or if some neighboring breeder will cooperate. You can then try more than one combination and compare results. Also, there is less possibility that you will lose time because your bitch presents you with an all-male litter, or one in which the only female is the poorest of the lot; for once again, it is better to choose a bitch for the next step in your program.
>
> Obviously, since you are seeking to establish show type in blacks, you will want to select a female puppy who represents an improvement over her dam in this respect. At this stage, type is of greater importance, but if the choice between two puppies is otherwise equal, or the variation a minor one that can easily be corrected, always choose the better colored one.
>
> In order to fix the desired improvement of type if it is obtained, the bitch (or bitches) selected from the first generation cross should be mated back to a salt

and pepper closely related to her sire and of equally good quality. This might be his own sire, making a grandsire-granddaughter breeding which is often very successful. Or it could be his uncle, a full or half brother, a nephew or even a son or grandson. In any case, the emphasis should be upon the most prepotent lines in the pedigree.

The result of this second generation color cross is decidely less predictable than was the first as far as color is concerned. Approximately half the litter will be salt and pepper, or perhaps there may even be one or more black and silvers. Also, if any recessives have been introduced there may be mismarkings or other color faults to a greater degree than is likely in the first generation. Then, considering the sex ratio, especially if the litter is small, there is a good possibility that there may be no more than one black bitch, if any. Unless other litters are available, either within the kennel or through cooperation with another breeder, this may mean waiting in the hope of better luck in the next litter.

If a good black bitch does appear in this litter, she will of course be three-fourths salt and pepper breeding. At this point there is a choice between a further mating to a salt and pepper, once again selected to maintain quality and continue the line breeding, or if there is one available, breeding to a black male of similar breeding. The decision depends on the judgment of the breeder and the results so far obtained. If the black color continues to be good, continuing the line breeding to the salt and pepper side may be the best decision in the long run. Even if the quality of the black is not all that it might be, this may still be the best choice.

After establishing a uniform type, with a number of individuals at hand for further breeding, emphasis in selection may then be shifted to color. The problem then becomes one of retaining the desired type while using the strongest colored individuals to improve the black color. If the type is sufficiently established, one may then try going back to one of the first generation cross. The mating of a homozygous to a heterozygous black should result in half the litter being homozygous. Which individuals are homozygous can then be established by test matings, preferably with salt and peppers, to see whether any salt and peppers are produced.

When test-mating to salt and peppers has identified a homozygous black of acceptable quality, the breeder will have come a long way toward accomplishing his objective. Several such blacks of both sexes should make it possible to breed black to black and obtain 100 percent black puppies. The problem from that point on is to maintain both type and color quality. This requires sufficient available stock to allow for proper selection and culling of inferior specimens.

12

The History of Black and Silver Miniature Schnauzers

THE HISTORY of the black and silver (B/S) Miniature Schnauzer is less clearcut than that of salt and peppers or blacks. One of the very distinct differences between solid black and B/S is that the blacks are genetically dominant while the B/S are recessive. In simple terms this means that a black parent can pass on this color gene regardless of the other parent's color, whereas both parents must carry the B/S gene to produce a puppy of that color. Two B/S parents, each having two B/S genes, will produce only B/S and cannot transmit the dominant black or salt and pepper (the latter is dominant over B/S, but is in turn recessive to solid black). Due, however, to modifying factors about which we know too little, the quality of the black portion of the coat may vary, and some sprinkling of salt and pepper or pure white hairs may be present, as well as undercoat that is less than pure black.

It appears that the original Marienhof import, Ch. Amsel v.d. Cyriaksburg carried the B/S gene. Her dam, Peppi v. Hohndorf, was listed in the German stud book as "black and brown," while Amsel's daughter, Fiffi of Marlou, and the latter's daughter, Abigail of Marienhof, were registered as B/S. Abigail, as the granddam of Ch. T.M.G. of Marienhof, appears many times in the pedigree of CH. DOREM DISPLAY.

Ch. Tiger Bo Von Riptide shown winning the Terrier Group at the Kennel Club of Beverly Hills in 1968, under Australian judge Charles DeGroen, handled by Daisy Austad.

The T.M.G. son, Ch. Inka of Aspin Hill, finished in 1938, seems to be the first B/S champion recorded by the American Kennel Club. Ch. Gretchen v. Harter was the first B/S champion bitch. California-bred, she finished in 1940, and according to her owner, kept good color throughout her life. If there were any post-war champions of this color before 1967, the AKC has no record of them.

It was purely by chance that Ch. Tiger Bo Von Riptide emerged. His dark salt and pepper sire Ch. Melmar's Jack Frost clearly carried the B/S gene, also producing the B/S bitch Ch. Black Magic of Mary-O. This pair when mated produced the first litter from champion B/S parents, and the first such combination to produce a B/S champion—Ch. Tiger Bo's High Mark, finished in 1969. A repeat breeding produced the short-lived Ch. Bruhil Sticky Wicket.

Tiger Bo, owned in California by Sue Hendricks, did much to stimulate interest in this color through his success in the show ring. He was seen on both coasts, initially causing quite a sensation at the AMSC Specialty in February 1966 where at 13 months he won an Open class of 15 under the great all-rounder, Alva Rosenberg. Defeated in the challenge, he had to settle for Reserve, and repeated at Westminster—the first B/S to score so well at these events. More important "firsts" would soon be earned, beginning with his Best of Winners over 45 class entries at the Southern California Specialty where his sister, Ch. Kelly Girl Von Riptide, was Winners Bitch. While still in the classes Tiger Bo became the first B/S Group winner, topping a quality entry at the Kennel Club of Beverly Hills in 1967, handled professionally by Daisy Austad, who also finished High Mark. Tiger Bo became the first B/S to sire three B/S champions, all from champion bitches line-bred to Jack Frost.

The first serious attempt to develop a B/S line began in 1955 by Mrs. Jackie Walsh (now Olsen) of Chicago. Her success with this color was based on intense line-breeding from the salt and pepper bitch Sugar Cookie. She carried 12 lines to DISPLAY, seven through Ch. Dorem High Test, three through Ch. Dorem Tribute and one each from Ch. Diplomat of Ledahof and Ch. Meldon's Merit.

Cookie is the maternal granddam of the first B/S Canadian champion, Walsh's Frosty Charmer, CD, who, indeed, is this color variety's kingpin stud, with more than half the B/S champions throughout the world carrying lines to him. Further development of this extraordinary line occurred here and in Canada simultaneously as a result of a single breeding.

The key branch involved was that of Ch. Dorem High Test. When the salt and pepper Cookie daughter Walsh's Peanuts was mated to the B/S Walsh's Frosty Beau, she produced Charmer, who carries ten lines to High Test. Walsh's Frosted Cookie, from a Cookie daughter bred to a Cookie grandson, nearly doubles the lines from High Test, and when bred to Charmer quadrupled the lines to him.

The offspring of the Charmer-Frosted Cookie breeding set the trend for B/S, with Can. Ch. Walsh's Frosty Spaceman going to Sharon Tomanica (Tammashann) in Michigan, and Sylva Sprite Ceratina going to Joanna Griggs (Sylva Sprite) in Canada.

Mrs. Griggs began breeding B/S in 1964, importing Charmer and then Ceratina from Mrs. Walsh. An additional import was made in 1968, but this time from England. Although British-bred for several generations, Can. Ch. Eastwight Sea-Voyager, CD, carries many lines to DISPLAY, particularly through Canadian-bred Cosburn exports, primarily from the Ch. Benrook Beau Brummell branch. Being uncropped, Sea-Voyager became the first and only B/S Canadian champion with natural ears.

I saw Sea-Voyager on one of his rare showings in the United States. He was a first-class Miniature Schnauzer on all counts, and had the best pair of natural ears I have ever seen, before or since. His coat and color were excellent and his attitude superb. He would have been easily finished in the United States had his owner persisted. Sea-Voyager, in fact, could finish just as easily today!

It was inevitable that Ceratina would be put to Sea-Voyager, and the result was all that could have been wanted, and more. Am. & Can. Ch. Sylva Sprite Snowy Mittens became the first B/S to earn both titles. He combined the substance and soundness of his dam with the refinement and showmanship of his sire. His success on the Montgomery County weekend in 1970, where he was Best of Winners at Devon, has yet to be duplicated by a B/S.

**Can. Ch. Walsh's
Frosty Charmer, CD**

**Can. Ch. Walsh's
Frosty Spaceman**

**Can. Ch. Eastwight
Sea-Voyager, CD**

Am. & Can. Ch. Sylva Sprite Snowy Mittens shown going Best of Breed at the Canadian Specialty, March 26, 1972, under Sam Lothrop, Jr., breeder-owner handled by Dr. Dorothy Griggs (Sylva Sprite).

There were dozens of Sylva Sprite Canadian champions finished over the next decade, and the large majority were B/S descending from Snowy Mittens. They were rarely exhibited in the states, and Mrs. Griggs explains why:

> Our showing in the U.S. is extremely limited. Since all our dogs are house dogs, we never had the heart to let them be professionally handled, with the kennel and cage life that goes with it. And so out of necessity we showed in the U.S. only rarely when able to take a holiday.

These rare occasions frequently proved fruitful. At the Paul Revere Specialty in Massachusetts in 1967, the B/S Can. Ch. Sylva Sprite Benjamin was Best of Winners, and his B/S half-sister, Can. Ch. Sylva Sprite Frills and Jade, Reserve. Both descend from Sea-Voyager and Ceratina.

A series of exports to the Continent began with a Sea-Voyager - Frills and Jade daughter, Swiss Ch. Schnauzi's Sybil. Frieda Steiger of the Schnauzi Kennel in Switzerland imported several other B/S in the early 1970s, all essentially from similar breeding.

American B/S champions descending from Snowy Mittens trace mostly to his son, Gough's Frosted Bonanza, who carries half solid black background. He is the sire of two B/S champions, including Am. and Can. Ch. Britmor Sunnymeade Frost, Am. CDX and Can. CD. Bred, owned and shown by Karen Brittan (Britmor) of Minnesota, Frost owns several "firsts." He is the first B/S with both bench and obedience titles in two countries, as well as a C.G. (Certificate of Gameness). With his Canadian Best in Show win in 1983, he became the first B/S to achieve this high honor in Canada.

Bob and Nancy Berg (Bo-Nanza) claim the most B/S champions descending from the Snowy Mittens son, Frosted Bonanza. His daughter, Bo-Nanza's Delightful Delsey, was the first to claim three B/S champion offspring, albeit one being a champion in the Netherlands. Dutch Ch. Bo-Nanza's Frosted Queen was exported to Mme. L. Huwhert of Belgium, while the Bergs retained her brother, Ch. Bo-Nanza's Frosty Lone Ranger. He is the sire of their most recent B/S champion, Ch. Bo-Nanza's Frosty City Slicker who carries three lines to Frosted Bonanza.

Frosted Bonanza claims one top producing sire among his descendants. His B/S great-grandson Ch. Aljamar Hot Ice, CD has sired six champions (two Canadian) to date in all three colors.

The exclusively American-bred branch from Can. Ch. Walsh's Frosty Spaceman is brought forward principally through his B/S son (and great-grandson) Am. & Can. Ch. Tammashann's Town Strutter. His only B/S champion offspring, Ch. Karma's Moonlight Shadow, is out of his B/S

Ch. Bo-Nanza's Frosty City Slicker

Ch. Tammashann's Town Strutter

granddaughter, Ch. Sercatep's Frost N Flash, CD, who claims two other B/S champions, all bred, owned and shown by Karin and Mark Jaeger (Karma) of Michigan. Their littermate B/S Ch. Karma's Image of Eclipse and Ch. Karma's Royal Flash are the most intensely line-bred, color-bred B/S to date, carrying nine lines to Charmer.

Debbie and Del Herrell (Sercatep), also in Michigan, have developed an extraordinary line of B/S, tightly line-bred on Charmer. This color variety's top producing sire is their B/S Ch. Sercatep's Strut N Proud (9 Chs.) with eight B/S champions to date. He is a half-brother to Frost N Flash, both by the salt and pepper Ch. Glory's Eager Beaver (4 Chs.).

The Charmer branch claims two additional top producing bitches. Pine Needles Sercatep Pride bred by Nancy DeCamp (Pine Needles) has four B/S champions, all by Strut N Proud. Margo Heiden (Sycamore), also in Michigan, bred four B/S champions from her Charmer great-granddaughter Sycamore Sassafras, Am. and Can. CD. One of these is the record-setting Am. and Can. Ch. Sycamore Solar Eclipse, whose AKC title quest included a Group 1st and a Best at the Columbus Specialty in Ohio—the first B/S to top a Specialty. In 1982, professionally handled by Richard and Arlene Smith (Richlene), his record-setting accomplishments included a repeat at Columbus, Best at the Chicago Specialty, plus 15 additional Bests of Breed, nine Group placements and three more Group 1sts. As No. 8 (Knight System) he set a record point total for B/S. Solar Eclipse is the sire of the Karma champion littermates, with the prospects for more.

Ch. Sycamore's Solar Eclipse shown going Best of Breed at the Columbus Specialty, November 13, 1981, under Roger Hartinger, handled by Richard Smith.

**Ch. Karma's
Image of Eclipse
with Mark Jaeger.**

**Ch. Sercatep's
Strut N Proud
with Debbie Herrell.**

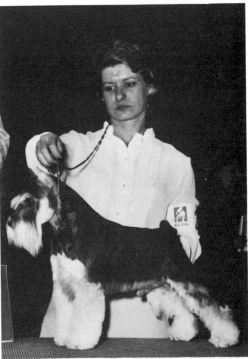

Ch. Ro-Sean's Maiden Warrior shown going Best of Breed at the Milshore Specialty under Robert Condon, handled by co-owner Carol Garmaker (Repitition).

Solar Eclipse carries a line to another black and silver family developed in the early 1970s by Susan Carr (Eclipse), along with June DiCiocco and Geraldine Senerote (Cobby Land). The key dog was the salt and pepper Ch. Blythewood Winsome Lad (4 Chs.). He is the double grandsire of the champion B/S brothers, Ch. Eclipse Trethaway's Coaldust and Ch. Eclipse Shadow of the Son. Shadow became a top producing sire with five champions, including two B/S, Solar Eclipse and Ch. Eclipse Dark Side of the Son, the latter claiming Winsome Lad as his only great-grandsire.

In the last decade a salt and pepper bitch registered simply as Jobie has had a marked effect on B/S as well as salt and peppers. There are 13 B/S champions to date, and even more salt and pepper champions intensely line-bred from Jobie. She served as foundation bitch for Carol and Kurt Garmaker's Repitition Kennel in Nebraska. Their first B/S champion, Ch. Repitition's Midnight Cowboy, carries three lines to Jobie. Their best producing salt and pepper sire, Ch. Repitition's Best Beau (6 Chs.), carries two lines to her. The B/S Ch. Rampage's Waco Kid, bred by Jan Ramel (Rampage) and owned by

Ch. Ro-Sean's Weekend Warrior shown going Best in Show under Alice Lane, handled by his co-breeder and owner Sean O'Connor (Ro-Sean).

the Garmakers, appears to be the heir apparent of those descending from Jobie. He is the sire of this color variety's first and only AKC Best in Show winner.

Sean O'Connor (Ro-Sean) in Wisconsin began a breeding program in the late 1970s that has produced two record-setters. His foundation bitch, Aljamar Fanny May, has produced three B/S champions to date, all from sires descending from Jobie. His first homebred, Ch. Ro-Sean's Maiden Warrior, finished at nine months, is this color variety's top-winning bitch. In 1982 she started out the year by winning the Milshore Specialty in Wisconsin—the first B/S bitch to top a Specialty. By year's end she had earned 11 Bests of Breed, 18 Best Opposite awards, plus nine Group placements, handled by the Garmakers.

"Like mother—like son" was the story of Ro-Sean, as Maiden Warrior came forth with another record-setter in her B/S son Ch. Ro-Sean's Weekend Warrior, by Waco Kid. Like his dam, he finished as a puppy, twice gaining Specialty majors. In 1984 he was owner-handled to Best in Show at the Indianhead Kennel Club over 669 entries—a most impressive "first."

Black and silvers, clearly on the rise, have captured most of the possible awards. What still remains is top wins at Parent Club Specialties. There has yet to be a B/S winner of an AMSC Specialty—sweepstakes or regular classes.

In 1981, after nearly three years without a new B/S champion, there appeared a virtual bonanza with a record ten new champions; in 1985 there were 14. That is nearly one half of the total of 55 which had been recorded since Ch. Inka of Aspin Hill in 1938.

Why the boom of '81 and '85? This has not come easily, and has taken breeders many years of careful selection to achieve these results. They not only had conformation on which to concentrate, but must always keep in mind a true black color what will hold, and with the proper amount of markings.

Alice Gough, who has enjoyed particular success in breeding, conditioning and handling champions of all colors, offers these special hints on grooming blacks and black and silvers:

Ideally, both the show dog and the household pet should be groomed alike. Since many blacks and black and silvers have salt and pepper bloodlines behind them and may acquire a lighter or dull undercoat, clipping will usually give an undesirable appearance. Many advocate stripping leg furnishings well in advance of the body coat, to minimize the possibility of the leg hair turning that undesirable "reddish" color. Even clippered or scissored areas under the tail or on the head will often take on a "mousy" appearance (showing the color of the undercoat). Occasionally banded hair will occur at the colic line on the throat. Double stripping this area helps, and may eliminate it in future coats.

Good, hard-coated blacks need more attention spent on furnishings. Keep them well oiled to prevent breaking, remembering to wash them with a mild shampoo frequently to prevent dust and grime clinging to them, adding to the chance for breakage. The soft-coated blacks are usually "dripping" with furnishings, although the color is less likely to be jet black. These soft coats should be double stripped; that is, hand stripped to the bare skin (keeping a "Tee Shirt" on until the coat peeks through), and then stripped again in each section. This hard work will be rewarded with a much harsher coat and less undercoat.

In the black and silver coat, the same types of body coats may be present, and deserve the same treatment mentioned above. However, the furnishings present a unique problem. Observe the dog from the rear, noticing that most black and silvers have a black overlay on furnishings, usually on the outside of the hind legs, which gives the optical illusion of the dog tracking narrow. We prefer to put the black and silver down by chalking all furnishings to the elbows and hocks as one would for a salt and pepper, thereby lightening the "overlay."

We suggest stripping in three stages. Approximately ten weeks prior to showing, we take off Stage 1, from behind the shoulder blades, down the sides to directly behind the elbows, straight back to one inch in front of the tail, taking the hindquarters down to two fingers above the hocks, with a small amount of fringe on the anterior of the leg, up to the loin. Stage 2 is taken off eight days to two weeks later, depending on the season of the year and the rate of hair growth of the individual. This area involves from the shoulder blades anteriorly up the neck and down the shoulders to two fingers above the elbows. The tail and the inch or so in front of it are also stripped now. Stage 3 is done six weeks prior to showing,

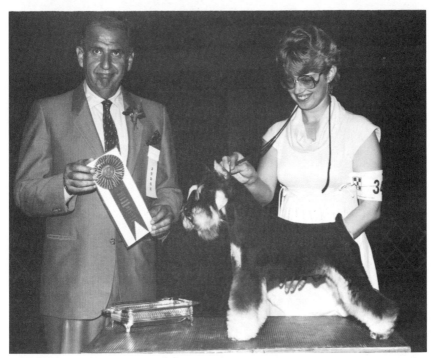

Ch. Rampage's Waco Kid shown going Best of Winners at the Gateway Specialty, June 3, 1983, under Louis Auslander (Alpine), owner-handled by Carol Garmaker (Repitition).

with the head stripped bare (cheeks and throat may also be stripped at this time if desired).

If you did not strip the cheeks and throat area along with the head, this area should be clipped with a #10 blade two weeks prior to showing. Also clip the "butterfly area" under the tail, and the underside from the ubilicus on back, avoiding the inside of both hind legs. Ears may be clipped if needed, and all inside hair pulled out of them. Nails are trimmed and the pads checked for excess hair. Eyebrows are shaped and legs are "barber poled." Inside legs are trimmed to give the appearance of a well-defined arch. Thinning shears may be used to blend clippered areas with the stripped coat on the front of the chest, to give a tight, straight look.

On the day of the show, for blacks, we wash furnishings with a no-rinse shampoo; blow damp-dry, add a protein hair thickener, finish drying, comb and check to see if adequately "barber poled." Check the dog gaiting as well as in stance.

For the black and silvers, we delete the protein hair thickener and apply a greaseless white night cream, and then work in all the chalk the furnishings will take, allowing them to dry completely, brushing out all residue, combing and checking to see if they are perfect, both standing and moving.

Since blacks and black and silvers are very striking, we hope all owners will take the extra time to make sure he is well presented and a credit to the breed.

215

13

The Miniature Schnauzer
in Canada

ALTHOUGH MINIATURE SCHNAUZERS are among the more popular breeds in Canada, the numbers being bred continue to be small compared to activities in the United States.

The first Canadian champion appears to be the German-bred, American-owned Nette v. Mumlingtal in 1933. Anne Eskrigge (Anfiger), breed historian par excellence, claims this first. Nette descendants include the famed record-setting producer Am. and Can. Ch. Sorceress of Ledahof.

The first homebred Canadian champion was the Misses Cluffs' Ch. Bendigo of Clearbrook, from an American-bred Wollaton sire and dam. It was a slow start, with only one other titlist, Am. and Can. Ch. Handful of Marienhof, finishing before World War II. He is the sire of the first Canadian-bred to achieve an AKC title—Audrey Firman's Ch. Droessel of Fuerstenhof.

A small nucleus of breeders in the Montreal and Toronto area accounted for the remaining "firsts" before the war years brought a halt to their activity. Edwin Wright of Montreal bred the first Canadian champion claiming parents with Canadian titles. Ch. Winwel Love-In-Bloom was sired by Thomas Wylie's Ch. Silvermist of Marienhof out of Mr. Wright's Ch. Kathie Khan of

Am. & Can. Ch. Cosburn's Aristocrat

Marienhof. The Silvermist daughter, Strathburn MC Alpha Ann, appears to be the first Canadian-bred to produce an AKC champion in Mac Mar Miniature Model.

Mr. Wylie's Strathburn establishment appears to have been the only really active breeding kennel during the 1940s, owning six Canadian champions, two of them also AKC champions. The first Miniature Schnauzer to win a Canadian Terrier Group was Mr. Wylie's homebred Ch. Strathburn JP Beta Misty in May 1948. In October that year, Mrs. Evashwick's Sorceress became the first to win Best in Show, and DISPLAY, in 1949, became the first male to attain this honor. From this point forward, the breed would depend exclusively on DISPLAY both here and in Canada.

Beginning with the formation of the Miniature Schnauzer Club of Ontario on September 26, 1951, the Toronto area became the center of breed activity. Mr. and Mrs. William Gottschalk were among the founders and served as club officers for several years. This club's first Specialty was won by their Am. and Can. Ch. Benrook Beau Brummell, and in 1952 by their Beau Brummell son, Am. and Can. Ch. Cosburn's Aristocrat—the first Canadian-bred AKC

Am. & Can. Ch. Jonaire Pocono Gladiator shown going Best of Winners at the AMSC Specialty, February 11, 1962 under Alva Rosenberg, handled by Mrs. Hugh Simpson (Rosehill).

champion. Aristocrat duplicated the win two years later under the American breeder-judge Robert Kerns, Jr. (Wollaton).

In 1955 the club was renamed the Miniature Schnauzer Club of Canada, with Toronto continuing to be the center of activities. Mr. and Mrs. Gottschalk's Cosburn Kennel by this time had received broad recognition. As the breeders of Ch. Cosburn's Esquire, their influence is felt world-wide (see BEAU BRUM-MELL branch).

Several successful prefixes emerged during the 1960s, including Caldora, Rosehill, Sylva Sprite and Tannenbaum. The leading sire during this period was Am. and Can. Ch. Jonaire Pocono Gladiator with 14 Canadian champions. Few stories can match that of Gladiator's. Bred by Mr. and Mrs. Specht (Jonaire), he was purchased as a puppy by William Marriot of Ontario, then 92 years of age. Mr. Marriot's daughter, Mrs. Hugh Simpson (Rosehill), had been winning well in the breed, and would handle Gladiator to titles on both sides of the border. At age 94, Mr. Mariott was able to see Gladiator complete his AKC title at the 1962 AMSC Specialty in New York, where Alva Rosenberg awarded him Best of Winners over 53 class entries. Gladiator is a triple great-grandson of Beau Brummell, and the dozens of Rosehill champions over the next three decades would extend this branch from DISPLAY to the present. Gladiator sons and daughters dominated the 1960s, the following gaining Top Schnauzer status: Ch. Rosehill Poco's Impression, Ch. Rosehill Coco Chanel and Ch. Graham's Gladiator Trademark.

One of Gladiator's first champion offspring was Jo-An-Alaur's Anastasia (ex Cosburn's Heide), foundation for Joan Morden's Tannenbaum Kennel in Ontario. Another breeder with nearly three decades of activity, Mrs. Morden claims a remarkable record of having finished one of every four puppies bred, all tracing to Anastasia. Her first homebred litter, by Ch. Handful's Blue Teal, produced Chs. Tannenbaum Blue Chip, By Golly and Lillibet, each, in turn, champion producers when line-bred to Esquire.

By the early 1970s, third and fourth generation Tannenbaums were enjoying successful show careers. Best known perhaps is Ch. Tannenbaum Purse Snatcher, Top Schnauzer in 1972 and the first of the breed to win three Bests in Show in Canada. Having earned his Bermuda title at six months and four days of age, he is believed to be the world's youngest champion. Ch. Tannenbaum Sunday Punch kept the ball rolling as Top Schnauzer for the next two years.

Lately, Mrs. Morden, an all-breed judge, has limited her breeding in favor of international judging commitments. However, with the 1985 littermate champions, Tannenbaum Newsboy and Morning Edition, the record of one champion for every four dogs produced at Tannenbaum continues.

Doris Hayes of Caldora Kennel was the first to bring Miniature Schnauzers into prominence in Western Canada, beginning in the mid-1950s. The most famous of the dozens of Caldora homebreds was Am. and Can. Ch. Caldora Returning Ace, who held the honor of being Canada's Top Schnauzer for four years. Mrs. Hayes was honored six years running as the Club's "Breeder of the Year" in the 1960s.

The Sylva Sprite Kennel was established in Ontario in 1959 by Joanna Griggs and her daughter Dr. Dorothy Griggs. They have become Canada's premier breeders with over 80 homebred, owner-handled champions to date, including some 30 black and silvers. Their most famous homebred, Am. and Can. Ch. Sylva Sprite Snowy Mittens, was Top Schnauzer in 1971, and his get, and theirs, have been leading winners to the present. Mittens continues to be Canada's leading sire of black and silver champions. No Canadian breeders have had a broader impact on bloodlines world-wide than Sylva Sprite. This influence is documented in the chapter on black and silvers, as well as those on Great Britain and other countries.

In 1968, Cherrylane Kennel was formed by a young teenager named Martin DeForest. However, when Martin left home to attend the university, priorities were realigned and breeding and showing were curtailed, but not his keen interest. Being a long-time admirer of the Blythewood dogs, it was Joan Huber whom he contacted for a fresh start. He acquired a number of first-class animals, including Am., Can. and Bda. Ch. Blythewood National Newsman,

Can. Ch. Sylva Sprite Twilight Blue became the third Sylva Sprite homebred to achieve Best in Show honors, receiving the nod from the classes under Winnifred Wartnow, owner-handled by Dr. Dorothy Griggs.

one of ten champions from matings of Valharra Prize of Blythewood to Ch. Blythewood National Anthem. Newsman was the winner of four U.S. Specialties in 1982, including AMSC Montgomery County, handled by Joan Huber —the first Canadian-owned dog to achieve this honor. He then finished his title in Bermuda with three straight Group 1sts. In 1983, Newsman was the Top Schnauzer in Canada, with a Best in Show and many Group wins, and in 1984, the top sire. With 15 Canadian and three AKC champion get that year, it was the best record ever achieved by a Canadian-owned sire. To date, the list of champion Newsman offspring exceeds two dozen—a Canadian breed record.

Several other Blythewood dogs would go north of the border to finish under the Cherrylane banner. Ch. Blythewood Thunder Cloud is the sire of five champions, most notably the homebred Ch. Cherrylane Thunderbolt, out of Am. and Can. Ch. Blythewood National Asset. Thunderbolt completed his Bermuda title in spectacular fashion, winning four Groups and two Bests in Show. His tragic death occurred when he had all but completed his AKC title.

Blythewood would also figure prominently in the formation of Mrs. E. M. Lee's Handsworth Kennel in Quebec and Lynda Berar's Naibara Kennel in Alberta.

Handsworth breeding was founded on Am. and Can. Ch. Jasper's I'm A Sweetheart, a double granddaughter of Ch. Blythewood Main Gazebo. Bred to Ch. Blythewood His Majesty, she produced the first and only littermates to achieve both AKC and CKC titles. One of these, Am. and Can. Ch. Handsworth Topsy Lee, enjoyed remarkable success in the United States handled by Joan Huber. Her title quest included major wins at two Specialties, and in 19 shows as a champion, she won Best of Breed 15 times, BOS three times—out of the ribbons only once. Mrs. Lee's initial import, Am. and Can. Ch. Blythewood Blue Max, was 1969's Top Schnauzer, and leaves champion descendants.

Mrs. Berar's foundation bitch came from Handsworth, and carried several generations of Blythewood breeding. Naibara's first homebred champion, Naibara's Something Special, by Ch. Sky Rocket's Bound To Win, was Top Bitch in 1976. Two years later her son Ch. Naibara's Midnight Special would lead the breed.

Am. & Can. Ch. Blythewood National Newsman became the first Canadian-owned Miniature Schnauzer to win a Montgomery County AMSC Specialty, October 1982. The judge is Alice Downey and the handler is breeder Joan Huber; Jinx Gunville presents the club medallion.

Can. Ch. Naibara's
Midnight Special
with Lynda Berar, and (below) her
son, Can. Ch. Naibara's It's Hard
To Be Humble, winning a Group
under Margaret Young.

In less than a decade, 32 champions claim the Naibara prefix, the majority of them breeder-owner handled. Sires from the Ruffian branch would continue to be the mainstay in the Naibara breeding program to the present. In 1984, the Midnight Special son, Ch. Naibara's It's Hard To Be Humble, finished third in breed standings with a Group win and several placements. The fact that he is uncropped makes his record unique, as he is believed to be Canada's first homebred champion with natural ears!

Armand and Jaclin Gratton (Frontenac) kept the breed to the fore in Quebec since the early 1970s. They introduced slightly different bloodlines than those already established by importing at 8½ months, Postillion Pirate's Pearl. She was finished within a month. Pearl is intensely line-bred to Ch. Marwyck Pitt-Penn Pirate, but also carries many lines to the Ruffian branch through her Helarry background. She proved to be a remarkable producer, with eight

---

Can. Ch. Frontenac's Cannon winning Best Puppy in Show under Vincent Perry, handled by his breeder-owner Armand Gratton (Frontenac).

champion get, including Ch. Frontenac Franc Pirate, also the dam of eight champions. Pearl's most successful son is Am., Can. and Bda. Ch. Frontenac's Big Foot, the sire of six champions to date. Pearl's influence is best measured by the fact that over 40 Frontenac champions descend from her.

The Grattons have also exported breeding stock to Denmark and Belgium, most notable among them being Can. and Int. Ch. Frontenac Pierre D'Asterix, a breed winner in Finland, Germany and Denmark, and a Best in Show winner in France. Pierre is owned by Mr. and Mrs. Henry Carlsen of the Asterix Kennel in Denmark, renowned breeders of Giant Schnauzers.

Massawippi Kennel is owned by Mr. and Mrs. S.I. Clark of Ontario. They began breeding in the early 1970s, basing their program on American-bred sires from the Ruffian and Diplomat branches. Their foundation bitch, Massawippi In For A Penny, is by Bound To Win, and has given them seven champions from three different sires. Penny's most successful offspring is her son Ch. Massawippi Troubadour, by Ch. Sky Rocket's Victory Bound. Troubadour is Canada's all-time top winning Miniature Schnauzer, with a record of 125 Bests of Breed—over 60 of these without defeat. The Top Schnauzer for 1981 and 1982, he went on to win three Bests in Show, 35 Group 1sts and over 60 other Group placings. At five years of age he had already sired ten champions including five Group winners and two Specialty winners.

Robert and Dorothy Moggach's Gay Meadows Kennel has been active since the mid-1960s, and has provided breeding stock to many others in the Ontario area.

Rosemary Duncan began her Hexenbraus with Can. Ch. Gay Meadows Clover Honey. She gave Hexenbrau two champions, and several more have emerged in succeeding generations. Mrs. Duncan added another Gay Meadows, this one a black and silver. Can. Ch. Gay Meadows Piped In White is by a Sylva Sprite sire and a Tannenbaum dam, so carries many generations of all-Canadian breeding. He has also added to the champions bred at Hexenbrau.

The Wheelwood Kennel was established in the mid-1970s by Irmgard Wheeler in Ontario. She has the distinction of being Canada's sole breeder of champions in all three colors. Based on a salt and pepper Rosehill bitch, Wheelwood has line-bred tightly within the Diplomat branch, especially to Ch. Landmark's Masterpiece. The blacks gain their color from Italian Ch. Malya Gunter, and the black and silvers from Snowy Mittens. The most recent Wheelwood champion is the black Ch. Wheelwood's Man In Black, who finished at the 1985 Specialty.

The partnership of Rene Germain and Earl Reidy (Pepperwood) and Lory and John Ross (Tanyetta) was the first to bring in Penlan lines. A line-bred trio from Carolane was imported in 1978, foremost among them being Am. and Can. Ch. Carolane's Star Warrior, a champion producer. All carry lines to America's super sire, Ch. Penlan Peter Gunn.

The 1980s have seen a resurgence of interest, and a host of new breeders are making their presence felt in all the provinces.

Can. Ch. Massawippi Troubadour, Canada's all-time top winning Miniature Schnauzer, is handled by Murray Clark for breeder-owners Mr. & Mrs. S. I. Clark (Massawippi).

Ernie Sellers has worked exclusively with Penlan stock since 1980, finishing his first homebred, Ch. Jena's Jazz Baby, in 1981. He then purchased Am. and Can. Ch. Penlan Penny Stock, getting his next two homebred champions from her breeding to Ch. Penlan Promissory. Both Ch. Jena's Juris and Ch. Jena's Justiciar finished from the Bred-by class. Penny was next bred to Ch. Penlan Peter's Son, who came to Jena in 1984 to live out his retirement years as his companion.

Sensation Kennel was established in 1981 by Irene and Paul Wessler, with their foundation, Ch. Frontenac Cleopatra's Pearl, being purchased as a puppy. She produced four champions, the most noteworthy being Ch. Sensation's Andante, by Troubadour. Andante was then bred to Newsman, giving them two more champions, including Ch. Sensation's Cheer Leader, who, in turn, has also produced two champions. In four years, Sensation has racked up eight champions, all finishing with Group placements.

Cestrian Kennel began in 1981 with the purchase of the line-bred Naibara bitch, Koerad's Midnight Serenader. She became Pam and Les Hallam's first champion, and produced, by Troubadour, their first pair of homebred, Group-winning champions. A repeat breeding gave them another pair of champions, including Ch. Cestrian Dusty Shadow, Best of Breed at the 1985 Specialty.

Catherine McMillan (Minuteman) of Saskachewan has bred three champions from Naibara's Be My Valentine, sired by Newsman. Ch. Minuteman's Go Dog Go has a distinguished record of 60 Bests of Breed, 10 Group 1sts and a Best in Show.

Blacks and black and silvers are clearly the specialty at Kathleen Todd's Stargazer Kennel in Manitoba. Founded on the all-color-bred black, Ch. Suelen Evening Stargazer, purchased from the partnership of Marilyn Laschinski and Janice Rue (Suelen), she would get two champions, one black and one B/S, from her first litter, bred to the B/S Ch. Rampage's Waco Kid.

Blythewood figures prominently in three recent establishments. Sue Ailsby of Regina has bred five Dragonair champions from her Acclaim daughter, Can. Ch. Blythewood All Dressed Up, all sired by Newsman.

The Caix Kennel of Lesley and David Salson is the well-known home of many top-winning Standard Schnauzers. Expansion into Miniatures was initiated with the purchase of Am. and Can. Ch. Cherrylane 24 Kt. Brat (Newsman-Asset), along with a Newsman son from Sensation, and a son of Ch. Blythewood Shooting Sparks from Blythewood.

The partnership of Tim Doxtater and Dom Emslie (Annfield) in British Columbia is another venture founded on Blythewood imports: Can. Ch. Blythewood National Sequence and Can. Ch. Blythewood Shenna of Annfield.

With American and Canadian bloodlines continuing to overlay, the progress expected on both sides of the border should be comparable.

Can. Ch. Cestrian's Dusty Shadow is Best of Breed at the 1985 Canadian Specialty under Clover Allen, handled by Murray Clark. Joan Morden (Tannenbaum), Club President, presents trophy.

**Can. Ch. Wheelwood's
Man In Black**

**Am. & Can. Ch. Penlan
Penny Stock**

14

The Miniature Schnauzer in Great Britain

Ch. Enstone Cito

THE MINIATURE SCHNAUZER was introduced to Great Britain just a few years after the original Marienhof imports began to make their mark in the United States. British breeders faced several handicaps not experienced by their American counterparts, accounting for the breed's slower progress. The six-month quarantine required by British law added to the difficulty and expense of importing foundation stock. The most obvious handicap was the Kennel Club's rule forbidding the showing of dogs with cropped ears. Since virtually all the German stock imported were cropped, they could not be exhibited. This would have provided a strong base on which to educate both breeders and the public as to the correct type and charming qualities of the breed.

Miniature Schnauzers suffered the same identity crisis in Britain as here, first being placed with their larger cousin, the Standard Schnauzer, in a single club. It was not until 1967 that both sizes were moved from the Non-Sporting Group to the Utility Group, where they have remained. Only in America are Miniature Schnauzers shown in the Terrier Group.

The breed was not given separate registration until 1932, and for a brief period the British Kennel Club changed their name to *Affenschnauzer*. The Club's first Challenge Certificates (CCs) were actually awarded to the breed under this name. Following a strong protest from the German Club, the breed has been called Miniature Schnauzer since 1936.

The 1933 edition of the Crufts show, which is equivalent to our Westminster Kennel Club event, was the first to give the breed separate classes. Three years later, in 1936, this show offered a set of CCs for Miniatures. The Bitch CC was awarded to the black Enstone Beda, eventually becoming the first black champion in the breed. The Dog CC also went to a homebred from Mr. W.H. Hancock's Enstone Kennel. Enstone Cito, a salt and pepper, was to become the breed's top winner of the post-war period with eight CCs.

There were seven champions made up in the four-year period preceeding the outbreak of the war in 1939. Two of these were German imports, including the breed's first English champion, the salt and pepper bitch, Ch. Crowsteps Grafin Heinzelmannchen. Mrs. Simmons of the Crowsteps Kennel imported more than a dozen Miniatures from the Continent in the mid-1930s, most being heavy in Heinzelmannchen blood.

Led by the Enstones and Crowsteps, along with Mrs. Langton-Dennis's Offley dogs, a firm foundation was layed. The Offley dogs were the first to carry American blood, albeit just a generation or two from similar Continental ancestry.

In 1933 Mrs. Langton-Dennis imported the American bitch Gretel of Allsworth, a daughter of Ch. Gretel of Marienhof, one of the nine champions in the various matings of Ch. Lotte v.d. Goldbachhohe to Ch. Cuno v. Burgstadt. Before leaving the States, Gretel of Allsworth was bred to Ch. Porgie of Marienhof, whelping three puppies in quarantine. One male, Simon of Offley, played an important part in the breed's post-war development.

The interruption caused by the war took its toll, and the breed during this period reached a low ebb. In 1946 when Championship shows were resumed, registration figures for the year amounted to only 47. Four years later the numbers grew to 76, the Kennel Club by then offering six sets of CCs for the breed.

The number of CCs allotted used to depend on annual registrations in the breed. The middle 1950s saw figures average about 150, advancing to around 500 in the middle 1960s, and today approaching 1,000. Currently, with a continuing rise in popularity, Miniature Schnauzers are granted 25 sets of CCs, including three at Specialty shows.

Dondeau Favorit Heinzelmannchen together with his son (right) Ch. Dondeau Helios, and daughter (left) Ch. Dondeau Haphazard.

Breed progress in Britain can be divided into three natural periods: pre-war, post-war to the mid-1950s, and the mid-1950s onward. A select group of American imports would play a vital role, particularly during the last three decades.

America's super sire of the 1950s, CH. DOREM DISPLAY, would prove equally important in bringing British lines forward.

The Quarrydenes of Mrs. Milson provided the main link between pre- and post-war periods. Mrs. Milson bred and owned 12 champions and provided foundation stock for several successful breeders. The first post-war champions were the littermates, Ch. Quarrydene Gabriel of Dondeau and Ch. Quarrydene Gaby of Dondeau, bred by Mrs. Milson, but owned by Donald Becker. Their dam, Quarrydene Gelda, a Simon descendant, held the record as the breed's top producing dam for over 20 years, with five champions from three different sires.

Mr. Becker bred or owned 14 champions between 1948 and 1970, based on the Quarrydene stock so rich in Enstone and imported Heinzelmannchen blood. He imported Dondeau Favorit Heinzelmannchen who tied in well with bloodlines already in Britain. Favorit was the first sire to produce four English champions.

The first post-war American import, Minquas Harriet, would also figure prominently in Mr. Becker's breeding program. Harriet, whelped in 1944, carried four lines to Ch. Marko of Marienhof and one to Ch. Priscilla of Marienhof, who carries similar lines as Ch. Porgie of Marienhof, the sire of Simon. Harriet, when mated to Pickles of Offley (who carries three lines to Simon and two to Simon's sister) produced Ch. Dondeau Hamerica—the most American-bred English champion of the post-war period.

The last Quarrydene champion, finished in 1962, introduced Dorothy Owen to the breed. Ch. Quarrydene Frances of Settnor is behind all the 11 champions bearing Mrs. Owen's Settnor prefix. The last, made up in 1974, was her great-great-great-granddaughter, Ch. Sao Selena of Settnor.

The new group of fanciers that came to the fore after the war saw the need to add the advanced American breeding that seemed to produce more style and showmanship.

Douglas Appleton imported two American-breds which were to play an important part in bringing the breed forward. The first, Ch. Rannoch-Dune Randolph of Appeline, was a double grandson of Ch. Delegate of Ledahof (a son of the great DISPLAY), and carried some of the same lines as Harriet. Uncropped, Randolph finished his championship in 1953 and won six CCs. In spite of his show successes, he sired only a few litters, but with significant results.

Bred to Doreen Crowe's Deltone Delilah, a double Hamerica granddaughter, Randolph sired Ch. Deltone Appeline Doughboy, a cornerstone sire.

Ch. Deltone Appleline Doughboy

Doughboy met with great success both in breed and all-breed competition, matching the long-standing record set by Cito, with eight CCs. The next entire decade would be Doughboy's, as his offspring almost exclusively dominated the breed classes.

Between the years 1950 and 1972 the Deltone prefix was associated with 18 champions, while 27 English champions came from either a Deltone sire or dam. The majority of present-day champions trace to Doughboy and the Deltone stock stemming from him. He is recognized as being one of the first to stamp his offspring with consistent and recognizable type.

American-bred dogs would continue to effect the breed through the 1960s. Douglas Appleton imported from Canada, Appeline Cosburn's Pickwick Peppers, line-bred to DISPLAY, and carrying Dorem, Benrook and Ledahof background. He proved to be a perfect tie-in for Pamela Morrison-Bell's developing Eastwights, founded on Deltone Delmanhatton, a Doughboy daughter out of Deltone Nevada, a Rudolph daughter.

The Eastwights continue to be Britain's top producing kennel within the breed. To date, 24 champions carry the Eastwight prefix, with only two not being homebred. Miss Morrison-Bell continued to concentrate on American bloodlines, using a son of Ch. Wilkern Tony From America with Delmanhatton, to get Ch. Eastwright Sea-Nymph. Peppers was used on Sea-Nymph, resulting in two champions. She produced a third when bred to yet another American-bred, Ch. Sternroc Sticky Wicket.

Tony and Wicket added further to the concentration of DISPLAY blood. Tony was imported by Mrs. Creasy of Roundway fame. His dam, Wilkern Nicolette, was, like Rudolph, a grandchild of Ch. Delegate of Ledahof. Tony's sire, Ch. Tweed Packet of Wilkern, was out of a litter sister to Delegate. Nicolette carries yet another line to DISPLAY on her sire's side.

In 1954, Tony became the first Miniature Schnauzer to win a Group at a Championship show. He also won several Bests in Show at all-breed Open shows. Although Tony sired two champion sons, his line was brought forward to the present through daughters. Roundway Anklet, the top producing dam to date in the breed, is intensely line-bred to Tony. Three of her six champions were sired by the Peppers son, Risepark Northern Cockade, and three from the American-bred Ch. Risepark Bon-Ell Taurus.

Beginning in 1960, yet another line to DISPLAY was added when Pamela Cross-Stern returned to England from living in America. She brought with her the first American champion to be imported. The father-son brace, Ch. Nicomur Chasseur and Ch. Sternroc Sticky Wicket, produced some record-setting results. Wicket became the first to sire eight champions, four out of Audrey Dallison's Gosmore Peaches and Cream, a Doughboy great-grand-daughter. These included Eng. & Aust. Ch. Gosmore Wicket Keeper, the first Miniature Schnauzer to go to Australia, and Ch. Gosmore Opening Batsman, winner of 24 CCs, the breed record for nearly 20 years. Mrs. Dallison also bred Ch. Gosmore Hat Trick, by Wicket out of a double Tony granddaughter. Hat Trick was to hold the record for bitches with 16 CCs for some 12 years.

232

Pamela Morrison-Bell at home with (L to R) Ch. Eastwight Sea-Wren, Ch. Eastwright Sea-Charmer and Eastwright Sea-Commodore.

Ch. Risepark Bon-Ell Taurus

Mrs. Dallison's Gosmore "Cricket Team" played a large part in helping the breed to become better known during this period of growth. She captured national press and television interest with Wicket at Crufts, where he was benched "Not for Competition," with his own private detective in attendance. The cricket theme used by Mrs. Dallison for all her dogs sired by Wicket did much to draw attention to the breed.

Among those becoming interested in the breed around the middle 1950s was Peter Newman, starting with two Doughboy puppies, Deltone Delouisiana and Ch. Deltone Delaware. These two produced Risepark Ha'penny Breeze, the dam of two champions. Mr. Newman's Risepark prefix was to play a significant part in the breed's history, particularly through a series of American imports, beginning with Ch. Risepark Bon-Ell Taurus.

Bred in California, Taurus carried a concentration of DISPLAY, principally through Ch. Diplomat of Ledahof, full brother to Delegate. This provided yet another American branch from DISPLAY, and the resulting type, another variation on the theme. Taurus sired five champions, three out of the top producer, Roundway Anklet. The most successful of the trio was Ch. Risepark Toreador, the sire of Pam Radford's and Dori Clark's homebred Ch. Iccabod Chervil. He, in turn, sired seven champions, including Fred and Phyl Morley's Ch.

234

Ch. Risepark Toreador with his trophies.

Ch. Iccabod Chervil as a veteran at eight years of age.

Ch. Castilla Linajudo with his Crufts trophies.

Castilla Zambra, the dam of history-making Ch. Castilla Linajudo.

First shown in 1979 at eight months, Linajudo won his first CC and Best of Breed, and never looked back. Shown only once in 1982, he captured his 31st CC—a breed record. In between, Linajudo became the first Miniature Schnauzer to win a Best in Show at Championship show level—and he won two! In addition he was three times Reserve BIS, including Crufts in 1980. He won the Utility Group nine times (another breed record) and was Reserve twice. These wins gave Miniature Schnauzers a tremendous nationwide boost, and set the stage for further top level successes which quickly followed.

The Morley's Zambra would also produce Ch. Castilla Diamante, owned by the partnership of Radford and Clarke, the top winner of 1983 with 10 CCs and two Group wins. She was sired by yet another Risepark American-bred, Ch. Irrenhaus Impact At Risepark.

The impact made by Taurus is nothing short of phenomenal, with nearly half of the champions finished since 1970 being his descendants. The Taurus son, Toreador, is in charge of the largest percentage of champions descending from this line. The Iccabod partnership finished the first of their seven champions to date in 1974. Their homebred Toreador son, Ch. Iccabod Chervil, quickly earned top producing status as the sire of seven champions, including Ch. Castilla Zambra, the dam of the famed Linajudo and Diamante.

Toreador daughters were highly prized by several new breeders during the 1970s. Tom Fennybough's Toreador daughter, Fernery Honeysuckle, gave him Ch. Fernery Fantastic, the sire of Linajudo. A trio of line-bred sisters by Toreador were to have a significant place in the breed's development. The three Catalanta bitches, Catalanta Miss Lucy, Miss Lissette and Little Sparkle, were bred by Sid and Gil Saville, and are out of a Taurus daughter.

Miss Lissette went over to Mrs. Furst-Danielson in Sweden, where she was mated to her American-bred Ch. Starfire Criterion Landmark. A dog from the litter was returned to Risepark where he became Ch. Jidjis Min Cato At Risepark, the sire of eight champions including the good producer Ch. Catalanta True Luck of Risepark, out of Catalanta Miss Sparkle.

Malenda is the prefix of Glenys Allen, who started off with Catalanta Miss Lucy, and has bred six champions to date. Her Miss Lucy granddaughter, Ch. Malenda Mimosa, was Best of Breed at the Club Championship Show in 1978 under the American judge Olive Moore of Travelmor fame.

William, Olive and Jennifer Moore of Trenton, New Jersey have had a far-reaching effect on contemporary British bloodlines. When Janet Price Callow returned home to England after spending several years with the Moores, she came with Ch. Travelmor's Fantazio and Riversedge Petite Pebbles. Fantazio brought with him yet another tail-male branch from the great DISPLAY. The pair when mated produced the aptly named Ch. Buffels All American Boy of Deansgate, the breed's all-time top producing sire with nine champions to his credit.

Buffels was owned by the Deansgate partnership of Pamela McLaren and Elisabeth Cooke. His major influence was through the Fernerys, Malendas and Eastwights, and subsequently, the Arbeys of Betty and Archie Fletcher. They started with the Buffels daughter Ch. Short and Sweet of Deansgate, a Taurus granddaughter, who gave them three champions by Eastwight sires. To date the Fletchers have made up nine champions, their latest being Ch. Arbey Sugar and Spice, the first champion sired by the cropped American-bred Skyline's Leader of Risemount.

The Travelmor people have for several years acted as host to American dog fanciers attending Crufts. They have made many friends on their annual visits and have shared many experiences with their British counterparts. A particular friendship with the Iccabod partnership has reaped remarkable rewards. In the early 1980s, two cleverly named Travelmors were sent over to Iccabod. The first, Ch. Travelmor's From U.S. To You, had truly regal

**Ch. Travelmor's
From U.S. To You**

Ch. Travelmor's U.S. Mail

background. Her dam, Ch. Reflections Lively Image, is a top producer in the U.S. with seven American and two English champions to date. She, in turn, is sired by the breed's all-time top sire in America, Ch. Penlan Peter Gunn.

Breed history was made in 1982 when From U.S. To You became the first bitch to win Best in Show at a Championship event in Britain. She was to win 19 CCs in just over a year to become the breed's top winning bitch to date.

The Moores later sent over the dog, Ch. Travelmor's U.S. Mail, personally selected as a ten-week-old puppy by Pam Radford. Another out of Lively Image, he also brought with him the top winning Skyline bloodlines, as the son of yet another American super sire, Ch. Skyline's Blue Spruce. Not to be outdone by his half-sister, U.S. Mail also became a Best in Show winner, topping over ten thousand entries at Birmingham City and winning Best at the Group show and All-Schnauzer Specialty in 1984. As this is being written, the offspring of the BIS winning Travelmor pair, Ch. Iccabod Travellers Tail, is making his presence felt on all levels of competition. In addition, U.S. Mail has further served notice as the youthful sire of English, Irish and Australian champions.

In recent years several other new prefixes have come into prominence. John and Susan Smedley have had three Best in Show winners at Club Championship shows, two by Rimmick homebreds. To date they have made up five champions including Specialty winning Ch. Rimmick Ricochet, the Utility Breeds Group show Best in 1979.

Philip and Suzanne Bagshaw's Brynmor prefix has yet another American-bred connection via Swedish Ch. Barclay Square Maximin Minx. Imported by Benny Blid, Minx spent some time with the Bagshaws before joining him in Sweden. Before going she produced three champions from two litters. The first, by their Brynsmor Joker, of Eastwight breeding, resulting in the brothers, Ch. Maximin Isbyorn, owned by the Smedleys, and Ch. Maximin Graben of Deansgate, owned by Deansgate, both champion producers.

238

Ch. Irrenhaus Impact At Risepark

The breed's only other Championship show Best in Show winner to date comes from this family in the Graben son Ch. Deansgate Truey Nuff, bred at Deansgate and owned by Dorothy Webster. Truey Nuff was BIS at Blackpool's Golden Jubilee Show in 1983.

It appears that a fourth "period" in British breed history is emerging with the 1980s, based on a new influx of American breeding with related bloodlines. Ch. Skyline's Blue Spruce, so intensely line-bred within the Diplomat branch, already has a dominant position in these emerging bloodlines. He is the sire of Ch. Travelmor's U.S. Mail, as well as Andy Walker's Skyline's Leader of Risemount, who is doubly bred on Spruce. Ch. Irrenhaus Impact At Risepark, whelped November 9, 1980, carries three lines to Spruce and has served notice as an important sire with six champions to date, including the top winning Diamante. In 1985, yet another Irrenhaus import was made up by Peter Newman. Ch. Irrenhaus Aims to Please Risepark carries four lines to Spruce, being a daughter of the inbred Spruce double grandson, Ch. Regency's Right On Target.

The future holds promise for these emerging new American bloodlines. Only time will tell which will achieve prominence and play a significant part in the breed's future.

The Color Varieties in Great Britain

Interest in blacks has always been limited. Almost three decades separate the breed's first black champion, Ch. Enstone Beda, from the next to finish, Ch. Jovinus Malya Swanee.

Mrs. Jo Reynolds can take full credit for the maintenance of blacks in the post-war era. Foundation for the Jovinus blacks was Redenhall Hella, rich in Enstone blood. Mrs. Reynolds had to turn to Italy for improvements, importing Swanee from Mrs. Possi's Malya Kennel. He was well received, winning Best in Show at the Miniature Club Specialty in 1963. This was the second time Mrs. Reynolds was to do so with a black. The bitch, Jovinus Risotto, was Best in 1961 and became the dam of the first British-bred black champion since Beda. It was the combination of Swanee and Risotto that produced Ch. Jovinus Replica. Finished in 1969, she is the last of this color variety to gain an English title.

The further efforts of Mrs. Reynolds, along with those of Wally Butterfield, Phyl and Fred Morley, and more recently Gill Barwick, have kept the color alive. However, they continue to lag far behind the advancements, based on the same bloodlines, being made in America.

The same can be said of the black and silver variety, but here the British have been severely handicapped. Not until June 1985 did the Kennel Club officially recognize the black and silver color. The relevant color clause now reads:

> All pepper and salt colors in even proportions, or pure black or black and silver. That is, solid black with silver markings on eyebrow, muzzle, chest and brisket and on the forelegs below the point of elbow, on inside of hindlegs below the stifle joint, on vent and under tail.

Pamela Morrison-Bell can claim much of the credit for advancements made in black and silvers throughout the world. The Eastwights obviously carried the black and silver recessive, as they would appear from time to time.

The arrival of Eastwight Sea-Voyager in 1967 marked the recognizable advent of this color, but his effect had to be realized in America. Sea-Voyager came over to Joanna Griggs of Sylva Sprite in Canada, where he quickly finished his Canadian title.

Sea-Voyager played a significant role in this color variety, siring three Canadian champions, including Am. and Can. Ch. Sylva Sprite Snowy Mittens, the first and only Canadian-bred black and silver to achieve both titles. Snowy Mittens sired eight Canadian champions and has eight American black and silver champion descendants, principally through his son, Gough's Frosted Bonanza.

Lines from Sea-Voyager are sprinkled throughout the Continent. The Snowy Mittens son, Sylva Sprite Entity went to Switzerland where he joined earlier Canadian exports of this color. Switzerland had been the first country in Europe to recognize the color; the Pinscher-Schnauzer Club in Germany recognized it in 1976, and it should soon be internationally accepted.

The British Miniature Schnauzer Club celebrated its Silver Jubilee Year in 1984 and pulled out all the stops in presenting its 25th Championship show. The Club's current membership is around 300, and a third of these sat down to a champagne luncheon. The Club's president, Miss Morrison-Bell of Eastwight fame, was the anniversary judge. She selected as her Best in Show the American-bred Ch. Travelmor's U.S. Mail. The Bitch CC and Reserve BIS was Deansgate I Am Mai, who at four years of age was made up at this show.

Ch. Catalanta True Luck of Risepark with Peter Newman.

Peter Newman, a vice-president of the club, circulated for the first time his long-awaited Club-sponsored *Breed Booklet*. To this writer it is a most comprehensive and remarkable work. The term "booklet" seems so much an understatement of its true value.

This chapter is written almost exclusively from materials provided in Mr. Newman's extraordinary work. Those that have enjoyed and/or expanded their knowledge of the breed as a result have Peter to thank.

241

15

The Miniature Schnauzer in Australia

$\mathbf{A}$NY COMMENTARY on the Australian dog scene deserves a bit of a geography lesson as well. Australia is approximately the size of the United States, but has only one-twentieth of the population. Sydney is the center of Australia's most populous state, New South Wales (N.S.W.), boasting 5,000,000 residents, and the most dog-related activities. The state of Victoria is next in population, and its center is Melbourne. The Melbourne Royal Show can be compared with our Westminster and England's Crufts. This spring event annually attracts over 6,000 dogs and lasts for 10 days. Just before Melbourne Royal finishes, the Perth Royal starts. As it cost some $1,200 in 1985 to fly the 2,000 miles west, there are not too many people flitting cross-country to show dogs. Even the distance between Sydney and Melbourne seems to prohibit many fanciers from out-of-state exhibiting.

In Australia, Schnauzers of all three sizes compete in the Utility Group, along with Boxers, Dobermans and the like. They follow the same pattern as in England, with Miniatures, Standards and Giants all in competition at the two Club Specialty events each year.

Miniature Schnauzers were first introduced to Australia in 1962, by Mrs. J. Rees of the Casa Verde Kennel in N.S.W. and Mrs. C. Cerini of the Koniglich Kennel in Victoria. England would supply the original stock, and continues to be the main source of new bloodlines. The key dog, however, would still be the "all-American" super sire, CH. DOREM DISPLAY.

Gosmore Wicket Keeper, from the famous Gosmore "Cricket Team" (see BRITISH chapter) was the first to earn an Australian title. Mrs. Rees also imported a pair of bitches for his court, resulting in several Casa Verde champions.

Mrs. Cerini began with an English-bred, CC-winning Wicket Keeper son, Deltone Deldario. He became an Australian champion within 10 weeks of his first show appearance, and was Best in Show at the first Schnauzer Club of Victoria Specialty in 1967. At seven years of age Deldario won the Breed at Melbourne Royal, and went on to further successes as a veteran. Blessed with the incredible longevity enjoyed by the breed, he died in 1980 at 18½ years of age.

Doreen Crowe of the famed Deltone Kennel in England was the principle supplier of breeding stock throughout the 1960s. The first bitch imported by Mrs. Cerini became Australian Ch. Deltone Delsanta Delia. She lived to be 13½ and is behind virtually all the Koniglich champions to the present. Other Deltones were added to the Koniglich roster, including Deltone Delsanta Doric, Deltone Deldaryl, and in 1972 Eng. Ch. Deltone Delduque—all becoming Australian champions and producers of champions.

Mrs. E. Templeman started her Tempo Kennel in May 1963 with the English import Sheenhart Honeysuckle, making her a champion the next year. Her daughter, Ch. Tempo Dasheba, by Deldario, became the first Victorian-bred champion. Honeysuckle provided only a slight variation on the theme, being a granddaughter of Wicket Keeper's brother Gosmore Middle Stump. Mrs. Templeman also imported Eng. Ch. Courtaud Pannyann Pampas, after he was Best of Breed at the Schnauzer Club of Great Britain Show in 1966. His dam is a daughter of Eng. Ch. Deltone Deldisplay, and traces in tail-male line to the American-bred Eng. Ch. Roundway Tony From America. In more recent years Mrs. Templeman has turned to Eastwight stock, importing and finishing Ch. Eastwight Sea-Cookie in 1977. He is a son of Eng. Ch. Buffels All American Boy of Deansgate.

Mrs. A. Ralph of the Fernlands prefix in Victoria also started with East-wight stock, importing Eng. Ch. Eastwight Sea-Lord and finishing him in 1974. These two Eastwight dogs played a prominent role in current breed development as both were used extensively, producing many champions. Mrs. Ralph, along with Lady Elizabeth Froggatt, imported Eng. Ch. Dengarse Take By Storm, who also traces in tail-male to all American Boy. He was Best in Show at the Schnauzer Club of N.S.W. in 1980, and has proven a top sire. Next to join the Fernlands was Courtaud Conqueror, a son of American-bred Eng. Ch. Irrenhaus Impact At Risepark. He has been used at stud in New Zealand and his offspring are doing well in that country. In 1985 Mrs. Ralph imported from California, Baws All American Girl, of Valharra and Skyline breeding. She was mated to Conqueror and produced a litter. Unfortunately, the bitch was killed in an accident in November that year.

In 1979 S. Walker and M. Brown of the Vabec prefix imported the bitch

Ch. Guadala Brunhilda

Eastwight Sea-Rythm and bred her to Sea-Cookie. Vabec Sea Joletta from this litter was purchased by B. Dennis and J. Lamping. After gaining her championship she was bred to Take By Storm. Of this litter, three were shown and soon were titled.

The Schonhardt Kennel was established in 1974 by M. MacLeod-Woodhouse in N.S.W. based on Eastwight stock already in Australia. Mr. N. Champion of Thornor Kennel provided Schonhardt with Ch. Thornor Suchi and Ch. Thornor Kakak Kechil, and many champions descend from them. Kechil is the dam of Ch. Schonhardt Copy Boy, three-time CC winner at the Club Specialty, in addition to a host of top awards including a Specialty Best, all-breed Reserve Bests, 7 Group wins and 54 Group placements. Also a successful sire, Copy Boy claims two Best-in-Show winners among his six champion get, and has progeny in New Zealand, Hong Kong, Japan and even the United States.

The Guadala Kennel of S. & J. Tiltman in South Australia was founded in 1980. Their foundation bitch, Ch. Eastdon Aurora Belle, bred by R. Ritzau, has given them three litters with champions in each, including two Best-in-Show winners. Bred to Ch. Schonhardt Copy Boy, Belle produced Guadala's most successful show bitch, Ch. Guadala Brunhilde. She was the breed leader in '83, winning Best in Show at the South Australian Autumn Festival under American judge Michelle Billings. That year she won four Groups, was once runner-up to Best in Show, and was Best South Australian Bitch at the Royal Adelaide Show. Breed wins at Melbourne Royal and Sydney's Spring Fair in 1983 are proof of the truly national nature of her achievements.

Ch. Starborne Brackens Boy

Until 1980, the only American bloodlines found in Australia came via British lines, due primarily to the stiff quarantine restrictions placed on all imports. Dogs entering Australia must do the full English quarantine, and then face a further two-month government kennel quarantine on their arrival. If they come in through Hawaii, they must do seven months there and then three months in Australia. All dogs from the American mainland must go through either England or Hawaii. It is an expensive and time-consuming process.

Mr. A. Bracken of the Starborne prefix in N.S.W. was the first to bring in American dogs directly from the mainland. He imported a breeding pair from Blythewood, both sired by Ch. Blythewood National Acclaim. They were cropped and unable to be shown, but a mating of the two produced excellent results. At the N.S.W. Specialty in 1981, under Vincent Mitchell, famed handler of the Gosmores in England, all three Starbornes from the Blythewood litter scored well. As puppies, Starborne High Acclaim was awarded first and Starborne Brackens Boy second out of a class of seven entries. Starborne Miss May won her class as well. A year later, Anne Rogers Clark, famed American all-arounder, awarded Best of Breed at Sydney Royal to Brackens Boy and reserve to High Acclaim. During the remainder of the year the three Starborne dogs were to earn many top wins, each gaining their titles. Mr. Bracken has since imported two other Blythewood dogs of similar breeding. A National Acclaim daughter, Blythewood Prize of Starborne, came over uncropped and quickly earned her title.

The offspring of the Blythewood imports have enjoyed continued success. A mating of High Acclaim to Ch. Vabec Sea Joletta resulted in Ch. Barbouze

Ch. Barbouze Rockafella

Hot Toddy and Ch. Barbouze Tia Maria. High Acclaim sired V. Fitzgerald's Ch. Varbruin Star Dynasty who won several Groups and Sweepstakes as a puppy, and as a mature bitch was Best in Show at the N.S.W. Specialty on two occasions. Brackens Boy was bred to B. Dennis and J. Lamping's Ch. Varbruin Love Flight, producing Ch. Barbouze Rockafella, CC winner at the Victoria Specialty at six-and-a-half months of age.

During 1982-83 M. MacLeod-Woodhouse imported from England yet another son of American-bred Impact. Rimmick Rikardo became a champion and has sired champions. The American connection was further strengthened in 1983-84 when Schonhardt imported from Hawaii, and quickly finished Ch. Hi-Crest Schonhardt Triumph-Hi and Ch. Hi-Crest Schonhardt Hi-Spring, both sired by Ch. Sunshine Indigo. In 1985 Schonhardt added the record-holding Best-in-Show winner Ch. Hi-Charge of Hansenhaus, the maternal grandsire of their Triumph-Hi.

Further American imports arrived or are due in Australia in 1986. From the Skyline Kennel, the uncropped Skyline's Down Under and Ch. Skyline's Every Witch Way will go to B. Dennis and J. Lamping. Two more Skyline dogs were imported by S. & J. Tiltman. Both Skyline's Snap Judgement and Skyline's Silver Screen have American champion parents, the former by the famed cornerstone sire, Ch. Skyline's Blue Spruce. Silver Screen, while in quarantine in England, was mated to the Blue Spruce son, Eng. Ch. Travelmor's U.S. Mail. The Tiltmans also purchased Regency's Thunder Down Under, by the Blue Spruce son, Ch. Regency's Right On.

In Victoria, P. & T. Nicholls have imported from England Ichabod Friendly Sky, who claims Group-winning parents: Eng. Ch. Travelmor's U.S.

246

Ch. Hi-Crest Schonhardt Hi-Spring

**Ch. Hi-Crest
Schonhardt
Triumph-Hi**

Mail and Eng. Ch. Castilla Diamante. D. Lilley, also of Victoria, imported and recently finished yet another U.S. Mail offspring, Ch. Castilla Illustrado, further strengthening the Blue Spruce line in Australia.

Blacks and Black and Silvers

As in England, the interest in blacks has been limited. Mrs. Cerini's Koniglich prefix has been the main producer of blacks since the early 1960s. Virtually all black champions to date carry lines to Mrs. Cerini's first black import from England, Jovinus Rigoletto. Here again, longevity was evident, as he lived to 17½ years of age. He became the first black to achieve an Australian title, and through his inbred son, Koniglich The Groom, has many black champion descendants in America. In Australia, Rigoletto descendants include the two-time Victoria Specialty Best-in-Show winner Ch. Koniglich Jakreisel, CDX and Ch. Koniglich Banjora, the Specialty winner in 1979.

Mr. & Mrs. J. Finn of the Elimbari prefix in N.S.W. took up the cause in 1979, importing from England the essentially American-bred Black Anfiger of Ripplevale, of Anfiger and Kelly breeding. He made up his championship and was Best in Show at the N.S.W. Specialty in 1982, only to die as a result of minor surgery a few weeks later. He did leave a champion son and daughter, and one of his sons, Elimbari Benji Black, is the sire of Ch. Bastram Black Tacker and Ch. Manziller Black Onyx.

To replace the loss of Black Anfiger, Gill Barwick sent the Finns another black dog, Ripplevale Black Investor, intensely line-bred on the Kelly blacks. He was never shown, but has a champion daughter from his first litter.

The blacks should be given a boost in 1986 with A. Bracken's purchase of a dog and bitch from the Kelly line. Both are being shown in the USA uncropped, and Kelly's Black Gem of Starborne earned championship points during the 1985 show season.

Black and silvers have been bred in Australia for quite some time but, as in England, were not a recognized color for the show ring. Following the standard change in England recently, the Australian National Kennel Club is expected to revise the Australian standard to include the color.

Eastwight imports can take credit for most of the black and silvers bred in Autralia to date. They have been bred in New South Wales by Schonhardt, Elimbari and Kolokov, in Queensland by Vabec and in South Australia by Guadala, all these lines having a predominance of Eastwight breeding.

The Miniature Schnauzer in Australia seems to have a great future with the introduction of so many new bloodlines, both from England and the United States.

**Ch. Koniglich
Kipps Kitt**

**Ch. Koniglich
Braford**

**Ch. Koniglich
Deldanilo**

16

The Miniature Schnauzer
in Other Countries

THE POPULARITY of the Miniature Schnauzer has risen steadily throughout the world in recent years. Today there are national breed clubs in both hemispheres.

The *Federation Cynologique Internationale* (FCI), located in Brussels, is recognized as the governing body by dog clubs throughout the world. Although each country has its own system for awarding a national title of champion, only the FCI can award the title of International Champion.

Each year the FCI sponsors a "World Show," designating the best dog and bitch of each breed as that year's World Champion. In the last decade show sites were truly international—Mexico City, Tokyo, Amsterdam—and in 1981, the homeland of the Miniature Schnauzer—Dortmund, West Germany.

There were 9,000 dogs shown in the four-day event with over 100,000 spectators visiting the grand *Westfalle Halle*. There were breed classes for all three color varieties, bringing out an entry of 112, with broadly international background. The single American ambassador was Ch. Valharra's Extravagant Erik, bred by Enid Quick and exhibited by his owner Erika Kalogeras. This

Ch. Valharra's Extravagant Erik winning Best in Sweepstakes at the Southern California Specialty under Yvonne Phelps (Sole Baye) owner-handled by Erika Kalogeras. Club President Margaret Blakley (B-Majer) presents trophy.

"once-in-a-lifetime" experience was chronicled by Mrs. Kalogeras, and provides remarkable insights into the international nature of the breed today:

> In 1981 I exhibited Erik at International Shows in France, Belgium, Germany and the Netherlands, several Schnauzer Specialties and the World Show. I found a number of differences between the FCI shows and the American variety of shows. For one, Erik was in a "Companion Dog" Group and not in the Terrier Group. The shows were all benched so that we were unable to leave until the show was over. Since the open class begins for dogs at age 15 months, Erik, who was one year when we arrived, was shown in the Youth (*Jungend*) Class, where ages range from 9 to 15 months. Schnauzers cannot be chalked and must stand for judging without being stacked. Erik and I learned very quickly and he won the class in each of the 10 shows entered. He won Best of Breed twice and at the World Show earned the title of Welt-Jungendsieger (*Youth Champion*).
>
> Everywhere Erik showed, he was a traffic stopper and a popular subject for amateur canine photographers. In Germany, the ancestral home of the Schnauzer, there was considerable resentment of the American version of the breed. There was

251

grudging admiration of Erik's sturdy conformation, coarse coat, perfect scissors bite and movement—and uniform disapproval of his abundant beard and leg furnishings. Several judges suggested stripping the legs so the harsh hair would grow in. However, one German judge admitted that he had not seen a better dog in the whole of Europe. In the other European countries we visited, Erik was accepted enthusiastically with only occasional negative references to the leg hair.

During part of my stay in Europe, I was a guest at the home of my Belgian breeder friends, M. and Mme. Louis Huwaert, who had purchased three American Miniature Schnauzers. Their black and silver dog, Dorovan's Midnite Star, a multiple European champion, won the World title at Dortmund. Another American male, Leroy Anfiger, won the black World title. This dog was prepared in the European style, which proves that our dogs can win either way. In all, American-breds won three World Championships and three Reserves out of seven entries. There is little doubt that European Schnauzer lovers will remember 1981 as the year the American Minis invaded and conquered the Continent.

In 1982 the Japan Kennel Club hosted the first FCI meeting ever held in Asia. Following the meeting, the Tokyo World Show was held for three days, bringing out 1,860 dogs—60 of them Miniature Schnauzers. Although the catalog shows only Japanese exhibitors participating, the entry was "All American." With the exception of a single entry sired by a British-bred Risepark dog, all others carried solid American backgrounds.

The last decade has seen a real boom in dog activities in Japan; the emphasis has been on smaller dogs, with Miniature Schnauzers among the most popular. California breeders have been the basic suppliers of breeding stock, sending over several first-rate champions that have gone on to win Japanese titles and top awards on all levels. Such west coast prefixes as Allaruth, Baws, Bokay, Hansenhaus, Skyline, Sole Baye, Walters and Winsor are well represented.

For several years in the 1980s, the Watanabe family set up a breeding kennel in Southern California, based on select purchases of stock from Baws, Hansenhaus, Ruedesheim, Sole Baye and Walters. The Watanabes were interested in all colors, and found that Dolores Walters could provide them with related stock that would produce them. They made Japanese champions of the black, Am., Can. and Mex. Ch. Walters' Dazzling Black, and the B/S, Walters' Ebony Snowman. Hichibei Kurashiki made up the salt and pepper Walters' Irish Treasure, thus making Mrs. Walters the first breeder of Japanese champions of all three colors.

Before returning to Japan the Watanabes finished several American champions, including Tomei homebreds. Foremost among them was the multiple Group and Specialty winner Ch. Tomei Super Star. This Peter Gunn son was purchased by Carolane in 1984 and is siring well for them.

The site for the 1985 World Show was Amsterdam, featuring over 10,000 entries. Even here, close to the birthplace of the breed, all the major winners carried predominantly American bloodlines. There are, in fact, very few Miniature Schnauzers outside of their homeland that do not descend from America's super sire, CH. DOREM DISPLAY.

The British began importing American-bred stock as early as the 1930s,

Black and silver in Switzerland in the mid-1970s. (L to R): Ch. Tribute's Tuxedo Junction, imported from Canada; Ch. Schnauzi's Sybil, all English and Canadian breeding; Ch. Schnauzi's Dinah, a combination of English, Canadian and Swiss breeding. All are owned by Frieda Steiger, Schnauzi Kennel, Switzerland.

---

and continued to refresh their basically European lines with new imports to the present. Their success is chronicled in the British chapter.

One of the first Europeans to import modern American stock was Frieda Steiger of the Schnauzi Kennel in Switzerland. Her original imports in the late 1960s were from Joanna Grigg's Sylva Sprite Kennel in Canada, and were principally black and silver. Frau Steiger was instrumental in bringing recognition to this color on the continent of their birth. Until the mid-1970s, black and silvers could only be shown in the United States and Canada. Frieda had the honor of breeding the first B/S champion recognized by the Pinscher-Schnauzer Klub of Germany (PSK). In addition, Schnauzi's Pyewacket and Schnauzi's Nanette, in May 1976, became the first of their breed to be awarded the PSK Jahrsieger titles. Both were Swiss champions, as Switzerland was the one country on the continent that recognized B/S right after their importation. Both Pyewacket and Nanette are sired by the Canadian import, Swiss Ch. Tribute's Tuxedo Junction, bred by David Ross of Toronto.

The foundation dam of the Schnauzi line is Swiss Ch. Schnauzi's Sybil, whelped in Switzerland, but bred in Canada, as her dam, Can. Ch. Sylva Sprite Frills and Jade arrived in whelp to Can. Ch. Eastwight Sea-Voyager, CD. European lines were also maintained, based on the B/S bitch, Kitty von Stedeke, bred by the Countess Claudine dePret.

In 1977, the first year in which B/S could earn CACIB awards from FCI, the Pyewacket son, Schnauzi's King, owned by Peter Marx, won the B/S Bundessieger title in Essen, Germany. Frau Steiger's 10-month-old Pyewacket daughter, Schnauzi's Melissa, won the Youth Siegerin title, and her recent Israeli import, Chatifa Barluz, the Youth Sieger title. At three French shows that year, Schnauzi's Nanette became the first B/S to earn the FCI title of International Champion.

Many more Schnauzi champions followed, all based on stock descending from the B/S sires, Sea-Voyager and Can. Ch. Walsh's Frosty Charmer, CD, both owned by Sylva Sprite. The recognition of black and silver by the PSK and FCI prompted Joanna Griggs to relate her feelings:

> In Switzerland and Germany, severe restrictions are placed on the breed. No interbreeding of colors, and no registration of black and silvers having a salt and pepper or black parent is allowed. The reason for these restrictions is not clear since all black and silvers breed true irregardless of the color of their parents, and experience has shown that excellent specimens can come from salt and pepper parents.
>
> These restrictions will accomplish something that is probably not intended, and the black and silver will be a distinct variety, not only in color but also in type. The European Schnauzer is very different from our Schnauzers, mainly because judges emphasize different points. In Europe coats must be extremely hard, without a trace of tan or yellow; furnishings should be hard and lighter than the body coat, but pure white furnishings are not desired.
>
> Some judges do not want "American-type" Schnauzers in the show ring and often say so! To conform, breeders strip or severely trim the furnishings. The Standard for the black and silver is more in line with our Schnauzers, and since black and silvers almost exclusively have been imported from the United States or Canada, they are very much our type. They have better bone, better toplines, more angulation and generally have more elegance. Due to the ban on interbreeding of colors, this difference will remain very much in evidence.

Vive la difference was the European response, and American bloodlines of all colors have since become highly prized by continental breeders.

The first American-bred black to enjoy success on the continent in recent years also made his home in Switzerland. In May 1979, Anne Eskrigge (Anfiger) sent over Leroy Anfiger to Beatrice Zingg. A breeder-exhibitor throughout the 1970s, her Rattlerhof blacks, exclusively of continental breeding, were among the most successful in Europe. Leroy was an instant success and the leading black of 1979 while still a yearling. The next year he completed his International (FCI) title and was Best Miniature of all colors at the PSK Specialty in Germany, topping an entry of 80. Leroy was also an instant success as a sire, with champion descendants throughout Europe.

Oddly enough, Frau Steiger would find a needed outcross in Israel, where Izchak Schkedi had begun a black and silver line in the late 1960s based on Israeli Ch. Geelong Dandy, bred in New Jersey by Randolph Higgins. The Barluz B/S are

Ch. Sylva Sprite Entity

Ch. Chatifa Barluz

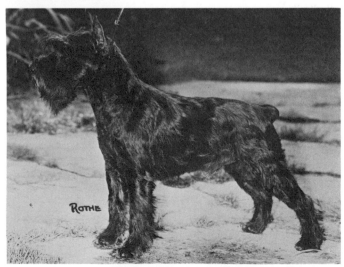

Ch. Leroy Anfiger

essentially American breeding, but provided outcrosses to English Eastwight and Italian Barbanera lines. Mr. Schkedi also imported the B/S Gough's Frosted Black Jack from the well-established Gough's Kennel in Minnesota. The Barluz B/S, based on this pair of American-bred sires, is sufficiently established so that Barluz breeding is found throughout Europe and the Scandinavian countries.

The Klondaike Kennel of Nils and Bodil Jordal in Denmark, originally founded in 1974 on English Eastwights, had developed its own blend using the best from the Swiss Schnauzis, the Israeli Barluz and several American imports. From Janice Rue of Illinois came the highly successful B/S Best-in-Show winner Int. Ch. Aljamar Op Art of Klondaike—a champion of Denmark, Luxembourg and Germany. As a son of essentially Italian-bred Ch. Aljamar Tommy Gun, he owns a truly international pedigree. The Jordals, equally involved with salt and peppers, also turned to America for stock, importing Walters' Nugget of Klondaike, in 1984 making her the first American-bred salt and pepper to earn a German title. Nugget also earned a Danish and International title. In a decade of breeding the Jordals have bred about 100 puppies and 21 of these are champions. Recent additions include the salt and pepper Carolane's Starfire, of essentially Penlan breeding, and their first venture in black, Skansen's Black Gem, both earning Danish titles. Gem is an in-bred daughter of Ch. Walters' Black Bandit.

Dolores Walters in California was foremost among breeders of all colors willing to export her best around the world. Walters dogs of all colors can be found throughout the Scandinavian countries, as well as Belgium, Italy, Japan and Taiwan. The salt and pepper Walters' One Shot, a half-brother to Nugget, both by Ch. Ruedesheim's Landmark (5 Chs.), was imported by Grethe Hansen of Denmark, earning his Danish title and topping 46 salt and peppers at the World Show in Amsterdam. CACIB certificates in Dortmund and Copenhagen put him well on the way to his International title.

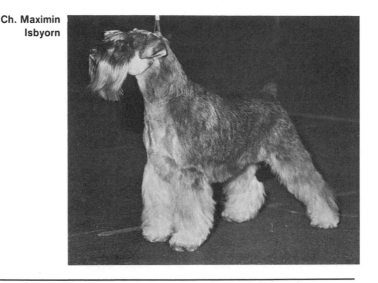

Ch. Maximin Isbyorn

Sweden and Finland abound with Walters breeding. Mari Saari of Finland has imported four of them, in all three colors, making Swedish and Finnish champions of the black male, Landmark's Raider, and the B/S male, Greer's Dazzlin Frost (a son of Japanese Ch. Walter's Black Frost). In 1979, Christina Lundstrom exhibited her black American-bred male, Gough's Ebony Edge of Knight, to Swedish, Finnish and Norwegian titles. Millie Olsson of Sweden has also concentrated on blacks, enjoying success with Walters' Black Flash, Best in Show at the Swedish Jubilee Show in 1982. Mona Bengtsson and Jette Larsen are also working with Walters dogs in Sweden.

The most prolific producer of Scandinavian champions is the Maximin Kennel of Benny Blid in Sweden. Here again, the American influence is a dominant factor, as this kennel is based almost exclusively on a pair of salt and pepper imports from Barclay Square (see TRIBUTE chapter).

Barclay Square Maximin Midas and Barclay Square Maximin Minx were quarantined in England in 1978 before finally making their home in Sweden. Minx stayed on even longer, producing two litters from which came three English champions. Shown only four times in Sweden and Finland in 1980, Minx earned both titles, and then produced a final litter containing the Specialty winner, Ch. Maximin Super Trooper. Through her children and grandchildren, Minx has had a profound impact on English and Scandinavian breeding. Midas was shown ten times in Sweden, winning nine Bests of Breed, including a Specialty, and once going BOS. As a sire, Midas produced about 50 puppies, 11 of them Swedish champions, six of these going on to produce another generation of champions. Most notable among the Midas sons is Ch. Maximin Smiling Yankee, Sweden's first multiple Best in Show winner, and the breed's record-holding sire with over 20 champion get. At the World Show in Amsterdam 1985, the Danish-owned Yankee daughter, Ch. Graskaggs Irma La Douce, was the best salt and pepper bitch.

In Finland, Soile Bister's Trixer Kennel is the foremost importer of champions, with American bloodlines the dominant factor. Founded on English Deansgates and Swiss Schnauzis, several American imports were added in the 1980s. From Bob and Nancy Berg's Minnesota-based Bo-Nanza Kennel came three black and silvers. Bo-Nanza's Trixer Frosty Pony earned Finnish and Swedish titles, and topped all colors at the Finnish Specialty in 1984. Already a successful sire, his son Trixer Voyager went to Frau Steiger and has CACIBs in Switzerland, France and Germany. Bo-Nanza's Frosty Gambler and Bo-Nanza's Trixer Frosty Song, both by Ch. Bo-Nanza's Frosty R Jr., followed, Gambler earning his Finnish title. Mrs. Bister recently added some salt and pepper Penlan breeding, gaining Swedish and Finnish titles on Penlan Princess of Trixer.

Other Penlan and Bo-Nanza dogs, as well as several of Walters breeding have gone to new Finnish breeders in the 1980s, so that current Scandinavian bloodlines are virtually "All American."

Belgium, home of the FCI, also has breed enthusiasts which have chosen American bloodlines. Madame and Monsieur Louis Huwaert of Brussels began with two Bo-Nanza black and silvers, earning a Dutch title on Bo-Nanza's Frosted Queen, a litter sister to the Bergs' Ch. Bo-Nanza's Frosty Lone Ranger. The Huwaerts then went to Dorothy and Ivan Mayberry's California-based Dorovan Kennel for their next B/S. Dorovan Midnite Star, sired by the B/S Ch. Valharra's Captain Midnite, offered a total outcross to established European-American B/S lines. He completed his International title in 1980, shortly after turning 15 months of age, and was Best Miniature at Courtrai, Belgium that year.

In Spain, Mr. A. Madueno of Madrid is recognized as the breed's founding father, bringing in breeding stock from Britain in the early 1970s. English Ch. Dengarse Pirates Treasure, and his Canadian-bred dam, Rosehill Pirates Silver, and later Eastwight Sea Ballet and Eastwight Sea Gem, all became Spanish champions. They formed the foundation for a host of Kilimanjaro champions, and are behind virtually all Spanish champions to the present.

Mr. F. Martinez Guijarro claims Spain's most successful winner and producer in International and Spanish Ch. Miky Kilimanjaro, the winner of 14 Bests in Show. A Miky son, Ch. Don Pedrin del Escarambrujo, owned by Mr. A. Lacoma, has scored many successes, as has his brother, Ch. Tono del Escarambrujo, owned by Miss Saizar. Tono was Best of Breed at the second Spanish Specialty in 1983.

The first Championship Show of the Schnauzer Club of Spain was held in 1982, judged by Heinz Holler, President of the German Pinscher-Schnauzer Klub. Best of Breed was Mr. Guijarro's homebred Ch. Beauty of Maidenhead. She is from the litter out of Pirates Silver, imported in whelp to Dengarse Yankee Spinoff. Tono and Beauty, bred together, produced the most recent star, Mr. J. Martinez Solano's Ch. Catalina de C'an Jack.

The first Spaniard to import an American champion was Mr. A. Pons, in 1984, quickly making Marmac Pretorian a Spanish champion as well. Pretorian, bred by Ralph Martin of Texas, represents a viable outcross to the predominantly

Ch. Trixer Voyager

Ch. Trixer Vampire

**Ch. Bo-Nanza's
Trixer Frosty Pony
with Soile Bister.**

**Ch. Marmac
Pretorian
with Maripi Wooldridge.**

Dengarse, Eastwight and Risepark British lines based on Mr. Madueno's original imports.

Elsewhere in the western hemisphere, outside the United States and Canada, the breed is still comparatively rare. American breeders continue to enjoy dog-show vacations to Bermuda, Puerto Rico, Mexico and even to South America, taking along their current homebred to exhibit at these annual events. Usually three or four shows are strung together so that a title can be earned on a single trip.

A small number of breeders in Mexico and South America have finished champions and have even made up International (FCI) champions. The Schnauzer population, while admittedly small, consists mainly of dogs from the United States.

Juan Aguilar of Medellin, Columbia imported Bandsman's Round-Up after he had won a Group and nine points as a yearling, shown by his breeder Carol Weinberger. He earned his Columbian title in 1980 with several Group placements.

Jose Machline of Sao Paulo, Brazil enjoyed extraordinary success in 1982 with Am. and Braz. Ch. Sole Baye's Sound-Off, bred by Yvonne Phelps. In his first four Brazilian shows he won four Groups and two Bests in Show. Mrs. Phelps has the distinction of having bred BIS dogs in two hemispheres, having exported to Japan the BIS-winning bitch, Japanese Ch. Sole Baye's Sunbeam, owned by Dr. Nagatomo. Sole Baye's Sunrise, a sister to Sound-Off, is also a Japanese champion, and Sole Baye has also sent two bitches to Canada—Can. Chs. April and Karusel of Sole Baye.

For the most part, the Miniature Schnauzer has become established on a limited basis in Africa with stock imported from England. The first recorded Rhodesian champion, Liza of Albright, returned to England in 1967, winning the Veterans Class at the Schnauzer Club Open Show when nearly eight years of age.

More recently, South Africa has developed a nucleus of breeders. Johan and Edith Gallant, well established as successful breeders of Giant Schnauzers, began importing Miniature stock in the early 1980s, based on a blend of Eastwight from England, Schnauzi from Switzerland and Klondaike from Denmark—all essentially black and silvers carrying American lines. In the fall of 1984 Marcia Feld of Illinois exported alternative bloodlines in the form of the B/S male Feldmar All-American Boy, linebred on the B/S Ch. Aljamar Hot Ice, CD. Shown five times, he was Best Puppy at each, going on to three Bests of Breed, one BOS and a Reserve. At his fifth show at nearly a year of age, he was second in the Utility Group. The Gallants plan further imports, including a black bitch from Feldmar.

Among the furthest travelled are the trio of Walters-bred Schnauzers introduced to Taiwan in the summer of 1982. Dr. S.J. Shiow, Dean of Studies at the Chung Shan Medical College, imported the salt and pepper Walters' Seeyou-around, a son of the B/S Japanese Ch. Walters' Ebony Snowman, along with two black females, one of which produced, while in quarantine, the first litter to be born in Taiwan.

Other countries have had Miniature Schnauzers of which to be proud, and more than likely they will carry, somewhere deep in their pedigree, the name of the great American sire, CH. DOREM DISPLAY.

17

The Miniature Schnauzer in Obedience

MINIATURE SCHNAUZERS have been outstanding performers in obedience competitions even before the AKC first established rules for such trials. Mrs. Slattery's Ch. Mussolini of Marienhof, after only ten days of training, won first in a Novice class of eleven at Philadelphia, November 1935, followed by a second at Baltimore a few weeks later. Since the AKC did not award CD (Companion Dog) degrees until the following year, Mussolini never officially gained the title. Perhaps an "Honorary" CD should be his, not only as the breed's first obedience winner, but also the first combined bench and obedience winner. Royally bred, Mussolini was from a litter of four champions, including the prolific sire, Ch. Marko of Marienhof (13 Chs.).

The trend for "beauty and brains" was officially initiated by Ch. Shaw's Little Pepper, CD in the early 1940s, trained and shown by his breeder-owner Marian Shaw.

Since 1936, some 3,000 Miniature Schnauzers have gained their CD degrees, and on the higher levels, they are consistently among the top ten performing breeds. In the fifty years since trials have been recognized, over 100 Miniature Schnauzers boast titles in both rings.

The versatility of the breed was never more graphically illustrated than by the mid-1950s career of Ch. Mein Herr Schnapps, UD, the first to acquire championship and UD (Utility Dog) status. Mrs. Edward Getz recalls how it changed her life:

> Schnapps was eight weeks old when we got him. How little we realized at that time how he would change the course of our lives. Our introduction to obedience was purely accidental. Until this time we had never participated in this satisfying endeavor. Before Schnapps was a year old, he had earned his CD degree and appeared on television to demonstrate the attributes of a well-trained dog.

At that time we decided to also show him in the breed ring. His recognition of the difference between the obedience and show collar is almost unbelieveable. While showing for his championship, Schnapps attained his CDX and UD degrees. The first two degrees were earned in three straight shows, his UD in four shows. All obedience training and handling was done by my husband, Edward Getz, who also occasionally showed him in the breed ring. At one show, Schnapps took the Terrier Group and tied for Highest Scoring Dog in Show. By the time he was two-and-a-half years old Schnapps had completed his championship and UD degree. His average score for the three degrees was 196½.

In 1956, Schnapps appeared, by invitation, at Westminster as the highest scoring terrier in the nation for the previous year.

Schnapps was started in tracking but never finished, due to our negligence. But the training paid off. We were moving to a new home with a large ground area. In the process of clearing scrub trees, my husband lost the keys to the car. It was dusk. We started the impossible search for the keys. My husband gave Schnapps his scent and dispatched him to find the key case. In a very few minutes, Schnapps was back, keys barely showing from under his whiskers. Where he located them we will never know.

A trained dog is a joy. Our social invitations all include Schnapps, because he conducts himself like the gentleman and champion that he is.

One of his greatest joys is retrieving live ducks. This could be influenced by his love of water. He retrieves the duck in true hunting dog fashion, though often the bird is almost as large as himself. Schnapps has appeared at various Sportsmen's shows against true water dogs. His performance has been so outstanding it has proved embarrassing to owners of trained water dogs.

His many television and show performances, plus his unusual show record and hundreds of trophies, are not what makes him a great dog in our eyes. To us he's tops because he's a real buddy. His intelligence and fearlessness add to the fun of having him as a member of our family.

An old misconception was that if you trained your dog in obedience it would not do well in conformation. It is still heard from time to time, but the facts prove otherwise, particularly with the versatile Miniature Schnauzer. This is not surprising considering their working inheritance from their larger cousins.

The fact that first-class bloodlines continue to appear in the immediate background of most successful obedience dogs speaks highly for the breeders involved. This trend is clearly evident, beginning with Mussolini.

Since DISPLAY, several top-producing lines and families were equally involved in obedience work. DISPLAY, himself, sired a UD and four others with CDs. His sister, Ch. Dorem Shady Lady, CD, is the grand matriarch of the Phil-Mar family. DISPLAY descendants dominated in both rings from the 1950s to the present. His sons, Ch. Dorem High Test and Ch. Benrook Buckaroo, continued the trend, the former siring six obedience titlists, and the latter four. A few generations from them came Ch. Marwyck Brush Cliff, the new leader with seven. His record was short-lived, as eight obedience degree winners were sired by Ch. Applause of Abingdon, CD. It is interesting to note that Applause was sired by Brush Cliff's litter brother, Ch. Marwyck Scenery Road. All three are sires of five or

Winemaker's Miranda, UD

more bench champions as well—a bright and beautiful family, indeed!

Applause's record stood for nearly two decades, broken in 1985 by Ch. Sim-Cal's Personality Plus, CD, sire of nine obedience winners: 1 UD, 3 CDX, 1 CD, TD and 4 CDs. Theresa Klemencic's Sim-Cal breeding program in Pennsylvania has for over a decade produced dogs that compete successfully on all levels of competition, both bench and obedience. The foundation for most of their success was Blythewood Naughty Kelly, who claims top producing parents: Ch. Blythewood Chief Bosun (11 Chs.) and Ch. Bon-Ell Sandstrom (3 Chs.). Line-bred or outcrossed, Kelly produced pups with beauty and brains. Her son, Personality Plus, is by Ch. Blythewood His Majesty (11 Chs.). A daughter, Sim-Cal Lil Girl, from yet another top producing Blythewood sire, is the dam of a champion son, plus three CD dogs, bred to her half-brother, Personality Plus.

Winemaker's Miranda, UD is far and away the leading dam of obedience winners. In 1985 her seventh offspring earned a CD. She is also the dam of two CDX, plus Ch. Ellar's Only Amos, UD. Bred by Cheryl Wine, Miranda was purchased as a four-month-old show prospect by Lynne Boone in 1973. She is a double great-granddaughter of Ch. Caradin Fancy That (9 Chs.), and is tightly line-bred within the Diplomat branch. Her training for both conformation and obedience began almost immediately. She went High in Trial in her first outing and won her first point and second leg at her first show as an Open bitch. As Lynne tells it:

> She went on to sparkle in the obedience ring and show her obvious boredom in conformation classes. She managed to accumulate seven points inspite of herself,

and was High in Trial twice. A Dog World Award winner, she ranked as high as No. 2 nationally in comparatively limited showing. She was also one of the first Miniature Schnauzers to earn OTCh points, and at almost 13 is still active enough to work, which she sometimes demands to do.

The Ellar breeding program in South Carolina has been more versatile than most, as Lynne has bred several champions, all descending from Miranda, and is the first and only breeder claiming two uncropped champions, including Ch. Ellar's Argonaut, the first male in half-a-century. He is a grandson of Miranda on one side of his pedigree, and a great-grandson on the other.

Beginning on July 1, 1977 a new obedience title was created by the American Kennel Club. Unlike the CD, CDX and UD titles, in which a dog is competing only for a perfect score, the new title measures the effectiveness of a dog against the others competing. To gain the title Obedience Trial Champion (OTCh) a dog must win at least one Open B and one Utility B class, plus a third under at least three different judges. A total of 100 points is required for the title and up to 34 points are offered for each win, depending on the number of dogs competing in the trial. Dogs placing second gain up to 13 points in the same manner. The title OTCh is indeed a superior achievement.

Through 1985, six Miniature Schnauzers had passed this supreme test:
OTCh Sycamore's Splash of Frost
OTCh Bo-Nanza's Miss Dark Shadow
OTCh Liebling Fritz Von Schilling
OTCh Mistress Annie of Quancie
OTCh Pepperhaus Pfeisty Pfritz
OTCh Princess Pfeffer II

OTCh Princess Pfeffer II was the first, and her son, OTCh Pepperhaus Pfeisty Pfritz, was the third. Both were trained and shown by Marilyn and Bill Oxandale of Missouri. Their Pepperhaus prefix can be found on both bench and obedience champions. Pfritz has two successful brothers, Pepperhaus Watch My Dust, UD and Ch. Pepperhaus Karbon Kopy, CDX, the latter already the sire of several obedience winners, including a pair with advanced degrees. Pfritz, Kopy and Dust were sired by Ch. Penlan Paragon's Pride (30 Chs.), and owe much to the Phil-Mar heritage of quality and intelligence.

The versatility of the Miniature Schnauzer is best exemplified by the number of dogs that have achieved both bench championships and advanced degrees. Seven have achieved the highest level—a bench championship (Ch.) and Utility Dog (UD) degree:
Ch. Adam v. Elfland, UD
Ch. Dufferton Mack The Knight, UD
Ch. Ellar's Only Amos, UD
Ch. Frevohly's Best Bon-Bon, UD
Am. and Can. Ch. Jonaire Pocono Rough Rider, Am. and Can. UDT
Am. and Mex. Ch. Marmeldon's Pacemaker, Am. and Mex. UD
Ch. Mein Herr Schnapps, UD

The Gateway Miniature Schnauzer Club on May 31, 1985, was honored to have five Obedience Trial Champions at its Specialty. From left to right: Bill Oxandale and OTCh Princess Pfeffer II; Eunice Revsdale and OTCh Bo-Nanza's Miss Dark Shadow; Marilyn Oxandale and OTCh Pepperhaus Pfiesty Pfritz; Phyliss Fleming and OTCh Mistress Annie of Quancie; George Schilling and OTCh Liebling Fritz Von Schilling.

In addition, 16 Miniature Schnauzers have earned bench (Ch.) and Companion Dog Excellent (CDX) degrees:

Ch. Alinder's All Star of Mari Sam, CDX

Ch. Barhelm's Rollicking Rogue, CDX

Am. and Can. Ch. Britmor Sunnymeade Frost, Am. CDX and Can. CD

Am. and Can. Ch. Doman's Daiquiri, Am. & Can. CDX

Ch. Galewood's Princess Mitzie, CDX

Ch. Gough's Bicentennial Black, CDX

Ch. Hol-E-Oakes George, CDX

Ch. Liza's William The Conqueror, CDX

Am. and Can. Ch. Marwyck Gun Fire, CDX

Ch. Orbit's Lift Off, CDX

Ch. Penlan Peter Pan, CDX

Ch. Pepperhaus Karbon Kopy, CDX

Ch. Skipper of Furstenhof, CDX

Ch. Sonny of Oakridge, CDX

Ch. Tel-Mo's Ami Somethun, CDX

Am. and Can. Ch. Wildwood's Showboat, Am. and Can. CDX

Blacks in Obedience

Obedience winners have come in all three colors right from the beginning, although the ones mentioned so far have nearly all been salt and pepper. The first black winner of an obedience degree was Fred v. Schonhardt of Crystal, CD. Fred was also the first with imported parents to gain an obedience degree. A quarter of a century later, in 1964, Hamann's Falla became the first black to earn a UD. His CD was achieved as a puppy, and his CDX shortly after his first birthday.

One of the most successful black lines in both bench and obedience stems from Gough's Ebony Knight Longleat, CD. He is the sire of the lone black Ch. -UD, Ch. Dufferton Mack The Knight, UD. The only other black to achieve Ch. -CDX, Ch. Gough's Bicentennial Black, CDX, also carries a line to Longleat. The Longleat son, Ch. Woodhaven's Black Gough Drops (4 Chs.), although never shown in obedience, leads this color variety as a sire of obedience titlists with four CDX and five CD offspring.

Perhaps the most successful dual champion is Alice Gough's Best in Show winner, Ch. Gough's Ebony Royal Knight, CD, still producing, and already the sire of two CDX and four CD winners, as well as bench champions. The chapters on blacks and black and silvers tell of further successes of the Gough's family, obviously bred for both beauty and brains.

Black and Silvers in Obedience

Among black and silvers (B/S) it was Sambo of Cobb, UDT who set the pace. Mrs. Charles Cobb describes some of his less noteworthy talents with obvious delight:

> A little applause is all he needs, and he will, for example, flip his scent discrimination article up in the air a few times, catching it on the fly, parading around the ring, showing the spectators and judge that he did, indeed, find the right one, and finally returning it to Chuck. Just a little more encouragement from the audience and he will dash to the center of the ring, turn in all directions, and wag his tail in gleeful delight. He truly is a show in himself, and has done much to promote the breed in his own little way.

Virtually all the "beauty and brains" among B/S can be traced to Can. Ch. Walsh's Frosty Charmer, CD and the British-bred Can. Ch. Eastwight Sea Voyager, Can. CD. All the dual champions of this color carry lines to one or both. Two generations of dual winners currently exist: Ch. Aljamar Hot Ice, CD is the sire of Ch. Suelen Snow Flurry, CD, CG; Ch. Sercatep's Frost N Flash, CD is the dam of Ch. Karma's Moonlight Shadow, CD, who in turn has a CD-winning offspring.

All the records among B/S dual champions fell in 1984 to Am. and Can. Ch. Britmor Sunnymeade Frost, Am. CDX and Can. CD, earning his CG (Certificate of Gameness). He became only the third Miniature Schnauzer to earn a CG through the auspices of the American Working Terrier Association. He is a

Hamann's
Falla, UD

Am. and Can. Ch. Britmor
Sunnymeade Frost, CG,
Am. CDX and Can. CD

267

third-generation black and silver CDX, being out of Britmor Sassafrost Teaberry, CDX, whose dam is Hi Ya Gret, CDX. The fact that Frost was the first B/S to win a Canadian Best in Show proves his quality as well as his versatility.

The first B/S to achieve the OTCh title did so in 1985. Am. and Can. OTCh Sycamore's Splash of Frost, owned and trained by Homer and Shirley Horton, twice scored High in Trial. He is a brother to this color variety's top producing bitch, Sycamore's Sassafras, CD (4 Chs.).

Senior Citizens and Obedience

In the Des Moines Training Club, 1981 through 1985, four Miniature Schnauzers finished their UD degrees, trained and shown by senior citizens.

Arnie Arnold, at the age of 64, put a UD on Ms. Fritz. It was his wife Edith that decided to try obedience and put Ms. Fritz through obedience classes and entered the shows at the age of 62. Edith and Ms. Fritz went through the CD in three straight shows with scores averaging 196. Ms. Fritz at 3½ years of age faced retirement, but Arnie would have none of it and took over her training, earning CDX and UD degrees in short order.

Arnie then took on another Miniature Schnauzer, a black, given to him as uncontrollable—a dog that could not be trained or even housebroken. That was a lot of "poppy-cock," said Arnold, and Arnie's Char Kol Imp, UD "took to training like a duck takes to water." Imp's granddam was Klein Schwarz Madchen, UD, the first black female to earn a UD.

Sam Beck, another senior citizen at 64, has two UD girls, Mari Sam's Golden Girl and Mari Sam's Final Edition. Marilyn and Sam Beck enjoyed both aspects of the sport, Marilyn showing in conformation and Sam in obedience.

Bart Kooker, another youngster at 62, and Spritka's Cicis Michele Tracy, UD round out this club's unique group.

Why Formal Obedience Training?

Why, indeed, one might ask. And the reasons are many. Above all else, a well-trained dog is a pleasure to live with, and a credit to the breed. An obedience-trained dog will constantly be a point of pride, whether on a pleasurable walk or when visiting or being visited. Equally important is that it serves as a safeguard for the dog itself. A dog trained to obey his master will do so under any and all conditions. When an emergency does occur, whether on the street or in the home, a spoken command, readily obeyed, may be its salvation.

Shirley Willey, of Shirley's Schnauzers in California, has pioneered for bench and obedience, finishing several dogs to both titles. She relates an instance where training really paid off.

> I found obedience to be an asset in the time of disaster more than once. While living in Florida we had a tornado. Our room was rapidly filling with water. I put Beau and Ginger's training collars and leads on and put them on down-stays on the bed while I went for help. They were still there when I returned.

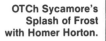
OTCh Sycamore's
Splash of Frost
with Homer Horton.

The next time was the February 1970 earthquake in Southern California. Beau woke me up seconds before the big shake, and I was fully awake when it hit. I put my four obedience dogs on down-stays on the bed, and my other dogs in crates for safety.

Although obedience work is great fun, it requires time and patience. Under no circumstances should a dog be physically punished in the process. It will spoil his desire to work, and no dog that works out of fear will make the grade either as a companion or in competition. Training should not be laborious, with sessions lasting no more than 15 minutes at a time. Each time concentrate on a specific requirement. Should a particular session be less than fruitful, do not lose your temper—tomorrow will be better.

For those who wish to train a dog with the object of seeking titles, they would be well advised to seek out a training class where others are preparing for the same goals. Most cities have dog clubs which provide such classes throughout the year. Individual breed clubs, when available, would provide a perfect outlet, both to learn about training and about your Miniature Schnauzer in general. It is a wonderful place to exchange experiences and problems unique to the breed.

The mechanics of training will not be discussed here, since many excellent books are available which cover the subject in depth.

Once you begin successfully training your dog and see how well he does, you will probably want to enter him in obedience trials held under American Kennel Club auspices. Rules and regulations for such events are always available through the offices of the American Kennel Club, 51 Madison Avenue, New York, NY 10010.

18

Breeding the

Miniature Schnauzer

IT HAS LONG BEEN SAID that "like begets like," and so selection remains the breeder's oldest tool. With bloodlines in Miniature Schnauzers being as tightly confined as they are to four main branches from a single individual, CH. DOREM DISPLAY, beginner's luck may find you have bred a top-flight puppy in your very first litter. This luck seldom lingers, however, as the ability to breed generation after generation of quality dogs comes only from careful planning and judicious selection.

A novice may feel that the study of genetics must enter into any thoughts of successful breeding. He would be surprised, however, at how little the subject of genetics is discussed. Wherever dog breeders get together to talk dogs, the discussion is more likely to turn to the various methods of breeding, such as inbreeding and outcrossing. These are the breeder's tools, and should be understood.

Inbreeding involves the breeding of closely related individuals: father to daughter, mother to son, brother to sister. Experience has indicated that inbreeding tends to set and perpetuate type. There are, however, many instances when like did not beget like, reminding us of the wide variety of genetic combinations possible in any given breeding. This explains the sudden appearance of a hidden recessive, and helps explain why inbreeding may have good and bad results. Inbreeding can, and has, produced wonderful results in skillful hands, but can produce harmful results when used at random. Wisely used, it is the most effective means of setting type. Misused, the results can be disastrous. Although the breedings do not result in "monster" puppies, as some people believe, they can and do double up on recessive genes that may be undesirable in nature—and there are many!

270

Most successful breeders will adapt a program based on various forms of line-breeding. The novice breeder would do well to follow their lead. Line-breeding is the mating of related dogs, such as half-brother to half-sister, grandsire to granddaughter, niece to uncle, or cousin to cousin - and there are more. We hear of closely line-bred, loosely line-bred or distantly line-bred dogs, but the terms have variable meanings.

The term line-breeding is generally applied to the mating of a dog and bitch sharing one or more common ancestors in the second or third generation. Grandsire to granddaughter or granddam to grandson is closely line-bred, and may by some be called inbred. A more accurate definition of line-breeding is perhaps that it is a succession of matings of related animals with a long-range plan.

Yet another course available is the outcross—the mating of purebred animals that appear to be unrelated or, more realistically, only distantly related. Outcrossing in Miniature Schnauzers is virtually impossible, unless German imports should find their way into the North American gene pool in future. Finding a pedigree among current show stock that does not have a single common ancestor in five generations is very unlikely.

Selection of Breeding Stock

In planning a breeding program that will be successful over a period of years, the first requirement is to have the type you want to produce clearly in mind. The shortest route to success would be to purchase a quality line-bred bitch from an established breeder who is producing the type desired. Hopefully this breeder will also serve as mentor, and will be of help to you as you go on. Perhaps you have already purchased a bitch as a pet and have decided to breed her. Before blindly plunging in, give serious thought to the difficulties and problems you face, and be sure before you get involved.

The responsibilities of the breeder are many. The bitch during her pregnancy requires special care. There may be many anxious hours before, during and after whelping. Caring for puppies over an extended period is very time consuming, and must be a labor of love. Frequent trips to the veterinarian must be included: you must plan for tail docking, and, probably, ear cropping. Then comes the most serious responsibility—placing the puppies in good homes.

If financial gain is a consideration, forget it! Few pet owners who raise a litter of puppies come close to breaking even, let alone come out ahead. A long-range breeding program will require considerable expense, and more time and energy than you might ever imagine.

If you are certain, and want to embark on a Miniature Schnauzer breeding program, a mentor—someone with broad experience—is almost a must. You will need all the help you can get, and would be wise to trust only one mentor until you have your own experience and knowledge on which to draw.

First up is the selection of a stud. The breeder of your bitch should have had a plan, even before she was born. Her potential suitor would probably have been chosen, and if her virtues and faults are identified as not being uncomplementary, that choice should be honored.

Many a novice, and even some experienced hands breed their bitches to the latest top winner, so that the pedigree will reflect this famous champion. Little thought is given to whether the parents physically complement each other. The list of top winners of both sexes that have proven unsuccessful as producers suggest either misuse or disuse, and the reasons are many.

Hopefully your bitch will have common ancestors on both her sire's and her dam's side. Selection should be based on deciding which is the most outstanding, and most prepotent for the qualities desired. Prepotency is too often loosely applied to animals less than deserving of this discription. Only a broadly used individual with an outstanding record as a producer of consistent quality and type is truly prepotent. As a novice, you would do well to use such a sire for your first breeding. Chances are his fee will be only slightly higher than others that may be available, and perhaps more convenient.

The Bitch In Season

A Miniature Schnauzer bitch can be expected to come into season, or heat, for the first time at from six to nine months of age. Some will wait until they are over a year old. Thereafter, they come in at roughly six-month intervals, although variations occur. A bitch should not be bred on her first season, and ideally, not until she is 18 months of age. Problems can arise if an older maiden bitch is bred. It is best that she be bred by the time she is three years old. There are, of course, exceptions to every rule.

The average heat cycle (estrus period) lasts from 14 to 21 days. A bitch approaching her season may display a certain amount of restlessness as well as an increased appetite. The first real indication is the swelling of the vulva, along with a discharge which is light in color and flow. As the season progresses, the flow increases and the color deepens to a bright red. After the eighth or ninth day the discharge decreases, changing in color to a pale pink or straw color. The vaginal discharge may vary considerably. In some bitches it is quite heavy, while so slight in others that it may go unnoticed.

A bitch is normally receptive and ready to breed from the tenth to the 14th day. Here again, variations occur, with successful breedings resulting as early as the seventh and as late as the 16th day. Some can happen even later, when the bitch is thought to be well out of season. The importance of strict confinement during this period must be stressed. Avoid neighborhood walks at this time unless you wish a series of unwanted suitors at your door step.

If a mating has been planned, and the bitch is to go to an outside stud, arrangements must be made well in advance. As soon as the bitch is noticeably in season, notify the owner of the stud dog and set the date that the bitch will be shipped or brought to the stud for mating. If she is to be shipped, plan on sending her at least three or four days before the expected mating.

Airline regulations and fees are many and varied. Weather conditions must also be considered, as many carriers will not accept dogs if temperatures are too high or low. You would be wise to get advise locally, as well as from the stud dog owner who may have many useful ideas on achieving the best and least expensive result.

Be aware of health regulations, as most carriers require a veterinary health certificate, as well as an airline crate. A conscientious stud dog owner will request that your bitch be tested for Brucellosis. This should be done as soon as the bitch comes in season. If she is due for booster shots, she should have them well before she is bred. Plan to leave your shipped bitch with the stud dog owner for several days after matings have been achieved.

That she should be in perfect health prior to mating is obvious. She should be neither too fat nor too thin, and completely free of internal or external parasites. Remember to avoid use of anti-mating (pills, powders or sprays) products at this time.

With a maiden bitch it is advisable to test that her vaginal passage is clear and there is no stricture. This can be accomplished by greasing and inserting, slowly and gently, your little finger to stretch the opening and passage. If this is not accomplished well before the mating, problems may arise. Be sure your hands are thoroughly clean before proceeding.

The Mating

Procedures for handling matings differ greatly. Some Miniature Schnauzer breeders accustom their stud dogs to mate on a table, while others feel the floor is safer. Whatever procedure is used, it is important that the stud dog be conditioned to allow himself and/or the bitch to be handled, and is not thrown off if you have to assist.

The atmosphere for a mating should be one of calm reassurance. Under no circumstances should the dog or bitch be hurt or frightened. The bitch should be on a leash when first introduced to the stud dog. They should be allowed to play and become more familiar. If the bitch shows any aggression, her muzzle should be tied. A stocking, or long, thin strip of cloth will do.

It is easier if two people attend a mating, one to hold the bitch firmly in place, particularly at the point of penetration. The other person, the more experienced, controls the back end of the bitch while assisting, if necessary, the work of the stud.

Sometimes an experienced stud dog will be reluctant to mate a bitch even though she appears ready. He probably knows best, and the mating should be postponed until he is obviously willing. If there is a decided difference in size, a small bitch may require a raised platform or mat. More likely, the stud will need the raised, non-skid surface in order to be at an easy height for working himself into the bitch.

As the dog penetrates the bitch, there is a knack in helping the stud follow through. This is accomplished by placing your palm under the stud's tail, pushing firmly and lifting upward. This lifts the dog's chest onto the bitch and raises the dog's back feet off the floor. He is then held in place for a minute or two while the penis swells, locking him into the bitch. At this point both are said to be "tied." A firm hold on the bitch is important as she may experience some discomfort. When they are safely tied, the stud may be turned by lifting one rear leg over the bitch. Care should be taken in this process to prevent any hurt to either. They may stand back-to-back for only a few minutes, but more normally, 15 to 30 minutes, sometimes even longer. In any case, wait until the separation occurs naturally, keeping a firm hold on both until this happens.

A bitch can be bred without the dog actually achieving a "tie." Some successful stud dogs never tie their bitches, yet regularly get them in whelp.

Artificial insemination is a fairly common procedure today, and experienced stud dog owners are always prepared should this be the only way to accomplish the task. Success may be less frequent, but failures are usually a result of some inadequacy or abnormality on the part of the bitch. Do not be put off, however, if this is the only possible way. Many owners of famous stud dogs have had semen frozen and banked for future use. Frozen semen has been successfully exported, and there are British litters achieved from this method.

Some stud owners will provide a second service, but this is unnecessary if all appeared to go well with the first mating. If there is some doubt, or there is particular pressure that the bitch be successfully mated, repeat the procedure 30 to 48 hours later.

The Pregnant Bitch

The gestation period, on average, is 63 days. Puppies born a week earlier, or more rarely a week later, can survive. They are less likely to survive the more premature they are. Count the day after the first mating as the first day, even when two breedings were achieved. This way you are not left wondering whether the bitch is going past her due date from the first mating or is only at her sixty-first day from the second mating.

Some bitches will reveal their condition early on while others keep you guessing. An observant owner may notice several days after a bitch has been bred that she is urinating more frequently. The condition will last only a few days and is attributed to a hormonal change which occurs at the time of actual conception. A marked personality change usually follows within two or three weeks. Your high energy bitch may become far more sedate, and require a lot more lap time, soaking up all the affection you have time to give.

It is not uncommon for a bitch to go off her food for a day or two during this early period, so do not be alarmed. This is rather like "morning sickness" in women. However, refusing food for several days is not normal and should be investigated by your veterinarian. Her diet, however, will never be more important and should be of the highest quality. As a precaution against calcium deficiency while pregnant and while nursing, vitamin supplements should be used in quality and quantity advised by your mentor or veterinarian. The latter should see the bitch some time during the pregnancy, so that he will be familiar with her condition should his help or advice be needed during whelping.

If a bitch is carrying a large litter, you may see a rounding of the abdomen as early as the third week, with the nipples becoming noticeably pinker, particularly in a first pregnancy. Typically, a slight distention of the abdomen will become apparent by the fourth week. In some cases, a bitch given adequate exercise, will keep a trim figure well into her sixth or seventh week, and in the case of a small litter, even later.

Watch the bitch's weight closely during the entire pregnancy. Ideally, she should be in perfect weight at the time of mating, so that changes are obvious. If she begins to appear thin over the shoulders or along the spine, increase intake accordingly, and consider two feedings per day. During the last four weeks, this may prove particularly prudent. As the pregnant bitch increases in size she will appreciate two or three smaller meals each day rather than a single large meal. A bowl of milk with a few dog biscuits before bedtime make a good "nightcap."

Normal exercise and established routine are a must during pregnancy. She should be left to set the standard, and allowed plenty of free or controlled exercise, whichever has been her routine. Just because she has full run of a fenced yard, do not assume that she is getting adequate exercise. She may just be moving from the shade of one tree to another. There should be brisk and lengthy walks started as soon as she is bred. There is nothing like regular roadwork to build up strength and stamina, both of which will be needed at whelping time.

Under no circumstances should you treat the pregnant bitch as an invalid, nor should you permit over-exertion, particularly in the final weeks. She will slow up quite naturally as her condition warrants. Her favorite chair, or even the stairs, may become an obstacle, where help is required as the load increases.

During the last week she should never be unattended, even in a fenced yard. As her time approaches, she will be seeking out a nest, and unsupervised may find an unreachable hideout under a garage or shed.

Preparations For Whelping

At least a week before the due date, the whelping site should be prepared, and the bitch accustomed to it. Choose a quiet place outside the mainstream of activity. Needless to say, if you have other pets, the whelping area must be off-limits to them. The box, itself, should be square and sufficiently large for the bitch to stretch out fully in it, with several inches to spare. A box about 30 inches square, with walls about 14 inches high seems ideal for a Miniature Schnauzer. A very satisfactory box can be made out of a good grade, lightweight plywood, sufficiently sanded so all surfaces are smooth. It is a good idea to have a rail around the inside, extending two to three inches from the side, and three or four inches from the floor of the box. This will help prevent the puppies from being crushed against the sides by a clumsy mother.

About a week before the bitch is due to whelp she should be bathed, with special attention given to her breasts. Use a mild soap or shampoo containing no disinfectants, and rinse thoroughly. The average Schnauzer carries little belly coat, but whatever there is should be carefully trimmed to make the teats accessible to the puppies. The hair around the vulva and from inside of the back legs should also be trimmed. After whelping, the bitch will have a discharge for several days, and shorter hair will be easier to keep clean.

Begin to accumulate other supplies which may prove useful during the actual whelping. A good supply of newspapers is a must. Layers of newspapers can best serve as bedding, being absorbent and easily disposable. The whelping box should be kept scrupulously clean, and the papers changed regularly. After the whelping, a rug or some other kind of sure-footed surface will be required so that the puppies can gain good traction while nursing. Thirty-inch squares of old mattress pads, cut to size, are excellent. They have enough body to lie flat, and are still washable.

Other needed supplies include clean towels, sterile blunt-nosed scissors, baby oil, cotton, Tincture of Merthiolate (or Iodine), sterile string, a heating pad or hot water bottle, a small cardboard box (other than the whelping box), a bit of brandy, some alcohol for sterilization, and an eye dropper for stimulating a sluggish puppy. These supplies should be set out in the whelping area so they are immediately available when needed.

When Whelping Begins

The most reliable indication that whelping is imminent is a continuous drop in temperature. Normal temperature is 101.5 degrees. When the temperature drops below 99 degrees it is almost certain that there is not much longer to wait. Other common signs that whelping is about to commence are refusal of food, shivering, panting, digging, wide-eyed staring, and a slight, sticky vaginal discharge. Any or all of these symptoms are normal.

When the temperature has settled at the 99° to 98° range, and the bitch's appearance has changed to what can best be described as "lumped up," expect labor within 24 hours. Now is a good time to notify your veterinarian that you may be needing his assistance. Be sure you have also established contact with an experienced breeder, should you need help.

The preliminary stages of labor—the panting and shivering, the digging and shredding of papers—can continue quite some time before the initial "breaking of water." The first puppy will be preceded by a water bag. If the bitch happens to be sitting as it is passed, you may not see the bag, only a spreading puddle. More likely it will appear from the vulva like a balloon. Allow it to break of its own accord. The first puppy should follow the expulsion of the water bag within four hours. More likely, you can expect the first born within a half-hour.

The actual labor is usually obvious. It consists of a fairly slow and steady straining, characterized by an arching of the back and raising of the tail, as if to

276

expel something. Note the time in which the first contraction occurs. If these hard contractions continue for more than an hour without producing a puppy, call for help.

Most likely a puppy will emerge after only two or three contractions, usually within ten to 20 minutes. Usually the puppy is presented headfirst in a sac surrounded by fluid. The puppy-filled sac will be followed by the cord and the placenta (after-birth), all as a single unit. The placenta is a blackish mass, almost as large as the puppy. It is vital that there be an after-birth accounted for each puppy that is born, as the retention of any may cause problems later. If the placenta does not follow naturally, grasp the cord closest to the bitch and gently but firmly pull until it emerges.

Opinions differ as to how much assistance should be given from this point forward. Some bitches resent interference, preferring to deliver and care for their young unattended. If she immediately breaks the sac with her teeth, and begins licking and nuzzling the pup until it squeals, leave her a moment to also bite the cord and eat the placenta.

If none of this is accomplished almost immediately, be prepared to break the sac, cut the cord and remove the placenta. The cord should be cut about an inch from the puppy, and the end tied with sterile string and dabbed with Merthiolate. The new puppy should then be gently but firmly rubbed with a clean, warm towel until it squeals and is breathing clearly. Rubbed somewhat dry, it should then be given to the mother. Further licking usually results in the puppy's first bowel movement, which is black. It is important that this occurs so that the puppy can digest the food that it is about to get from mother.

It is not uncommon for a new arrival to greet the world feet first! This is called a breech birth, and can cause some difficulty. Sometimes the sac ruptures during the passage down the birth canal and may be partially presented as two hind legs dangling from the vulva. If the rest of the body does not immediately follow with the next contraction, use a small towel or face cloth, dipped in warm water, and with gentle pressure, grasp the hindquarter, rotating the body very gently as the bitch strains. Pull in a downward direction if the puppy is coming tummy down; pull in an upward direction if the puppy is on his back. If you are not able to dislodge the puppy, and it slips back into the bitch, get her to the veterinarian quickly. Remember, however, that your efforts may save the puppy—waiting for help will surely limit its chances of survival.

The first puppy is often the largest, and can produce considerable pain in its delivery. The bitch, in her pain, may turn to bite this thing which seems to be causing it. You must be alert to prevent this. Also, if the contractions for the next puppy commence as soon as the first is expelled, she may be more concerned with her labor than with the newborn puppy. Your assistance will clearly be needed.

Should a puppy arrive that appears lifeless, or nearly so, stimulate it by vigorous but gentle rubbing. If this accomplishes nothing, immerse the puppy, except for the head, first in cold (65°) water, then in hot (100°) water, and keep

A three-day-old litter of black and silver puppies after tail docking.

alternating until the shock stimulates the puppy to gasp or squeal. A drop or two of brandy placed on the tongue may also help.

When the bitch becomes restless and concerned with the next arrival, move the puppy to a small cardboard box in which there is a heating pad or hot water bottle, covered with a towel. The bottom of the box should feel warm to the touch—not hot. Keep the box within the mother's sight. There is no need to add to her anxiety.

The timing of successive puppies will vary. Often two pups will arrive a matter of moments apart, and then there may be a longer wait for the next. Between deliveries, remove the top layer of newspapers and replace them so that the box will have a clean surface to receive the next puppy. Should more than an hour elapse in between puppies, when you are sure there are more, this is cause for only minor concern. If, however, the bitch is straining without success for more than 20 minutes, seek the advice of your veterinarian. She may require a Pitruitrin shot to help speed up the process. Sluggish labor is usually due to uterine inertia or lack of muscle tone, encountered more often in older bitches. Sometimes a short walk around the room or yard (on leash) will stimulate labor.

Remember that whelping is hard and often painful work for the bitch. During the whelping, offer her a small bowl of milk or broth. Also offer her a drink of water between deliveries. She may or may not want either, but offer it anyway.

Make certain that all puppies nurse as soon as possible, whether delivered normally or by cesarean section. It is also important that each puppy has an initial bowel movement. Watch for this black material to be passed by each

278

A five-week-old litter of black and silver puppies before ear cropping.

puppy. Usually the mother stimulates this action by licking the genital area. Thereafter, she will continue to do so for several days, eating all of the stools. This is her instinctual way of keeping her nest clean, and is quite normal and natural.

It is difficult to determine when a bitch has finished delivering a litter. The most obvious information comes from the bitch herself. Most often, a definite change occurs in her attitude and behavior. She will seem to relax, resting contentedly as she cleans and nurses her new family. If, however, another puppy arrives an hour later, don't be surprised—and above all, be there!

Once the whelping is definitely over, she should be given the opportunity to relieve herself, and then given privacy and quiet. The whelping box should be freshly covered with newspapers, topped by a clean pad or towel to provide traction for the crawling puppies. This is not the time for visits from the children or neighbors. There is plenty of time for sharing later on.

After the Whelping

The new mother should be fed as soon after whelping as an interest in food is shown. Keep the meals light for the first day or so. Cereal and milk three or four times a day, adding a raw egg yolk to one of these will do nicely. Rice with cooked chicken is a good transition from the milky feeds to her more usual fare. Her appetite may lag for the first few days, and she may have a slightly elevated temperature—above 102°. Take her temperature at least twice daily. It should be a normal 101.5° within four days. She will soon be eating and drinking normally while her puppies grow chubby and contented. Fresh water should be available at all times.

Miniature Schnauzers are a docked breed and this should be accomplished at between three and six days, if all the puppies are strong. Dewclaws should be removed at the same time as tail docking. Examine all four feet as dewclaws are frequently found on the rear as well as the front feet. Docking and dewclaw removal should not be attempted by a novice. Consult your veterinarian on this. Check the puppies' toenails frequently and cut them back when necessary. They can be as sharp as needles and can hurt the mother as the puppies nurse.

For the first few days your bitch may be reluctant to leave her new babies. If necessary, carry her out to relieve herself frequently, and clean her breasts with warm water after each trip.

The bitch's diet during the four or five weeks of nursing will depend on the size of the litter. She should be fed three or four times a day. For the first week she will need about one and one-half times her normal ration. By the second week it should be doubled, and with large litters it should be increased to three times the usual amount, and more, if necessary. Always offer more food if she quickly finishes a meal—she will know best if more food is required.

Puppy Size and Growth Rate

Puppies vary in size at birth and frequently in the rate of development Five to 6½ ounces at birth appears to be average in Miniature Schnauzers. Weight charts compiled by Dale Miller (Barclay Square) indicate that puppies maturing at a correct size weigh from 13 oz. to 1 lb. 3 oz. at two weeks old. At four weeks, puppies of correct size weighed 1 lb. 9 oz. to 2 lbs. 4 oz. At six weeks they should weigh from 2 lbs. 8 oz. to 3 lbs. 5 oz. The greatest uniformity seems to occur at eight weeks of age, with males ranging from 4¼ to 4¾ lbs. and females from 4 to 4½ lbs. In keeping charts for future reference, be sure the time of weighing is consistent, always either before or after feeding.

Post-Whelping Problems

Although problems after whelping are uncommon in the bitch that has had proper care, close attention should be payed to any rise in temperature (above 102°), or abnormal behavior such as weakness, restlessness, drooling or chomping of the jaws. Excessive consumption of water, followed by vomiting, is another sign of a potential complication. Get advice from your veterinarian should any symptoms persist. He will know how to treat any post-whelping problems such as eclampsia, mastitis, metritis or pyometra. Early treatment at the first signs of trouble is essential.

Weaning the Puppies

Along with more than doubling in size after the first ten days, expect the eyes to begin opening. The lids open gradually, beginning with slits at the inside corners. Sometimes the eyes are stuck-up initially. When this happens, gently wipe them with warm water until they are clean and open. Although seeing very little, all eyes should be open and clear by 15 days of age.

The third and fourth week in a puppy's life is considered the most crucial. Tests indicate that very rapid development occurs at this time. Clarence Pfaffenberger in his comprehensive work, *The New Knowledge of Dog Behavior* (Howell Book House, New York, NY), writes:

> At twenty-one days of age the puppy not only can start to learn, but will start whether he is taught or not. This change is so abrupt that whereas the puppy does not see (at least very little) or smell or hear at all on his twentieth day of age, within twenty-four hours he does all of these quite well. Naturally, he needs the security of his mother.

Mr. Pfaffenberger continues:

> This period of twenty-one to twenty-eight days is so strange to the puppy that at no other time in a puppy's life can he become so emotionally upset, nor could such an upset have such a lasting effect upon his social attitude.

If the puppies are to be moved to new quarters in another section of the house, this should be accomplished before or after the critical 21 to 28 day period. The bright lights, noise and confusion of family life may be fine for socializing older puppies, but not babies.

Weaning should not begin until after the puppies are 28 days old under normal circumstances. If the mother has an inadequate milk supply, you will of course start weaning earlier. Teaching a puppy to eat from a dish is started only as a supplement to mother's milk. Weaning is a gradual procedure. Baby cereals with a spot of honey in warm milk provide a good beginning. Each puppy should be started individually. Put your finger, dipped in the milk, into the puppy's mouth. As he begins to suckle or lap, place him within reach of the food until he laps by himself. It is best to do this when the puppies are hungry. They will catch on to lapping up milky foods right away, and will happily share the same feed pan with their littermates for two or three weeks.

At the end of the sixth week, puppies should be checked for worms and given their first immunization shot. Virtually all puppies are born with roundworm (ascarids), and worming procedures should be followed on the advice of your mentor or veterinarian. A schedule for future immunizations should also be set.

About 30 days after whelping the mother will start making herself less available for nursing. Most bitches ask for time off before then, and will enjoy some of their more usual activities, like free exercise, longer walks, lap time with you —any change from the confines of the whelping box. The mother will want to stay with the puppies during the night, at least for the first six weeks. Thereafter, if she still has milk, she will only visit them periodically, mostly for play. Most mothers love to play with their puppies, and all benefit from the relationship.

As the puppies depend less and less on mother for their supply of essential vitamins and minerals, these nutrients must be provided in the basic diet you are feeding. Seek advice from your mentor or veterinarian as to what supplements should be used.

A Cycle Ends and a New One Begins

By eight weeks of age, weaning should be complete, with no further nursing from mother. Separate feeding dishes should be used for each pup hereafter, not only to prevent squabbling, but as a check that each pup is receiving a full ration.

At this point the bitch has put her all into producing and caring for a fine litter. She deserves a rest. Although a new cycle will begin within two or three months, she should not be bred at the season immediately following a litter. There are special circumstance, of course, where breedings on consecutive seasons are valuable. In the case of "super moms," this should cause no problems. The bitch's age, condition and general health must, however, be the primary factor in making such a decision.

Ears — To Crop or Not to Crop

Schnauzers of all sizes are among the dozen or so breeds which are more frequently seen with cropped rather than natural ears. Since this is accomplished most usually at ten to 12 weeks, the breeder must decide whether to accept the responsibility or leave this to the new owner. Most prefer the former, and place their pet puppies after ears are cropped and completely healed.

The history of cropping falls into the realm of folklore, beginning centuries ago. The justification for this essentially cosmetic procedure has for over a century been a matter of esthetics and tradition. The fact that the large majority of Miniature Schnauzers are cropped speaks for the persisting desire to perpetuate this tradition.

As with tail docking, the ear crop has an esthetic objective. Both are thought to enhance the beauty of the individual by achieving a more distinctive look. As with length of tail, there are similar variations in the length and shape achieved in ear cropping. Each breed has its own style.

Several countries throughout the world have outlawed ear cropping, and in several of the United States, this procedure is illegal.

There is considerable risk and expense involved with ear cropping, and those who elect the procedure should be well informed. The decision should be taken only after you are completely familiar with the entire process, including the after-care required. Above all, seek out a "professional" who has a reputation for excellence—one who specializes in the breed. Your local veterinarian may not have the skills, experience or desire to perform cosmetic surgery.

Uncropped, untended natural ears are just as likely to stand straight up as they are to hang hound-like.

Natural Ears

Natural ears may not always do what you want "naturally." Uncropped, untended natural ears are just as likely to stand straight up as they are to hang hound-like. Getting them well placed, so that they break above the skull may take a bit of doing.

Since the 1930s, only an occasional uncropped Schnauzer appeared in the American show ring. Only a few (four as of 1985) have earned championship status, and these in the last few years. There are more and more dogs with natural ears being sold as pets, and a few breeders are electing to bypass tradition and leave all their homebreds uncropped.

On November 22, 1981 history was made when Jean Fancy (Fancway) gave Best of Breed to Ch. Regency's Equal Rights, making her the first uncropped Miniature Schnauzer to complete the requirements for an AKC title

since 1934. She was conditioned and shown by her owner, Beverly Verna (Regency). A year later, Ch. Skyline's Seventh Heaven finished on one coat, handled by Clay Coady for owner Carol Parker (Skyline). Lynne Boone (Ellar) is the only breeder with a brace of uncropped champions. Ch. Ellar's Wildflower finished in 1984 and Ch. Ellar's Argonaut in 1985, both handled by Sue Baines. Argonaut is the lone male among them.

All four carry Ch. Skyline's Blue Spruce (50 Chs.) as a common ancestor. Equal Rights is by the Spruce son, Ch. Regency's Right On (27 Chs.), and so is Seventh Heaven, the latter a Spruce double granddaughter. Wildflower carries three lines to Spruce, two through the Spruce son, Ch. Irrenhaus Blueprint (19 Chs.), and Argonaut has two lines to Spruce.

Each of these breeders took special pains to "set" the ears at various stages of puppyhood so that they would be well placed and carried. Some start setting ears at six weeks, others at eight to ten weeks. The ears will probably be pasted on and off until the age of five months, and in some cases up to nine months.

Since little attention has been given to breeding correct natural ears, those of the Miniature Schnauzer are quite varied in size, shape, thickness of leather, as well as placement on the head. Dogs with large, houndy ears will have little chance in the show ring. Those that hope to competitively exhibit an uncropped dog will be well advised to select a specimen with fairly small, well-placed ears that can be enhanced by "setting." Judges will expect ear carriage not unlike some of the other terrier breeds, breaking above the skull and held close to the cheeks.

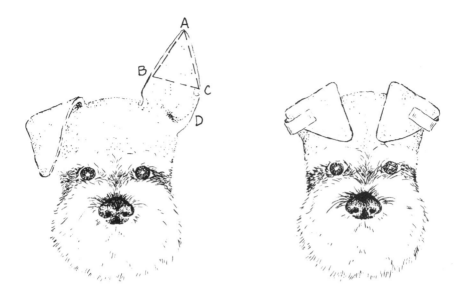

Setting Ears

Setting ears is a fairly simple process, and involves a minimum of materials. Needed will be a surgical adhesive, or any other glue that will hold fabric to fabric. Some wholesale pet suppliers carry a specialized glue produced specifically for setting ears. Tincture of Benjoin or mineral spirits are useful in properly cleansing the inner ear.

A conscientious breeder that sells a puppy with natural ears will have already begun the process at from six to eight weeks, and will be able to advise the new owner on the maintenance of the procedure. Several months with glued ears will not appeal to every new owner, but if a show career is in the future, it is almost a must!

To begin with, this is an entirely painless process, and the puppy will quickly become accustomed to the condition, and will enjoy the extra attention. Another pair of hands will be necessary in the beginning. Someone will have to hold the puppy's head to get the job done quickly and easily. With electric clippers, remove all the hair from the skull and ears, inside and out. The inner ear should be cleansed with dry cotton, and excess hair pulled from the ear canal. Repeat the procedure using Tincture of Benjoin or mineral spirits and allow to dry. Keeping the inner ear scrupulously clean at all times is imperative.

Keep a box of tissues handy as pasting can be messy. Study the diagram, noting the positions: A, B, C and D. Spread the glue on the underside of the ear flap from the tip (A) toward B and C. Lay the ear on the skull, the tip pointing toward the inside corner of the eye, and press. Hold the pup's head to prevent him from shaking the ear loose. Paste the other ear in a similar way. After both are clearly held fast, place a bit of surgical tape at position D, to hold the outer edge of the ears, at the fold. Check to see that there is ample space, unglued, to allow the ears to "breathe." Be sure the ears are placed symmetrically. The position can be changed by resetting. When you are satisfied with the set, hold the pup and brush him or otherwise distract him so that he does not shake his head until the glue is dry. This will take about five minutes. Should an ear come loose from the pup shaking or scratching, repeat the process.

The initial set will be maintained for three weeks, after which the hair on the ears and skull will have grown enough so the area can be easily cut loose. Carefully snip the hairs near the adhesive with the tips of the scissors until they are free. Clean the ears, inside and out, and clipper the same areas as before. Reset immediately unless some soreness or possible infection is found, In this case, correct completely before resetting

At about five months, when the front permanent teeth are in, leave the ears loose for a few days to see if they are as you want them. Some will be ready at this time, and will require no further setting, If they are lower than desired, or if an ear tends to "fly," reset them both. If an ear appears further away from the head than its mate, it should be pasted further onto the skull than its mate. This is the time when any corrections should be made. Ears that are not symmetrical in placement and carriage are a decided disadvantage in the show ring.

There is a simple technique for assisting the fold to crease at the desired position. Using a light oil (baby oil will do), between thumb and forefinger, gently press the fold as you would to crease paper. Press and rub the entire length of the fold. A few minutes of this from time to time will greatly increase your chances of achieving correct natural ears with a proper fold. This procedure can be done while the puppy is enjoying time in your lap. Use one hand for petting and the other for creasing an ear. The pup will love the extra attention. It should be relatively painless, but if you press too hard, the pup will let you know.

The skin may, on rare occasions, become allergic to the glue. Take the ears down and dust the affected areas with a medicated powder, allowing them to dry and heal. Dust the area several times the first day. Allow them to completely heal, then repaste.

The setting and resetting process can be continued as long as necessary up to a year of age. If the ears are not as you wish by then, their chances of ever being correct are slim.

**Ch. Regency's
Equal Rights**

**Ch. Ellar's
Argonaut
with Sue Baines.**

19

Grooming the

Miniature Schnauzer

A WELL-GROOMED Miniature Schnauzer is a delight to the eye, and should be a point of pride to the owner. The breed loses much of its character and charm if the coat is not properly maintained.

The grooming instructions in this chapter are intended to educate the new owner in all facets of grooming and general coat management. The instructions may appear lengthy due to their detail, but once digested and experienced, you will want to know even more.

The first-time owner will probably be dealing with a three- to four-month-old puppy, already with ears cropped and fully healed. If your puppy is uncropped, it is assumed that this is as you wish and the ears will remain natural.

The new puppy, purchased from a reliable and responsible breeder, will arrive with a multitude of instructions, hopefully even some on initial grooming. If you prove to be a worthy owner, that breeder may serve as mentor, providing a constant source for needed information and advice.

Purchased from a responsible breeder, your new puppy will have already had considerable experience, and will arrive in a neat and tidy condition. If it was agreed that yours is a "pet" puppy that will not be shown, chances are he will already be neatly clipped in a proper style, and maintenance thereafter will always involve electric clippers as your principal tool.

If there is to be a future in showing, be sure the puppy is not machine clipped early on, as this will make the required initial stripping process more difficult.

In either case, the grooming process should begin immediately. Proper training during puppyhood can mean the difference between an individual easily managed, leaving both hands for the grooming process, or one that leaves neither to do the job intended. Be kind, but firm. Keep the sessions brief in the beginning, and follow them with some reward, like a favorite tidbit or a brisk walk. There is much to be learned by you and the puppy during these first few months.

Tools and Equipment

Regardless of whether you intend to show or plan simply to maintain a well-groomed pet, certain basic tools and equipment are required. The advice of a mentor will prove invaluable in securing the best for the least. If this is not possible, another source may be a local grooming shop. The average pet store may not be equipped to handle your needs if you are planning to show your puppy. It may, however, be able to supply you with the address of, or catalogs from, wholesale pet supply houses. These are by far the best source for the sophisticated grooming gear needed. Another source may be at a local AKC-sanctioned dog show, where suppliers and vendors have booths for direct sale. The selection may not be as complete, and the prices will surely be higher than those offered through wholesale catalogs. You will, however, be able to see first-hand the large assortment of grooming paraphernalia available.

Consider the grooming tools and equipment to be a lifetime investment and buy the best you can afford. A grooming table with a restraining arm, two combs, two brushes, two scissors, nail clippers, stripping knives and a hand and/or electric clipper are all required items.

The Grooming Table

Grooming tables are manufactured in a variety of styles, each suited to special needs. They are readily available through wholesale catalog suppliers as well as some national chain stores. Along with the required grooming arm or post, this may be your most costly investment. If you are planning to show your dog, you will certainly need this equipment for working both at home and at the shows.

If you wish to improvise, the simplest solution would be to secure a piece of one-half to three-quarter-inch-thick plywood, approximately 18 inches wide and 30 inches long. This can be topped with rubber matting, and a clamp-on post can be purchased or even improvised if you are handy with plumbing supplies.

Grooming Tools

Combs

You will need two metal combs. One is the combination comb, like the Greyhound®, with both coarse and medium teeth. The points are sharp and go through leg and face hair without tearing them. The other comb should have fine metal teeth—from ten to 15 teeth per inch. It may be with or without a handle. This comb will have duller points and is used on the body coat, principally for removing undercoat.

Brushes

Two brushes are needed, each having a particular purpose, while a third, called a palm pad, might be a welcomed addition. The most important for general use is a wooden or rubber-backed pin brush—Safari #442® is a favorite with Schnauzer fanciers. This brush is excellent for daily brushing, removing a minimum of undercoat. You will need a slicker brush for the undercoat as well as for brushing leg hair and face furnishings. This is a small rectangular brush, approximately 2" x 4", with bent metal bristles and an angled handle. It must be used with caution as it can easily remove more undercoat or furnishings than desired.

Scissors

Two pairs are needed, one for straight trimming and the other for thinning. Straight-edged barber scissors, with at least three-inch blades, should be snub-nosed for safety. Thinning scissors come in two types—single or double serrated. I prefer the former, as it cuts half as much hair. However, the Skipper® "double duck" is excellent, having three-inch blades with 30 teeth on each blade. Carbon steel scissors are recommended rather than stainless, as they work better on dog hair and retain their sharpness far longer.

Nail Clippers

Guillotine nail clippers are best suited to the task—the Resco® clippers being most popular. A small metal nail file will also prove useful, between clippings and to soften edges immediately after clipping.

Stripping Knives

At least two stripping knives will be needed. One should be a coarse or medium knive having 12 to 18 teeth, for body work. A fine stripper with 20 to 30 teeth is necessary for working on areas which must be kept particularly short, like the head, ears and chest. MacKnyfe®, McClellan®, and Pearson® make excellent knives in fine, medium and coarse grades. The Lyon Grooming Comb® is particularly suited to removing undercoat.

Clippers

Although there are several varieties of hand clippers available—the type the barber uses for trimming—you will eventually want to invest in electric clippers manufactured by Oster®. Model A2 is the older design, while Model A5 is a more recent innovation. Both are excellent machines. The principal difference is in the A5's "snap-in" blade feature. If a pet trim is desired, this is a must. Even with show trims, it will come in handy in dealing with the throat, ears and belly. Most dogs after enjoying their show careers will eventually be maintained by clipping instead of stripping the body coat. Two or three blades will be needed—a #8 or #10 will handle body work most easily, while a #15 is used for areas to be kept shorter.

Miscellaneous Supplies

As you become more involved in the grooming process, several items will prove useful—actually necessary if you intend to show. Grooming chalk or powder comes in a variety of types; the choice is best left to individual taste. Cornstarch from the pantry shelf will suffice until you are familiar with other products. Working chalk or powder into the coat during the stripping process makes the hair easier to grasp. Baby oil can be used on tender, over-worked areas to avert burning or drying out.

The waterless-rinseless type of shampoos are best suited to cleaning the dog in part, rather than giving a full bath, which is seldom necessary.

Add a spray bottle to your paraphernalia. Filled with water, it can be used in a variety of ways. Cotton swab sticks also are useful, as are tweezers. Various hair products, such as cream conditioners, are also likely to be found in the tack boxes of most exhibitors.

The Miniature Schnauzer Coat

The Miniature Schnauzer has a double coat: the hard, wiry outer coat and the soft, dense undercoat. The recognized colors are salt and pepper, solid black and black and silver. The same basic grooming is used for all three colors.

The more popular salt and pepper color is distinctive and unique to the breed. Although the overall color is gray, it is produced as a result of "banded" hair. Banding occurs when an individual hair has one color at the root which changes to a lighter color, and to dark again at the tip. A properly banded salt and pepper coat can only be achieved by stripping or plucking the hair. This is also the only way harsh texture and correct color can be maintained. If the coat is cut or clipped, the main body coloring becomes an overall slate gray, varying in tone from light to dark, with the true salt and pepper color being lost.

The Stripping Process

The process of stripping, or pulling the hair out from the roots, may seem abhorrent to the uninformed. It is, however, quite natural to strip out the coat of a Miniature Schnauzer. If left to its normal cycle, the hair would eventually reach a length of two to four inches and die. Rather than shedding, the dead hair tends to linger half-heartedly. It does not break off, but eventually falls from the roots. The stripping process is only assisting the natural cycle, and can be relatively painless.

The finger method of stripping is best for beginners, as you learn the process. If the coat is blown (dead, and ready to be plucked), it will come out easily. Grasp the strands of hair between thumb and index finger. Pull in the direction of the lay of the coat. Repeat the process until one or two square inches have been removed. Then take a coarse or medium stripping knife and attempt to repeat the procedure. Instead of gripping the hairs between thumb and bent forefinger, grasp them between your thumb and the knife. Hold the knife perpendicular to the dog and grasp the hair as close to the roots as possible, pulling in the direction of the lay of the coat. Use an arm and shoulder pulling movement, not a wrist action. If you flex your wrist, you will cut rather than pull the hairs with the knife. Compare the hairs being removed from the finger stripping and knife stripping. If you are plucking, the hair is of uneven length. If you are cutting, the hair will be even in length. Remember to work a small area at a time until all the outer coat has been removed.

Stripping is a tedious chore—partly manual labor and partly an art. The cliche "practice makes perfect" definitely applies. The length of time consumed in hand stripping depends on three factors: proper tools and equipment, the cooperation received from the dog, and your own skills.

There is only one correct grooming pattern for a Miniature Schnauzer, but there are two distinctly different ways to achieve it. Whether hand-stripping, which is necessary if you wish to show, or machine-clipping, the overall look will be the same—only coat texture and color will differ.

Basically there are two approaches to stripping. One involves dealing with the entire body in one or two sessions, as would be done in clipping the pet. The other requires stripping in "sections" over a period of weeks. Artful "sectioning" is one of the basic requirements in bringing the Miniature Schnauzer into "show" coat.

The "One Strip" Method

The "one strip" method is clearly shown in DIAGRAM A and B. Essentially, all the areas which appear to be clean are removed within a week to ten days. A longer period will result in obvious strip lines and too much variation in coat length. No amount of skillful blending of the areas is very successful.

In handling the body section, begin at the base of the tail, but not the tail itself. Go up the back to the withers (base of neck), taking out the sides or rib section, but leaving the underbody fringe to be scissored later.

After completing the back and sides, strip the hindlegs to about an inch above the hocks. Never strip into the indentation of the hock joint.

At this point, the dog is half stripped, and if you are unable to complete the forward section at this time, it can be picked up in a few days. In completing the "one strip" method, you would continue to remove the forward section: neck, shoulders and head, as well as the tail.

In order to make these instructions as thorough as possible, time will now be given to some of the more professional methods used in preparing the body section for show purposes.

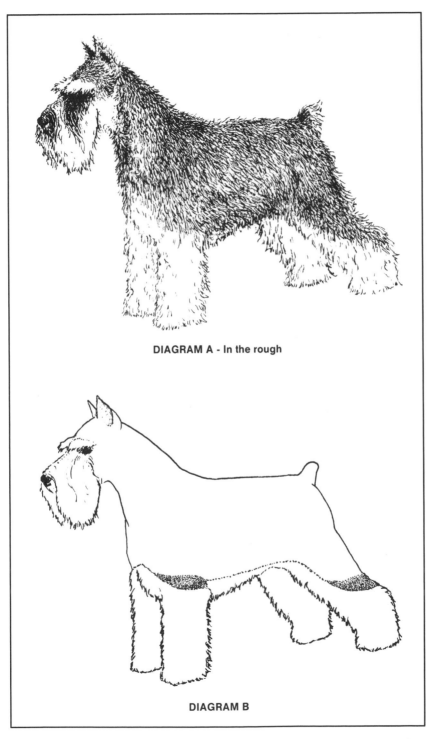

DIAGRAM A - In the rough

DIAGRAM B

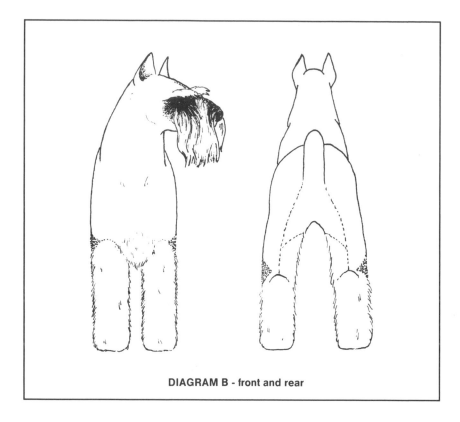

DIAGRAM B - front and rear

Stripping In Sections

Stripping in sections is the exhibitor's way of achieving the most desirable outline, based on variations of coat lengths. This process involves from eight to ten weeks, depending on the individual coat quality of your dog. No two dogs grow their coats at exactly the same rate, and it is not unusual for a dog to grow coat faster on one stripping than the next. Be sure that the period between sections does not exceed ten days, or the blending of the coat later will prove more difficult.

The following steps should be followed over a six-week period.

WEEK 1 - Remove all the body hair from behind the withers on the back and sides and on the hindlegs as described in the "One Strip" Method. DIAGRAM C illustrates the completed process achieved in the first week.

WEEK 2 - Beginning at the base of the skull, strip out an inverted "V," starting out with a width of about one inch. Gradually widen the strip as you work down the back of the neck until you join the section of the back previously stripped. DIAGRAM D shows the desired result.

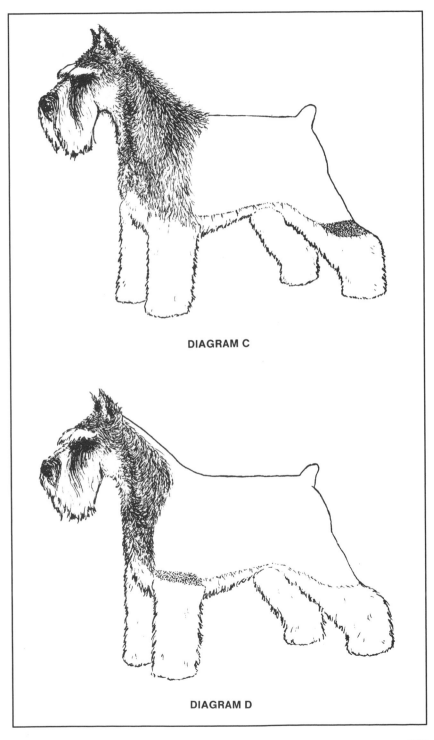

DIAGRAM C

DIAGRAM D

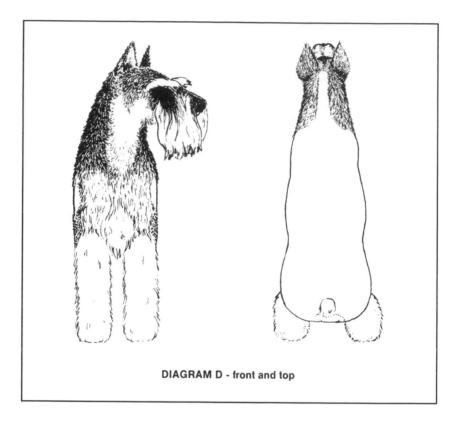

DIAGRAM D - front and top

WEEK 3-Take out the remaining hair on the sides of the neck and shoulders, down to an inch above the elbows. See DIAGRAM E and F. Be sure you do not strip or trim into the indentation at the elbow. This small area of hair just above the elbows is trimmed later in a process to be described.

WEEK 4-Study DIAGRAM G and H before beginning the work on head and ears. Study both the profile and top of the head as it should look when stripping is completed. A medium or fine knife will do the job, although frequent use of thumb and forefinger will give the best result. Remove all the hair in this area, including the undercoat. Start stripping from the back of the skull forward. As you bring your work to where the eyebrows begin, take considerable care in forming this line. With thumb and forefinger, strip out the area between the eyes, but not as deeply as on the skull. Strip out the sides of the skull from the outer corner of the eyes to the outer corner of the ears, leaving the sides of the cheeks and under throat for later.

Strip or clipper the ears at this time, using scissors to finish off the edges. The beginner will find ear stripping difficult as the area is particularly sensitive. Use a fine knife for these more difficult to handle short hairs, and use clippers if you must.

296

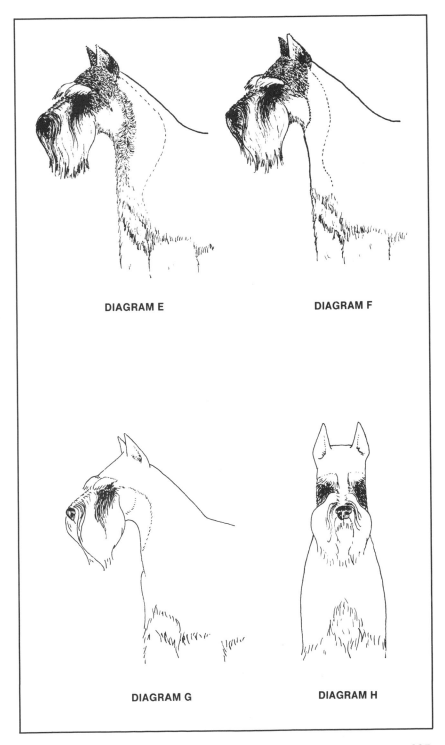

DIAGRAM E

DIAGRAM F

DIAGRAM G

DIAGRAM H

Whether cropped or natural, the inner ear should look neat and clean. Removing the hair with clippers is easiest, but some hand work near the ear canal is required. This is a sensitive area and using only thumb and forefinger can be very time consuming. A pair of tweezers will help, and a fastitious groomer will quickly learn their function.

WEEK 5 - At this point, the cheeks, throat and chest must be dealt with. The amount that is stripped, and that which is clipped is a matter of personal pride. These areas must be kept neat throughout the weeks of showing, as short, in fact, as the head. These areas will need constant maintenance during the show period, whether stripping or clipping. Be reminded that clipping will produce a softer texture, and a loss of the true salt and pepper color.

Using clippers, take out the hair under the throat. Before proceeding, comb the whiskers (beard) carefully forward and then grasp the beard and muzzle before bringing the clipping to within 1½ inches of the corners of the mouth. When in doubt, remove less rather than more—chin whiskers take a long time to grow.

With stripping knife or clippers, remove the hair on the chest to the point of the shoulders, leaving a small inverted "V" shape as shown in DIAGRAM H. Thinning scissors may be used to blend the joining-line between shoulders and chest, and between neck and throat.

WEEK 6 - At this point the undercoat will begin to show prominently. This should all be completely removed over the next two or three weeks, using a fine stripping knife or comb, and following the same pattern used for the outer coat. This process can do some damage to the new growth of hard hair if not done correctly. You may wish to use a fine (flea) comb first in order to learn the skills involved. The knife or comb should be held at a 45 degree angle, and with slight pressure, working in the direction of the natural lay of the coat.

This weeding out process must be continued as the new coat grows, otherwise the ingrowing coat will lift and separate quicker than it otherwise would.

Trimming Head, Beard and Eyebrows

The Miniature Schnauzer's head should give the appearance of being *brick-shaped* as illustrated in DIAGRAM I. All trimming is done to achieve this look, aiming at length and flatness of skull, cleanness of cheeks, as well as a keen and alert expression.

There is a tendency to leave an overabundance of whiskers as in DIAGRAM K, both in length and thickness. This detracts from the overall rectangular look which is desired. DIAGRAM L shows a dished-out look, where too much hair has been removed from under the eyes.

Before proceeding, be sure the beard and eyebrows are freshly washed and chalked. Facing the dog, comb the beard forward and with barber scissors cut a straight line to the outer corner of the eye. Where the clipping of the cheeks and the cutting of the beard meet, blending should be done with

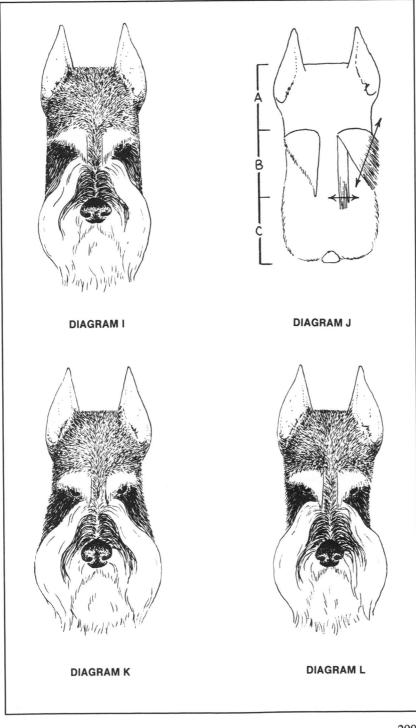

DIAGRAM I

DIAGRAM J

DIAGRAM K

DIAGRAM L

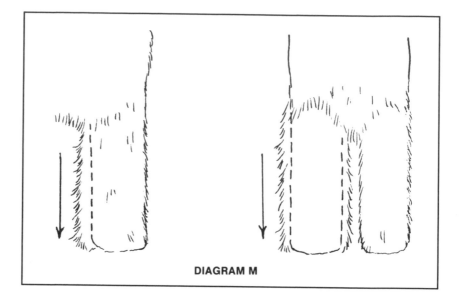

DIAGRAM M

thinning scissors. The area under the eyes and at the bridge of the nose should be carefully hand plucked should there be any "fuzzy" quality here. The darker mask, so desirable in the salt and peppers, should be carefully maintained. Finger-strip when it begins to look untidy.

Trimming the eyebrows takes special skills, and the process should be studied first-hand before any attempt is made. A word of caution: take off less rather than more, and give yourself some time to look at your work. More can always be removed.

Facing the dog, comb the eyebrows forward, but slightly outward. Trim close at the outer corners of the eyes. The length of hair left on the inside will depend on several factors. If the foreface is short, a little less eyebrow will give the effect of more length. If the foreface is longer than the skull, leave the eyebrows slightly longer. Longer brows are often left to disguise light, round or large eyes, reducing the amount of eye seen. Follow the pattern illustrated in DIAGRAM J for the basic technique.

Trimming Front Legs and Feet

The aim in grooming the front legs is to have them look solid, full and straight viewed from any angle. All Schnauzers are not blessed with heavy leg furnishings, therefore they should be kept as dense as possible. The texture of leg hair may vary from soft and silky to hard and brittle. But in each type, cleanliness and careful grooming will prevent loss of furnishings.

Dry clean and comb out the legs before beginning. Add chalk and backcomb the leg hair and then lightly comb downward with a palm pad. Before trimming, make sure the dog is standing in its natural show stance. An

300

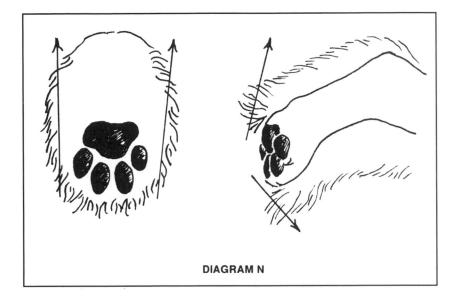

DIAGRAM N

honest appraisal of the front will pay off here, as you will want to minimize any fault that is present. Avoid creating a fault that isn't there! Poor blending at the elbows can create a pinched-in front or an out-at-elbow effect. Study DIAGRAM M before proceeding.

Standing directly over the dog and looking down on to the front legs, use straight scissors, pointing straight down. Trim in a circular manner all the way around each leg. This is called "posting," as the aim is to achieve a straight-as-a-post look.

The hair around the feet should be trimmed in a similar fashion, aiming at a round rather than pointed look. Lift each paw so that the pads are visible as shown in DIAGRAM N. Remove mats or any excess hair between the toes. Be careful not to carry your trimming to the top of the toes. The hair on top of the feet should be left full so that it can be blended evenly with the lower leg hair.

If your dog is not blessed with full furnishings, you will want to do some trimming at the same time (or before) the first week of body stripping. Sparse or brittle furnishings can be improved by limited stripping, using thumb and finger. Applying a light oil or lanolin preparation will help prevent brittle hair from breaking, and seems to encourage growth.

Trimming Hindquarters and Feet

The hind legs are prepared and trimmed in much the same manner as the front legs. Here again, be sure the dog is in his natural show stance, and assess his qualities and faults. Study DIAGRAM O and see what technique may be used to create the best possible look.

Backcomb the furnishings and then comb downward with the palm pad

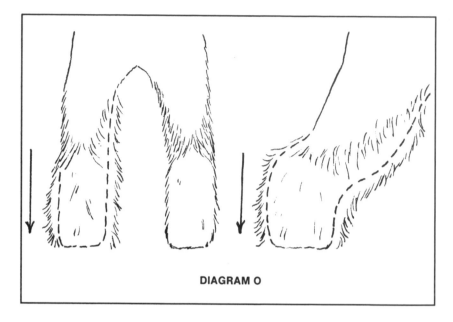

DIAGRAM O

or comb. In trimming the hocks, begin in the same manner, standing over the dog with the scissors pointing straight down. You want to achieve that straight-as-a-post look, and will trim the hocks in the same circular motion. The hair on the rear feet should be trimmed in the same manner, remembering that the rear feet are slightly smaller, and will be left a little fuller.

On the inside of the stifle, from the breech to the inside of the hock, trim any wispy hairs. On the outside of the stifle, trim along the natural contour of the stifle to blend into the hock. Make sure the finished scissoring of the rear is in balance with what you have accomplished on the front legs.

The true test of your trimming occurs when you move your dog. What efforts you have made to minimize faults while in stance may not be adequate on the trot. More work may be necessary, but extreme care should be taken. It takes some time to grow an inch of leg hair.

Trimming the Underbody Fringe

Comb the underbody fringe and then use the palm pad to box it out a bit. Using straight scissors, trim the hair at the tuck-up near the rear legs to about a half-inch in length. Trim toward the front legs, gently tapering your line, so that the hair is longer at the chest than at the tuck-up or loin. The chest hair should reach only to the elbow and should not appear to be overabundant.

Trimming the Tail

The tail and the area below the tail will need periodic trimming. This area should always be kept neat and close by either topping with a stripping

302

knife or thinning scissors. The tail itself should be rounded at the end, not pointed, and the length of hair kept in balance as further growth occurs.

Maintaining the Show Coat

Bringing your Miniature Schnauzer into show coat is only the beginning. To keep a show coat going longer requires considerable time and effort. The hair will constantly grow, and continued adjustments are required. The head, cheeks, ears and front section, as well as under the tail will need to be stripped or clipped almost weekly. The shoulders will need occasional blending and thinning, using the stripping knife. After the dog has been in full coat for a month, begin weekly thinning of the neck and body by finger stripping longer hairs as they appear. Hair between the pads and inside the ears should be cleaned out at all times.

Before each and every grooming session, reassess your dog, both standing and moving. Become more and more aware of his virtues and faults, and always trim with these in mind. Each grooming session is a learning experience, and often a revelation, as you discover some new way of providing a better balanced and more finished product.

There are no short-cuts to good grooming. Experience is the best teacher. No, experience is the only teacher!

Ch. Penlan Paperboy
A well groomed Miniature Schnauzer in prime coat.

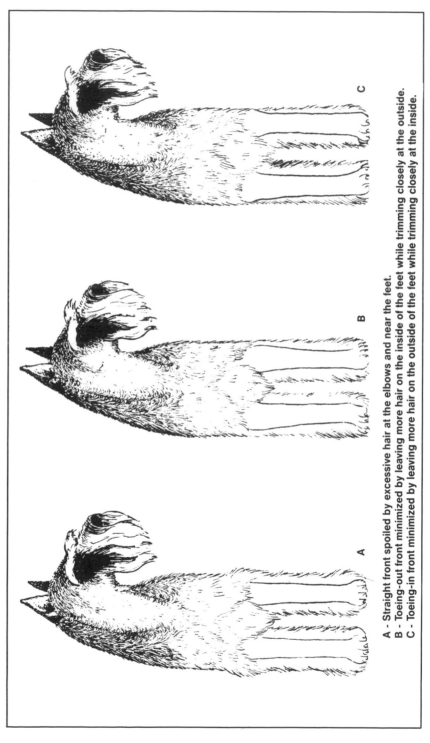

A - Straight front spoiled by excessive hair at the elbows and near the feet.
B - Toeing-out front minimized by leaving more hair on the inside of the feet while trimming closely at the outside.
C - Toeing-in front minimized by leaving more hair on the outside of the feet while trimming closely at the inside.

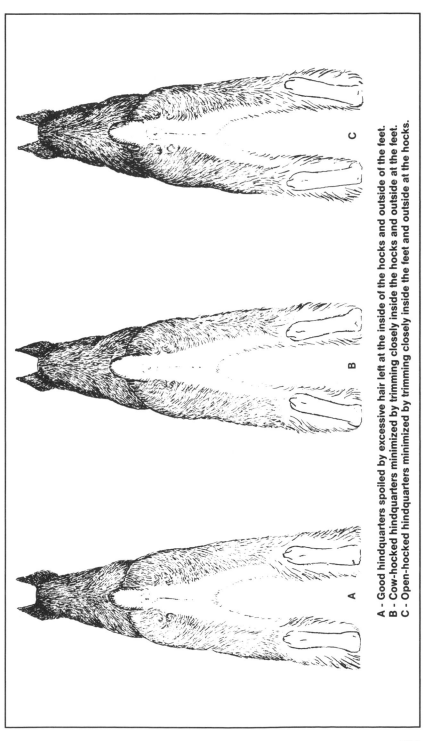

A - Good hindquarters spoiled by excessive hair left at the inside of the hocks and outside of the feet.
B - Cow-hocked hindquarters minimized by trimming closely inside the hocks and outside at the feet.
C - Open-hocked hindquarters minimized by trimming closely inside the feet and outside at the hocks.

20

Showing the Miniature Schnauzer

IF YOU ARE LOOKING for a sport that offers good fellowship as well as boundless competition, showing your Miniature Schnauzer may be just the thing. This challenging activity has been enjoyed by young and old throughout the world for over a century. It knows no barriers—class, color or creed.

It is a sport for all seasons—and all reasons. Showing dogs offers enjoyment and involvement for the single person as well as the whole family, and creates friendships that last a lifetime. Whatever your reasons, there is a great deal of pleasure and satisfaction in showing a well-bred dog, beautifully groomed and thoughtfully trained.

Providing your dog has been sensibly raised, and has typical temperament, there is no real reason why you cannot succeed to some degree right from the beginning. Like all sports, there are levels on which success can be measured. If your immediate goals are realistic, they are within reach. Only the chosen few become Olympians, Derby winners—or Best in Show at Westminster. Reaching the top in any endeavor takes talent, effort and, above all, perseverance.

Dog Shows

The conformation, or breed classes at a dog show are essentially a series of beauty contests—a process of elimination that ultimately results in one dog being selected as Best in Show. The level of competition will vary, depending on the type of show. On the highest level, Best in Show at the Westminster Kennel Club's annual all-breed dog show can be compared with victory at the Kentucky Derby. The 1941 winners of these events are known to this day. Ch. My Own Brucie is as famous a Cocker Spaniel as there ever was, and who has not heard of the great Whirlaway. Their breeders achieved a pinnacle that few realize, and that success represented decades of serious involvement.

Match Shows

Matches are held in many urban areas nearly every weekend, and most are open to all ages and all breeds. The match show is intended as a training

Inez Hartley examines Ch. Hughcrest Hugh Hefner while professional handler Clay Coady keeps him alert and in control, without interfering with the examination.

---

ground for the dogs, the exhibitors and even the judges. Experienced breeders take their puppies to match shows for ring education, as well as to see how they react to the experience. Here is where you and your dog can learn the procedure as well as benefit by watching those more experienced. Many of the more seasoned exhibitors will be helpful to newcomers and will readily share their knowledge.

Most entry fees at match shows are very reasonable and entries can be made on the day of the match. The form and procedure is very much like that of an AKC Licensed show where championship points are offered.

AKC Licensed Shows

In 1985 the American Kennel Club licensed over 800 all-breed shows and an additional 1,200 independent single breed (Specialty) shows. Entry fees for most shows range from $10.00 to $20.00, and must be included along with a properly filled out official entry form. All must be received by the show superintendent before the posted closing date, usual two to three weeks before the actual show.

When your entry is acknowledged, the excitement begins. The program will tell you what time your breed will be judged and in which ring. It will also show the number of dogs in each breed. It lists the breed, followed by four numbers. For example, it may read: *Miniature Schnauzers 12-14-3-2.* This means that there are 12 dogs (males) competing for the championship points and 14 for the points in bitches. The last two figures indicate that three champion males and two champion females are entered for Best of Breed competition, and are not competing for championship points. On the other hand, it may read: *Miniature Schnauzers 1-0-0-0,* which means that only your dog has been entered, and there will be no championship points offered.

Getting Started

The best way for a complete beginner to start is to enter a local match show where there is some assurance that other Miniature Schnauzers will be shown. If your first effort can be in the company of an experienced exhibitor you have already met, that would be most helpful. If not, seek out other Schnauzer exhibitors as soon as you arrive, and set up near them as there is much to be gained by observing their procedure.

From the moment you enter the show grounds you are creating the circumstance for making your dog show or not show. Above all else, you must make the entire experience as pleasurable as possible. A day at the dog show should be a joyful experience, not something to be dreaded.

If you have done your homework, your dog will take examinations, both on the table and on the ground, in his stride. He will be lead trained, and prepared to perform as expected in the show ring. Most judges follow the same pattern in ring procedure, so it would be wise to watch earlier classes under the same judge if at all possible.

Exhibiting may appear simple on the surface, but it takes a great deal of time and effort to have a dog looking and showing competitively. It *is* a competition, and to seasoned exhibitors the show ring is their "moment of truth." Here is where fanciers evaluate and compare the progress of their breeding programs with those of fellow breeders.

The chapter on Grooming will give you all the needed instructions on bringing your Miniature Schnauzer to the show looking his best. What follows is advice about training, handling and ring procedure.

Show Training

Start posing the future show dog on the table each time he is groomed. Teach him to allow you to place his four feet just the way you want them and to keep them that way. Then hold his head and his tail up and tell him to "stay" or "hold it," giving the command in a firm voice. If he does not obey and keeps moving, start all over from the beginning and keep at it until he understands just what you want. It will not take him long.

Open his lips and examine his front teeth and encourage members of the household to do so; then later, friends and strangers. Always be gentle. Have people lift up his front feet, run their hands along his spine and handle his hindquarters and hocks. Soon he will take this all as a matter of course.

You must start training your puppy to the show lead early. A soft slip lead is all that is necessary. He will soon learn that this lead requires a particular response. Hold the lead straight and fairly tight in your left hand, and train your Schnauzer always to walk on your left side. Never allow him to walk on the right side, and teach him not to cross in front of you.

You should attend as many dog shows as possible to learn the procedure in the show ring in order to teach your Miniature Schnauzer exactly what to do. If your dog knows in detail just what you require of him and thoroughly understands the routine, he will do his utmost to please without any uncertainty or bewilderment. You must, in turn, remain calm and collected and have confidence in yourself and in your dog. Most Schnauzers enter into the game of showing with zest and enjoyment and give of their best. They seem to sense that the other dogs are rivals, and with confidence in and affection for their handler, do their best to out-show their competitors. You must do your best as well.

Watch the professional handlers at the dog shows. See what they do and how they do it. Learn as much as possible of ring technique. Observe, for instance, that a good handler never comes between his dog and the judge, but always allows the judge a clear and uninterrupted field of vision. Standing or moving, you must always keep your dog in the judge's eye in the most advantageous manner.

Before you show your Miniature Schnauzer, make up your mind that you will meet other very good dogs in the ring. A knowledge of your dog's faults and virtues helps you to keep a balanced point of view. Study him against others in your own mind, study the printed Standard, study pictures of the best. Know just where your dog stands. Although your affections are involved, and you are justly proud of him, all the other exhibitors feel exactly the same way about their dogs. These natural sentiments have nothing to do with your Schnauzer's points as a show dog.

You may be sure, if you keep on showing, your Schnauzer will find his rightful level. If he is really good, and well presented, nothing can keep him down; if not, nothing can bring him up. In the course of a long show career, you will be knocked down at times unjustly, and, on the other hand, you may also win unjustly. Unless you can cheerfully take whatever comes, showing dogs may not be for you. Be a modest winner and a good loser. It pays.

Show Procedure

If you have entered an AKC licensed show, you will receive the *Schedule of Judging* and your exhibitor's pass in the mail. It is your responsibility to have your dog groomed and ready at ringside when your class is called. A few minutes before the scheduled time, check in with the ring steward who will give you an arm band with your dog's catalogue number printed on it. If you have entered the 6 months to 9 months puppy dog class, you will be among the first of the breed to enter the ring. When your class is called you enter the ring with the dog on your left and line up as the steward or judge directs. If you are a beginner or novice, try not to be first in line. This gives a little extra time to observe the judge's procedure.

Most judges follow a basic pattern in ring procedure. The first direction will usually involve the entire class being asked to move counter-clockwise around the ring once or twice. Hold the lead in your left hand, always keeping your dog between you and the judge. When the judge signals the class to stop, stack your dog, or use bait to keep him alert and in control until it is your turn to be examined. Miniature Schnauzers are usually examined on a table. After placing your dog on the table in a show pose, be prepared to have his teeth and bite examined. Some judges will ask you to show the mouth, others will do their own examination. While always having complete control of your dog, try to keep your hands out of the way during the entire examination.

Following this, the judge may ask you to move your dog, or he may go on and check the next dog, saving movement requirements for later. He will eventually want to see your dog gait in a pattern of his choice. He may ask you simply to take your dog "Down and Back"—straight away across the ring and straight back to the judge. Many judges will request various patterns: the "Triangle" in which the dog moves straight away down the ring, across to the opposite corner and back to the judge on a diagonal; the "T" pattern in which your dog moves straight down the ring, across to one side of the ring, back across to the other side of the ring, back to the center and then returning to the judge; the "L" pattern in which the dog moves straight down the ring, across to a corner, back to the center and back to the judge. He may want a second look and ask for a different pattern, so be prepared and listen carefully.

At the end of a requested movement pattern, stop a little distance from the judge, as he will want to see your dog standing free. He will be making a final check of ear-set and expression, as well as natural topline and tail-set. At this crucial point you will want your dog looking alert and showing his best. The name of the game is Dog *Show*, so teach your dog to show on command, either with bait (boiled liver is most commonly used) or with a ball or squeaky toy. When the judge has completed his individual examination of your dog, standing and moving, he will request that you take a position behind the other dogs already examined. If there are still others yet to be examined, take the time to work with your dog, straighting his beard and furnishings while also keeping him from getting bored. Here is where the bait or toy may again come in handy.

After all the dogs have been examined and gaited, the real competition begins, and a "third" eye would be helpful. Always keep an eye on the judge as well as your dog—and an extra eye on the competition if you can. The judge may ask the entire class to move again in unison, or he may ask only a few. Be ready! He may ask certain dogs to come together for further comparison. This is not a sparring match, and you must always have complete control of your dog. The judge will eventually make up his mind and send the first four placings to the designated markers and distribute the ribbons and any other awards offered.

If you win first in the class you must return for the judging of Winners Dog; if you are second, you may also be called for further judging for Reserve

Winners Dog, so stand by. After each class for males is judged, the steward will request that all first-place winners return to the ring for the judging of Winners Dog (WD). Here is where championship points are awarded, depending on the number of males in competition. If your 6-9 months puppy dog is selected WD, the second-place winner from that class is called to compete with the remaining class winners for Reserve Winners Dog (RWD). If the WD is disqualified for any infraction of the AKC rules, the RWD would then be credited with WD and awarded the points.

The classes for females follow in the same way, and after Winners Bitch (WB) and Reserve are selected the WD and WB compete further against champions for Best of Breed (BB). The judge will examine this class as he did all others. The final outcome will be a BB winner, a Best of Opposite Sex (BOS), as well as Best of Winners (BW). The BW award can be crucial, as there are frequently larger numbers in one sex. Example: in an entry of 4 dogs, 11 bitches, 3 male champions and 4 female champions, your 6-9 puppy dog might earn 2 points for WD, an extra point for BW (there are 3 points in bitches), and yet another point (4 point total) for going BB. In defeating all 15 bitches, he earns the scale of points (4) for the total number of bitches competing.

The Best of Breed Miniature Schnauzer is then eligible to compete in the Terrier Group. The best of each of the 26 terrier breeds are judged in much the same manner, with the emphasis being on which dog is closest to his own breed Standard. The best four will be given Group placements, and the Group 1st winner goes on to compete for Best in Show. If, by chance, your puppy is named Best Terrier, there may be an additional point awarded (total of 5). If there was a 5-point award made in any of the terrier breeds, your dog picks up the additional point by virtue of the superior win.

The final competition of the day will see seven finalists—the best Sporting, Hound, Working, Terrier, Toy, Non-Sporting and Herding dogs—the winner earning the coveted Red, White and Blue ribbon for Best Dog in Show.

How a Dog Becomes a Champion

Championship points (from 0 to 5) are awarded to the Winners Dog and Winners Bitch, with the possibility of additional points for defeating champions for the Best of Breed and Best of Opposite Sex. Further points may be earned by going on to Best Terrier or Best in Show. The maximum award possible at any single show is 5 points.

To become a champion, a dog or bitch must acquire 15 points under at least three different judges, and two of these wins must be *majors*. A major win carries 3, 4 or 5 points, and must be won under two different judges. A real "flyer" might earn three 5-point majors on a three-show weekend, but most show quality Miniature Schnauzers compete in 25 or more shows in order to achieve enough wins to earn the AKC certificate naming the dog a "Champion of Record."

Epilogue

YOU HAVE READ of the history of the Miniature Schnauzer in the United States and throughout the world. You have learned of and from the dedicated fanciers who have brought the breed to its present state. You can with a minimum of time and effort, connect your own Miniature Schnauzers to their proper sire lines and learn more of their families through studying the text and photos which accompany the charts.

You have been given a visualization of breed perfection, and hopefully a clearer understanding of how these qualities may be achieved, not only through breeding, but also through a higher degree of grooming and presentation.

The gallery of photos presented, both historic and contemporary, are intended for the pleasure of every reader, as well as to give a graphic record of breed progress.

In closing the pages of *THE NEW MINIATURE SCHNAUZER The Breed Since Ch. Dorem Display,* every effort has been made to touch on all facets of the breed that are important to dedicated fanciers, both old and new. The goal has been to combine all topics in print and picture that will have value in helping you better understand and appreciate this wonderful breed.